THE *SISSIFICATION* OF AMERICA:

A Fifty-Year Decline In American Exceptionalism

⊖

JOHN W. STEVENS

ISBN-10: 0615652719
EAN-13: 9780615652719
Library of Congress Control Number: 2012910047
CreateSpace, North Charleston, SC

This book is dedicated to my family and all Americans who desire to reclaim America and restore its virtues of exceptionalism to our government and its people, as well as fight to restore fidelity to the US Constitution.

Author's Note

Since the writing of this book, the United States Supreme Court has ruled by a slim majority, that ObamaCare is constitutional. In my opinion, on June 28, 2012, the fundamental principles of the US Constitution were significantly compromised by the egregious action of the Supreme Court. As a direct result, the individual freedoms of all Americans, as well as the constitutional principle of Federalism that protects the sovereignty of the nation's states, are in dire jeopardy. This is precisely what I feared could occur in our great nation as stated in chapter four of my book.

The November elections of 2012 are without a doubt, the most critical and pivotal elections in recent American history, and they will forever determine the fate of our country! It is my sincere hope and prayer that my book, *The Sissification of America: A Fifty-Year Decline in American Exceptionalism,* will inspire the majority of Americans to awaken from their sleep and elect a new president and a constitutionally conservative Congress in November of 2012. Only then will these two federal branches of government be in a position to come together for the express purpose of not only discarding ObamaCare, but also delivering a stinging rebuke to the United States Supreme Court.

John W. Stevens

Acknowledgments

The following people encouraged me in the writing of this book: Rita Stevens, Christa Stevens, Faith Riley, Tim Riley, Bethany Stevens, Carol Thurman, John Temple Stevens, Christian D. Stevens, Gwen Wright, Tianta Stevens, Michael Medved, Lori Borgman, Bobbi Korte, David Gillotti, and Suzanne Donovan-Marlowe.

Thank you for contributing your encouragement, feedback, memories, anecdotes, photos, and research.

Table of Contents

Introduction

The Merriam-Webster Dictionary defines the word **sissy** as "a timid or cowardly person." The following two humorous anecdotes aptly illustrate the definition and its antithesis most effectively:

Anecdote #1

QUESTION: ARE YOU A DEMOCRAT, REPUBLICAN, OR SOUTHERNER?

Here is a situation that may help you decide. Consider the following scenario:

You are walking down a deserted street with your wife and two small children. You are carrying a Kimber 1911 caliber .45 ACP, and you are an expert shot. Suddenly, an Islamic terrorist with a huge knife comes around the corner, locks eyes with you, screams obscenities, praises Allah, raises the knife, and charges at you. You have mere seconds before he reaches you and your family. What do you do?

Democrat's answering process:

"Well, that's not enough information to answer the question!
Does the man look poor or oppressed?
Have I ever done anything to him that would inspire him to attack?
Could we run away?
What does my wife think?
What do the kids think?
Could I possibly swing the gun like a club and knock the knife out of his hand?
What does the law say about this situation?
Does the pistol have appropriate safety built into it?
Why am I carrying a loaded gun anyway, and what kind of message does this send to society and to my children?
Is it possible he'd be happy with just killing me?
Does he definitely want to kill me, or would he be content just to wound me?
If I were to grab his knees and hold on, could my family get away while he was stabbing me?
Should I call 9-1-1?
Why is this street so deserted? We need to raise taxes, have paint and weed day, and make this a happier, healthier street that would discourage such behavior.
This is all so confusing! I need to debate this with some friends for a few days and try to come to a consensus."

Republican's answering process:

BANG!

Southerner's answering process:

BANG! BANG! BANG! BANG! BANG! BANG!

Click...Click.

BANG! BANG! BANG! BANG! BANG! BANG!

Click.

Daughter: "Nice grouping, Daddy! Were those the Federal Hydra Shok Personal Defense 165 — grain JHPs or the Winchester Personal Protection 230 — grain SXTs?"

Son: "Can I shoot the next one?"

Wife: "You are NOT taking him to the taxidermist!"

— Author Unknown

Anecdote #2

GOD IS BUSY

A United States Marine was attending some college courses between assignments. He had completed missions in Iraq and Afghanistan. One of the courses had a professor who was an avowed atheist and a member of the ACLU. One day the professor shocked the class when he came in. He looked to the ceiling and flatly stated, "God if you are real, then I want you to knock me off this platform. I'll give you exactly fifteen minutes." The lecture room fell silent. You could hear a pin drop. Ten minutes went by and the professor proclaimed, "Here I am, God; I'm still waiting."

It got down to the last couple of minutes when the Marine got out of his chair, went up to the professor, and cold-cocked him—knocking him off the platform. The professor was out cold. The Marine went back to his seat and sat there silently.

The other students, shocked and stunned, sat there looking on in silence. The professor eventually came to. Noticeably shaken, he looked at the Marine and asked, "What in the world is the matter with you? Why did you do that?" The Marine calmly replied, "God was too busy today protecting American soldiers who are protecting your right to say stupid stuff and act like an idiot. So He sent me."

The classroom erupted in cheers!

— Author Unknown

The author of this book, *The Sissification of America: A Fifty-Year Decline in American Exceptionalism*, is currently a conservative public school teacher in Southern California, instructing early American history to a rambunctious—yet inquisitive—species of eighth-grade students. I am also the assistant choral director at a local high school in my community. It is certainly not the purpose of this book to belittle the majority of hard-working and patriotic Americans. The purpose of this book is to painstakingly reveal to the American people, through an examination and comparison of our country's vibrant history up through our contemporary era, how a number of America's citizens, its federal government, and some of its various political, public, and private institutions have gradually led our nation down a precipitous fifty-year decline in the influence of virtues that once made America truly exceptional. What are these virtues? They are unique American virtues consisting of the following: a thriving work ethic, patriotism, honesty, self-determination, rugged individualism, a spirit of independence, capitalism, competition, education that is second to none, limited government, Godliness, and a Judeo-Christian rectitude of impeccable character. These virtues are still present in America today, but to a much lesser degree when compared to the years between 1620 and 1961.

So what precisely has occurred in America during the last fifty years that has significantly diminished our country's unique virtues of exceptionalism and their influence not only upon our own culture and society, but also upon our foreign friends and foes? The seven chapters of this book will answer this question. First, I will present to the American people the following credentials:

I am a veteran public school teacher with more than twenty-five years of practical teaching experience in the classroom. I possess a professional bachelor of music degree as well as a master's degree in education administration from the University of Redlands in Southern California. I also hold a specialized certificate in GATE (Gifted and Talented Education) instruction from the University of California-Riverside. I am a mentor teacher and have been presented with various awards over the years, such as GATE Teacher of the Year, a Redlands Unified School District School Board Commendation, a recognition from the Redlands Beaver Medical Clinic for outstanding teaching in the Redlands Unified School District, and a letter of commendation for my teaching accomplishments from a United States Senator, Barbara Boxer of California. In addition, many of my classroom living-history programs have garnered recognition and have been featured in various local newspapers over several decades. I have delivered professional presentations at a number of educational forums and universities throughout the state of California, such as lectures on the implementation of exemplary elementary and middle school pedagogical techniques at CAG (California Association of the Gifted) conventions as well as various schools of education, including the University of Redlands, California State University–San Bernardino, and the University of

California–Riverside. I have also been invited to speak before local public forums such as the Rotary Club, the Civil War Roundtable, and the California Republican Assembly. As a former GATE Site Coordinator at Clement Middle School in Redlands, California, I was instrumental in developing and administering a GATE program that served as an exemplary demonstration model for the state of California, through which I hosted visits from administrators and instructors from various school districts as well as a visit from the California state director of GATE instruction, La Donna Heine. While visiting Clement Middle School during a school wide PQR (program quality review), Mrs. Heine commended me for my leadership in making that school a demonstration site for gifted and talented education programs at the middle school level.

Such credentials, experience, and educational leadership serve as a fitting platform from which to address the issues raised in this book. As both a public school teacher and author, I have deliberately chosen to include a variety of very entertaining anecdotes within this narrative because they are not only engaging stories that people enjoy reading—whether they be fact or fiction—but they also put a human face on the controversial topics being presented. To be sure, I will not in any way present information that is politically correct because if I were to do so, I would be a willing accomplice to the very premise that imbues the title of my own book. I am known by my family, friends, colleagues, and students to be a most outspoken and feisty Irishman, and rarely do I hold anything back with regard to my conservative political views. Nevertheless, my history students continually get a big kick out of me every school year, and in the process, they learn a great deal about their country's history and the legacy our Founding Fathers left us, while also managing to have tremendous fun in class.

In 1916 an American Presbyterian minister, the Rev. William J. H. Boetcker, published a leaflet that listed his "Ten Cannots," which are a reflection of a number of American virtues that are highlighted in this introduction. Remarkably, his "Ten Cannots" are just as applicable today as they were during the early part of the twentieth century. Consider the following:

THE TEN CANNOTS

1. You cannot bring about prosperity by discouraging others.
2. You cannot help small men by tearing down big men.
3. You cannot strengthen the weak by weakening the strong.
4. You cannot lift the wage earner by pulling down the wage payer.
5. You cannot help the poor man by destroying the rich.
6. You cannot keep out of trouble by spending more than your income.
7. You cannot further the brotherhood of man by inciting class hatred.
8. You cannot establish security on borrowed money.
9. You cannot build character and courage by taking away man's initiative and independence.
10. You cannot help men permanently by doing for them what they could and should do for themselves.[1]

Well, my fellow Americans, you cannot help but occasionally reflect upon the words of Rev. Boetcker's "Ten Cannots" as you read the following chapters of *The Sissification of America: A Fifty-Year Decline in American Exceptionalism.*

John W. Stevens

THE NEW ENGLAND WAY

*I have but one lamp by which my feet are guided, and
that is the lamp of experience. I know of no way of judg-
ing the future but by the past.*

— Patrick Henry

Picture yourself in the following vicarious situation: You are secretly conducting church with family and friends in the privacy of
your own home in England, knowing full well that you are breaking
the law. The king's horsemen unexpectedly break open the door,
arrest everyone present, and proceed to cart you, your family, and
your friends off to prison—clapped in irons. After being released
from prison, a few of your family members and friends convince
you to join them as they decide to take a risk and permanently head
across the treacherous North Atlantic on a three–thousand-mile
journey to the New World, a journey fraught with danger. Family members pack what meager belongings they are permitted to
bring aboard a small, seaworthy vessel in order to embark upon
the venture together with the fellowship of other English Pilgrims.

Your family tearfully waves a final gesture of goodbye to relatives and friends who are standing on the dock as the ship slowly begins to leave the port of Plymouth, England. Gradually the shores of your beloved homeland disappear into the horizon, and you begin to question as to whether or not you have made a wise decision. Many Pilgrims have heard rumors that the Jamestown settlement in Virginia has not been very successful and that the casualty rates of your fellow countrymen have been more than fifty percent. You come to the swift realization that all emigrants on board the *Mayflower* will be forced to cope with the following likely scenario in Virginia: life threatening diseases, possible starvation, and imminent attacks from hostile Indian tribes. In all likelihood, the odds are that you will only have a fifty-percent chance of survival in the New World. And if that weren't sufficiently daunting, loneliness will assuredly take its toll on everyone's emotions because some of your family members and close friends have chosen to remain behind in the relative safety, comfort, and familiarity of England.

While embarking upon this perilous journey to the New World, the captain and crew of the ship see fit to confine all passengers, for the majority of the time, to the stuffy and cramped quarters below deck where it is dark and physically uncomfortable. The captain and his officers simply do not want you or the other passengers underfoot as the *Mayflower* is being sailed. During fierce storms, all Pilgrims are vomiting below deck as the ship violently thrusts everyone to-and-fro, and no one is permitted to wander up on deck for fresh air or to take care of personal necessities. One has no alternative but to wear soiled, smelly clothing stained with vomit and human waste because nobody has any fresh and clean clothing to change into, at least for the time being. You and your fellow passengers are seasick, thirsty, smelly, and filthy beyond all comprehension, and to add insult to injury, the captain and sailors aloft taunt, curse, ridicule, and hold all of the Pilgrims below deck in absolute contempt because they are offended by the sounds of prayer and psalm singing. The sailors refer to the Pilgrims as "glib-gabbety puke stockings," while another "Salt" on the *Mayflower* smugly remarks that he wants to "throw half of the Pilgrims into the sea."[1]

During a horrific turn of events, the main beam of the ship breaks in the tempest of a fierce storm! The Pilgrims are frightened beyond belief as all hands are about ready to perish and go down with the ship in the middle of the North Atlantic with absolutely no hope of rescue. All of the terrified saints are fervently praying for God's everlasting mercy and favor while even the most arduous and pigheaded sailors begrudgingly acknowledge that in all likelihood, they are about to meet their Maker. Fortunately, there are a number of skilled Pilgrim artisans aboard who think quickly on their feet and assist the ship's sailors with the repair of the main beam just in time by utilizing a great iron screw they had brought from home. They use it to help keep the beam in place, saving both the ship and all hands on board. The tempest, however, does produce a much-appreciated positive result. With newfound respect and appreciation finally being displayed toward the passengers by the captain and the ship's crew, it is of no small significance that the sailors do an about-face and wisely choose not to taunt and ridicule you and the Pilgrims any further on the remainder of the voyage to the New World.

After a long and arduous sail across the North Atlantic, and with a huge sigh of relief, the English emigrants finally make it to America, hoping to see their fellow countrymen greeting everyone on board the ship from the shores of Virginia. But the Pilgrims are frustrated to discover that the ship is off course, and the *Mayflower* must anchor off the virgin shores of Massachusetts rather than the shores of Virginia during November of 1620.

Thus were the real adventures of the Pilgrims as they departed England aboard the *Mayflower* and headed for America in the early seventeenth century. The preceding account of the Pilgrims' adventures is not at all reminiscent of the typical, romanticized version we often ascribe to that famous story of so long ago.

The Pilgrims and Puritans of Colonial America in the 1600s were anything but wimps or sissies. As a matter of fact, they were paragons of early British-American risk-takers who were willing to sacrifice virtually everything in order to establish a new home and way of life in Massachusetts, free from the tyranny of their king back in England. These courageous ancestors of ours settled the shores of what would become New England in order to escape religious persecution in the old country. Thousands of Puritans immigrated to Massachusetts as a result of the Great Migration from England because they were granted a royal charter to establish the Massachusetts Bay Company, and in 1630 the Puritans established the city of Boston, which would become one of New England's most prosperous communities. The prominent Puritan leader, John Winthrop, became the Massachusetts Bay Company's first governor, and it was Winthrop who would proclaim the following immortal words during the founding of the Commonwealth of Massachusetts:

> So shall we keep the unity of the spirit, in the bond of peace....Ten of us will be able to resist a thousand of our enemies....For we must consider that we shall be as a City upon a Hill, the eyes of all people are on us. [2]

This is certainly not a timid utterance of the will-o'-the-wisp, now is it? What precisely was John Winthrop proclaiming? Why would his profound words be quoted in various speeches addressed to the people of our nation hundreds of years later by two famous American presidents of the twentieth century? These are questions worth pondering and answering for a variety of important reasons.

The Puritans adamantly believed God was calling them to establish a new commonwealth in America that would be a scintillating example of success for the world to behold. John Winthrop's words were an emphatic, prophetic statement that would hold fast to this very day. Two popular presidents of the twentieth century, John F. Kennedy and Ronald Reagan, were inspired by John Winthrop's words as they both guided their administrations with the challenge and promise of his words. Kennedy and Reagan certainly were not ignorant of American history. In fact, they were acutely cognizant of the important influence American history would have on future generations, including their own. These two remarkable presidents were not the least bit reticent to publicly acknowledge the historical and positive legacy the Puritans bestowed upon this nation, to acknowledge the strong foundation they laid during the process, and to point the way for future generations as to how the Puritan "New England Way" could effectively guide elected leaders of contemporary America. For example, when President-elect John F. Kennedy stood before the political leaders of Massachusetts and delivered his "Address to the General Court of the Commonwealth of Massachusetts" on January 9, 1961, he said:

> Our governments, in every branch...must be as a city upon a hill, constructed and inhabited by men aware of their great trust and their great responsibilities.[3]

What a poignant statement made only a few decades ago by a popular American political figure. We need to acknowledge the fact that Kennedy was referencing a very significant moment in American history for the purpose of reminding the nation of the **puritanical** standards our leaders need to set and maintain, both at the state and federal levels. He was using Winthrop and our Puritan ancestors as examples for all of us to emulate. Kennedy was emphasizing the importance of our elected officials keeping the public trust and taking their civic responsibilities seriously while discharging their duties with the utmost integrity. If it was important and good enough for President Kennedy, it should be equally important and good enough for our current politicians of both political parties at all levels.

In Ronald Reagan's farewell speech to the nation in 1989, he also alluded to John Winthrop's words when he said,

> I've spoken of the shining city all of my political life, but I don't know if I ever quite communicated what I saw when I said it. But in my mind it was a tall, proud city built on rocks stronger than oceans, wind-swept, God-blessed, and teeming with people of all kinds living in harmony and peace, a city with free ports that hummed with commerce and creativity, and if there had to be city walls, the walls had doors and the doors were open to anyone with the will and the heart to get here. That's how I saw it and see it still.[4]

Reagan's words and sentiments really go directly to the heart and soul of America's core values and eternal optimism, don't they? It is important to call everyone's attention to these important points because many Americans, especially conservatives, are so weary of the current flood of cynics, political nay-sayers, and pundits who poke fun at candidates running for political office who occasionally choose to point out to the American people that there are elements of our past worth repeating and emulating. We have all heard these cynics, especially of the progressive persuasion, acrimoniously accusing their political opponents of desiring to build bridges to the past rather than the future, as if somehow the important lessons of our nation's past should be relegated to the ash heap of history. Contemporary progressive nay-sayers and elitists would have us all believe that the best of what our nation's past has to offer us no longer bears any meaningful significance to today's more enlightened and progressive society. Nothing could be further from the truth. Americans can take considerable comfort in the fact that both John F. Kennedy and Ronald Reagan did not ascribe to this kind of pap and crap. On the contrary, they brilliantly illustrated the necessity of linking the bridge of our past directly to the bridge of our future in order to keep our nation focused on what is truly important. The so-called "change we can believe in" current political leaders promote has nothing in common with the "change" the majority of the American people yearn for, which is, in reality, nothing but a sincere desire to return to the time-honored values of integrity, honesty, ingenuity, cooperation, bravery, and hard work once emulated by many of our ancestors in both public and private life. One of our Founding Fathers, Thomas Jefferson, once enjoined,

Honesty is the first chapter of the book of wisdom.

In my capacity as a history teacher, I admonish my eighth-grade history students to be vigilant with regard to learning life's harsh lessons from both the positive and some of the negative aspects of our nation's past. However, we must all sing our nation's praises and celebrate its good fortune, and we must learn to take our floggings from the occasional errors of our ways so that we may continually trim our sails and bravely confront the winds of uncertainty as we carry on with our proud ship of state—hoping that what is laudable about our past will ultimately guide and help keep us on a straight and proper course. That is what the strong of heart of all generations are supposed to do rather than give in to what is politically easy or expedient for the moment like a bunch of wimps who vacillate back and forth like blades of grass in a stiff wind. Both John F. Kennedy and Ronald Reagan were anything but examples of such dubious vacillating blades of grass. They guided our proud ship of state with a strong command of American history, with the courage of their convictions, and with decisive leadership skills and executive experience the American people could be most proud of.

This author is going to be quite frank, if not actually brutal here. In my personal opinion, one example of a wind-driven vacillating blade of grass is our current president, Barack Obama. He certainly ought not to be flogging our nation in public before world leaders on his international apology tours. President Obama's apologies to the world on behalf of all Americans for what he considers to be our nation's indiscretions or lack of humility that we have supposedly shown since 9/11 may sit well with smug European leaders and South American dictators, but it certainly does not sit well with me and many other proud Americans. How could it possibly be in America's best interest for President Obama to go cap-in-hand before various international leaders, dictators, and royal kingdoms, seeking their favor and forgiveness for what he deems to be our nation's shortcomings or for the previous policies and actions of President George W. Bush and his administration? Besides, the rest of the world is hardly in any position to judge or criticize America for acting in her own best interest and safety post-9/11, and we certainly do not need our current president making politically correct statements as he travels about the globe that may, in any way, give our astute enemies the remote impression that an inexperienced scaredy-cat is in charge of the White House. On the other hand, John F. Kennedy and Ronald Reagan were both strong of heart examples to us all. They both exemplified John Winthrop and his "City upon a Hill," and they were outstanding leaders who inspired and united the majority of the American people.

I can clearly recall a visit President John F. Kennedy once made to my hometown of Great Falls, Montana, in 1963, when I was a very young lad. I was with my best friend and his dad at the time, waiting for the president's motorcade to pass by our street, as all of the citizens were informed ahead of time as to the exact route Kennedy would take through town. As the president's convertible (the very one Kennedy would tragically be assassinated in a couple of months later in Dallas, Texas) began to slowly turn our direction off of Tenth Avenue South, my friend's dad quickly placed me on top of his shoulders. The assembled crowd was waving and loudly cheering the president as his motorcade slowly passed by, and I was truly blessed as President Kennedy pivoted to his right while sitting in his convertible, looked up and made direct eye contact with me for a brief moment. He beamed a big smile and winked at me as he waved to all of us while slowly heading north through town. From that moment on, even as a young child, I had a feeling of great pride in a national leader I instinctively knew I could trust. It is an image I can clearly visualize to this very day even though I am now in my late-fifties.

As an adult, I can now appreciate just how correct my initial feelings and instincts were toward Kennedy when I was a young child. After all, you might want to recall the fear we experienced as a nation during the Cuban Missile Crisis of 1962. President Kennedy stood up to Russia's despot, Nikita Khrushchev, as our two nations stared each other down and were at the brink of thermonuclear war. Kennedy did not bat an eye, nor did he shirk a good old-fashioned Irish fight while confronting the Soviet leader despite the immense pressure our president was under as he had to deal with the ominous threat of a possible nuclear attack upon our nation. As a matter of fact, Kennedy threatened Russia with full nuclear retaliation and total annihilation if it were to attack America. As fate would dictate, it was Khrushchev who acquiesced to the demands of President Kennedy when he eventually backed down from the confrontation and removed all of Russia's nuclear missiles from Cuba! President Kennedy announced to the nation that he could rely on America's "Ace in The Hole" if necessary. My father once told me when I was a young teenager that Kennedy was referring to our nuclear Minuteman missile defense forces of Malmstrom Air Force Base, which is headquartered in Great Falls, Montana.

The following excerpts are from a speech delivered by President Kennedy when he visited Great Falls on September 26, 1963. He delivered the speech at Great Falls High School Memorial Stadium, and the following excerpts were retrieved from the American Presidency Project on the Internet. As you read these excerpts, reflect upon Kennedy's remarks to the people of Great Falls and compare them to the current sentiments and apologies being made by President Obama as he travels about the world. The comparisons are most astounding to say the least.

Montana is a long way from Washington, and it is a long way from the Soviet Union, and it is 10,000 miles from Laos. But this particular State, because it has, among other reasons, concentrated within its borders some of the most powerful nuclear missile systems in the world, must be conscious of every danger and must be conscious of how close Montana lives to the firing line which divides the Communist world. We are many thousands of miles from the Soviet Union, but this State, in a very real sense, is only 30 minutes away.

The object of our policy, therefore, must be to protect the United States, to make sure that those over 100 Minuteman missiles which ring this city and this State remain where they are, and that is the object of the foreign policy of the United States under this administration, under the previous administration, and under that of President Truman. One central theme has run through the foreign policy of the United States, and that is, in a dangerous and changing world it is essential that the 180 million people of the United States throw their weight into the balance in every struggle, in every country on the side of freedom. And so in the last years we have been intimately involved with affairs of countries of which we never heard 20 years ago, but which now affect the balance of power in the world and, therefore, the security of the United States and, therefore, the chances of war and peace.

I know that there are many of you who sit here and wonder what it is that causes the United States to go so far away, that causes you to wonder why so many of your sons should be stationed so far away from our own territory, who wonder why it is since 1945 that the United States has assisted so many countries. You must wonder when it is all going to end and when we can come back home. Well, it isn't going to end, and this generation of Americans has to make up its mind for our security and for our peace, because what happens in Europe or Latin America or Africa or Asia directly affects the security of the people who live in this city, and particularly those who are coming after.

I make no apologies (emphasis mine) for the effort that we make to assist these other countries to maintain their freedom, because I know full well that every time a country, regardless of how far away it may be from our own borders—every time that country passes behind the Iron Curtain the security of the United States is thereby endangered. So all those who suggest we withdraw, all those who suggest we should no longer ship our surplus food abroad or assist other countries, I could not disagree with them more. This country is stronger now than it has ever been. Our chances for peace are stronger than they have been in years....

So I urge this generation of Americans, who are the fathers and mothers of 350 million Americans who will live in this country in the year 2000, and I want those Americans who live here in 2000 to feel that those of us who had positions of responsibility in the sixties did our part, and those of us who inherited it from Franklin Roosevelt and Theodore Roosevelt will have something to pass on to those who come, and our children, many years from now....

This is the record which this country has written since 1945, and it is upon this great record that I believe we now must build. This sun and this sky which shines over Montana can be, I believe, the kind of inspiration to us all to recognize what a great single country we have, 50 separate States, but one people, living here in the United States, building this country and maintaining the watch around the globe.

This is the opportunity before us as well as the responsibility. Thank you. [5]

Many Americans wish we currently had a man or woman in Washington, DC, exhibiting this kind of bold leadership and forthright character because we would enthusiastically embrace him or her in a heartbeat. Given what Kennedy addressed to the people of Great Falls in 1963 shortly before his tragic assassination, I think it is safe to opine that he would probably have supported President Bush's military intervention in Iraq during his presidency. On the other hand, would Kennedy have approved of President Obama's cap-in-hand approach with today's world leaders, offering apologies on America's behalf? You judge for yourself.

The following excerpts are from John F. Kennedy's 1946 Independence Day oration, "Some Elements of the American Character," presented in Boston, Massachusetts, while he was a candidate for Congress. They eloquently speak volumes in describing the American character the Puritans established with their "City upon a Hill." These remarkable excerpts of Kennedy's speech should remind current politicians, especially those who are progressive, as well as other like-minded liberal candidates who aspire to run for public office under the advice of their Machiavellian handlers, pundits, and other nay-sayers, that if we were to pay heed to the current cynicism they extol and to follow their standards of behavior and duplicitous vision of today, John F. Kennedy himself would not be fit to meet their own criteria of what a modern candidate should be or advocate on behalf of the American people. Enjoy reading these excellent excerpts of Kennedy's speech delivered just after World War II.

A nation's character, like that of an individual, is elusive. It is produced partly by things we have done and partly by what has been done to us. It is the result of physical factors, intellectual factors, spiritual factors. It is well for us to consider our American character, for in peace, as in war, we will survive or fail according to its measure.

...The informing spirit of the American character has always been a deep religious sense. Throughout the years, down to the present, a devotion to fundamental religious principles has characterized American thought and action. Our government was founded on the essential religious idea of integrity of the individual. It was this religious sense which inspired the authors of the Declaration of Independence: "We hold these truths to be self-evident: that all men are created equal; that they are endowed by their Creator with certain inalienable rights." Our earliest legislation was inspired by this deep religious sense: "Congress shall make no law prohibiting the free exercise of religion." Our first leader, Washington, was inspired by this deep religious sense: "Of all of the dispositions and habits which lead to political prosperity, religion and morality are indispensable supports."... Inspired by a deeply religious sense, this country, which has ever been devoted to the dignity of man, which has ever fostered the growth of the human spirit, has always met and hurled back the challenge of those deathly philosophies of hate and despair. We have defeated them in the past; we will always defeat them...

Another element in the American character is the idealism of our native people-stemming from the strong religious beliefs of the first colonists, developed as they worked the land... In recent years, the existence of this element in the American character has been challenged by those who seek to give an economic interpretation to American history. **They seek to destroy our faith in our past so that they may guide our future.** (emphasis mine) These cynics are wrong, for, while there may be some truth in their interpretation, it does remain a fact, and a most important one, that the motivating force of the American people has been their belief that they have always stood at the barricades by the side of God....It is now in the postwar world that this idealism—this devotion to principle—this belief in the natural law—this deep religious conviction that this is truly God's country and we are truly God's people—will meet its greatest trial....But, if we remain faithful to the American tradition, our idealism will be a steadfast thing, a constant flame, a torch held aloft for the guidance of other nations....

...From the birth of the nation to the present day, from the Heights of Dorchester to the broad meadows of Virginia, from Bunker Hill to the batteries of Saratoga, from Bergen's Neck, where Wayne and Maylan's troops achieved such martial wonders, to Yorktown, where Britain's troops surrendered, Americans have heroically embraced the soldier's alternative of victory or the grave....Wherever freedom has been in danger, Americans with a deep sense of patriotism have ever been willing to stand at Armageddon and strike a blow for liberty and the Lord....

...The right of the individual against the state has ever been one of our most cherished political principles. The American constitution has set down for all men to see the essentially Christian and American principle, that there are certain rights held by every man which no government and no majority, however powerful, can deny. Conceived in Grecian thought, strengthened by Christian morality and stamped indelibly into American political philosophy, the right of the individual against the state is the keystone of our constitution. Each man is free.

He is free in thought.

He is free in expression.

He is free in worship. (emphasis mine)

To us, who have been reared in the American tradition, these rights have become part of our very being....They were dearly won for us only a few short centuries ago and they were dearly preserved for us in the days just past. And there are large sections of the world today where these rights are denied as a matter of philosophy and as a matter of government....Eternal vigilance is the price of liberty. It was the price yesterday. It is the price today, and it will ever be the price. The characteristics of the American people have ever been a deep sense of religion, a deep sense of idealism, a deep sense of patriotism and a deep sense of individualism....May God grant that, at some distant date, on this day, and on this platform, the orator may be able to say that these are still the great qualities of the American character and that they have prevailed. [6]

Honest to God, if John F. Kennedy were still alive today, we would more than likely observe him speaking at various Tea Party rallies standing shoulder-to-shoulder with Glenn Beck on the steps of the Lincoln Memorial! If one were to hand an unsigned copy of this inspiring speech to current politicians and leaders of the Democratic Party, both at the state and national levels, would they even recognize precisely who it was that once delivered this vibrant oratory? Would they acknowledge that it was delivered by a prominent leader of their own party? Would they currently agree with it or would they regard the sentiments of the orator as being radically religious and extreme, thus exhibiting character attributes that are totally out-of-step with the American people while living hopelessly in the past rather than being a necessary political agent of "change"? Would Democrats erroneously presume it to be a speech being delivered by some conservative, radical, right-wing Republican politician or extremist Tea Party candidate who is supposedly attempting to establish a Christian theocracy in America and, therefore, ought to be publicly mocked and made an example of derision for the rest of the nation as has repeatedly occurred with conservative politicians such as Sarah Palin? One can only speculate, however, as this author reflects upon Kennedy's poignant speech delivered in 1946 as well as the tough-love speech he delivered in Great Falls in 1963, the issues he raised are just as pertinent to what is transpiring in America today as they were in Kennedy's day right after World War II, as well as during his own presidential administration.

There are some very important lessons Americans had better absorb from all of this, such as how quickly we tend to forget or ignore the important precepts of American history, even recent history, and the puritanical ideals and virtues great leaders such as John F. Kennedy and Ronald Reagan modeled for us while serving in public office. Indeed, as we currently observe the endless parade of secular-progressive politicians and their followers marching down mainstream American towns coast-to-coast and tooting their own horns, it is quite a tough and bitter pill for many of us conservative Americans to swallow while we observe how a significant number of our fellow citizens blithely tolerate the boorish behavior of current progressive politicians who foolishly mock American history rather than holding these offensive chumps' feet to the fire for their cagey attitudes and behavior! Well, as a nation, we continue to do so at our own risk and peril.

In 1980, Ronald Reagan was elected the fortieth president of the United States in an Electoral College landslide. You might recall that Iran had once held fifty-one Americans hostage during the Jimmy Carter administration of the late 1970s. Being the inept, weak leader that he was, President Carter was not considered a serious threat to Iran by the Iranian leaders, and they took their sweet time in returning American citizens to our custody—that is, until President Reagan took control of the helm. The Iranian Ayatollahs clearly understood that with regard to Reagan, they were dealing with an entirely different kind of president, and they clearly understood that Reagan would deal with them very swiftly and quite forcefully if they were to continue to tarry in returning our hostages to us, which, of course, they didn't once they were compelled to answer to this tough American Irishman. There was truly a restored sense of national pride with our new president, and we began to have confidence once again in ourselves as a nation that was sorely lacking during the Jimmy Carter administration.

Once again, too many Americans have currently forsaken another important lesson of the past: weakness and indecisiveness are by no means the manner with which to confront any foe. On the contrary, strength and fortitude are the primary means with which to effectively confront America's enemies. For example, if President Obama continues to proceed down a primrose wussy path while approaching the ominous nuclear threat Iran poses to our ally, Israel, much in the same manner as President Carter once approached the Iranian hostage crisis during his administration, it may be too late for another type of Ronald Reagan to step in and thwart the impending war that will certainly erupt in the Middle East should Iran be permitted to develop nuclear weapons and proceed to carry out its threat to use such weapons of mass destruction against the state of Israel. This is just one of many reasons why President Barack Obama needs to be fired by the American people in 2012, replicating what Americans did with Jimmy Carter in 1980.

The presidential administrations of Kennedy and Reagan both had flaws, such as Kennedy's Bay of Pigs fiasco and Reagan's Iran-Contra affair, yet both of these presidents decisively served the American people well despite their flaws, and they certainly led the nation with the courage of their convictions. While these two great presidents never claimed to be infallible, they nevertheless commanded the respect of most Americans as well as foreign friends and foes alike. What is particularly admirable about both Kennedy and Reagan is the fact that they instilled in the American people the necessity of occasionally reflecting upon our nation's history whereby we might wisely glean from it the very best of what it has to offer us so that America may continue to navigate the waters of rugged individualism, safety, and prosperity. Using "The New England Way" as a guide, Reagan and Kennedy proved to the American people that it was not necessary to do the following: politically reinvent the wheel; reject American capitalism; mock the virtues of our country's past; coddle and brownnose the various Muslim nations and their leaders; throw our trusted and reliable friend, Israel, under the bus; undermine our Judeo-Christian religious foundation and principles; or circumvent our Constitution while governing our great nation. In addition, both Kennedy and Reagan—presidents of opposing political parties—did not seek to emulate Western-style European socialism and pacifism in order to successfully accomplish their noble tasks as leaders of the United States.

Succinctly put, the majority of the American people have simply had enough, and that is precisely why the Tea Party movement is exhibiting early signs of tremendous success with regard to untethering this nation from the oppressive pole of left-wing radicalism which is tearing this nation apart under the disingenuous and corrupt leadership of the Obama administration. The historic midterm elections of 2010 bear this out, though it definitely will take a number of hard-fought election cycles to accomplish this Herculean feat. But it is definitely going to occur step-by-step, one election at a time! The 2010 election cycle is just the first conservative salvo in a long series of political battles between conservatives and progressives. Conservatives need to fight to the bitter end in order to restore common sense to our nation as well as return us to the kind of constitutional republic envisioned by our Founding Fathers!

Every year, I tell my eighth-grade students that we should all be proud of our American past, and I remind them of the old axiom coined by a Spanish-American pragmatic philosopher, George Santayana, that declares, "Those who cannot remember the past are condemned to repeat it." The American people desire to reside in a country where we are proud of who we are while remaining resilient in times of adversity. We live in the greatest country on earth, and we are not perfect by any means, but perhaps it is about time for all of the American people to reacquaint themselves with the vision both Kennedy and Reagan had for this nation. In the process, we would be reminded of the fact that John Winthrop and the Puritans miraculously accomplished precisely what they set out to do. They established a firm foundation upon which our great nation would rise throughout the centuries, and with this there can be no doubt or argument. However, millions of Americans do have some serious doubts and arguments with regard to the credibility, honesty, tenacity, and vision of some of our current batch of leaders and politicians. Politicians of both major political parties would be wise to remember the following impenetrable truth once spoken by President Abraham Lincoln:

> If once you forfeit the confidence of your fellow citizens,
> you can never regain their respect and esteem.

Unfortunately, a number of our current elected officials are not paying heed to Lincoln's admonition, much less the words of the great Puritan, John Winthrop, as recalled by Kennedy and Reagan. This is another valuable lesson we can garner from the 2010 midterm elections. Some of our elected representatives are letting the American people down big time as we are compelled to listen to and put up with their political sophistry while they whine and act like a bunch of sissies. The current emergence of the Tea Party movement and the liberals' arrogant and outrageous reaction to this grassroots movement as well as their unending castigation of its members and its message is proof positive of this. This is all part of the Democratic Party's playbook together with the complicity of its mainstream media minions! From 2008 to the elections of 2010, the Democrats couldn't really defend or justify their outrageous behavior and policies during their one-party rule as well as their obvious falling out of favor with the majority of the American people; therefore, their typical plan of attack was to marginalize Tea Party activists and somehow attempt to portray them as some type of frightening bogeyman who was about to pounce upon innocent and unsuspecting Americans. With their rhetoric, liberals were grasping at straws and hoping we would all be intimidated into falling for their duplicity. For example, former Speaker of the House Nancy Pelosi once referred to Tea Party members as "astroturf" and tried to marginalize the movement's message and influence with such offensive comments, but the Tea Party movement had the last laugh in 2010!

Here is another sobering observation concerning the seismic political shift towards common-sense conservatism that occurred during the 2010 elections. The American people rejected outright corruption that included closed-door meetings as well as the double-dealing shenanigans occurring between members of the 111th Congress and the Obama-Reid-Pelosi political machine. Such boorish behavior and actions were reminiscent of "Boss" Tweed and Tammany Hall of New York City during the mid to late 1800s. The insolent manner in which ObamaCare was crafted and passed by Congress is a validation of this fact. All of this corruption and abuse of the public trust by elected officials was wearing quite thin on the nerves of average Americans, and this is certainly one rickety old corrupt bridge to the past many of us didn't bemoan the loss of as we observed it going down in flames of glory in November of 2010. And conservatives are certainly going to remind the American people of this come Hell or high water throughout future election cycles.

Having said that, however, the following should serve as a stern warning and wake-up call to the Republican Party which has just regained control of the House of Representatives as well as greater numbers and clout in the US Senate: Americans have given Republicans another chance even though the decadent political machines are alive and well in America. We continually read about scandals occurring throughout the country with members of both political parties that would be grist for the daytime television drama mills. Wasteful, careless spending by Congress and the president is at an all-time high, to the mind-staggering sum of trillions of dollars, with absolutely no regard being afforded to the average American who sacrifices several months of his salary each year to feed these bloated piglets at the trough. The way many of us currently view things, it is as if our federal government and many of our state governors and legislatures hold the American people in absolute contempt while they smugly play us like finely tuned fiddles for the fools we sometimes are. After all, the American people in general must also be held accountable for a great deal of the mess we are currently in as we continually elect and reelect people who have absolutely no common sense and are simply out of touch with the needs and concerns of the majority of hard-working Americans.

Oh, to be sure, some politicians pay us lip service at election time only because they need us to get elected to office, shamefully promising the American people everything under the sun while buying our votes, knowing full well that these promises can never be paid for without driving the country into total bankruptcy. The trouble is, a number of Americans are often gullible and fall into the trap of some of these Johnny-Come-Latelies with their promises and political sophistry. Then the public wonders why the nation is mired in a thick black swamp of quicksand we have collectively created. Former Speaker of the House Nancy Pelosi once promised the American people Congress would drain this current swamp under her leadership, yet she and her cohorts effectively managed to broaden the dimensions of this foul swamp, and they were deservedly fired for doing so by the majority of American voters who were anything but gullible in 2010. The same can happen to Republicans in 2012, and it will happen if they do not govern in the manner with which they promised the American people during their campaigns of 2010. Our conservative mascot so fittingly applies in this case: we shall display memories like elephants!

Contemporary progressive Santa Clauses and tooth fairies should be entirely ashamed of themselves for what they have foisted on this nation between 2008 and 2010, but the humiliating reality is that they aren't. Even worse is the fact that these brazen big spenders make no apologies whatsoever for their policies. Immediately following their demise in November of 2010, Nancy Pelosi, as well as some Democrats who lost their seats in Congress, actually bragged publicly by confessing to the American public that they had absolutely no regrets for their policies and actions while serving in the 111th Congress! They just don't get it, and neither does President Obama! If there is one thing we can all be assured of, it is this: Should President Obama manage to win reelection in 2012 and is supported once again by a Democratic majority in both houses of Congress, the nation will most assuredly find itself reliving the national nightmare of the Obama-Reid-Pelosi team of 2008-2010.

The whole affair reminds me of a wonderful line in the humorous classic film, *Life With Father*, where the protagonist, Mr. Clarence Day, frustratingly remarks to himself quite loudly while pacing back-and-forth in his study after reading his New York newspaper: **"Why did God make so many dumb fools and Democrats?"** States such as California and New York are out of money, and they are billions of dollars in debt. They can no longer pay the bills, yet both states are still under the tightfisted control of progressives. In addition, the federal government is responsible for the following partial list of economic abominations over the course of the past several years: instituting TARP, attempting cap-and-trade (although this was ultimately rejected by Congress), taking over the banks, owning much of the car industry, holding more than 50 percent of Americans' home mortgages through

Fannie Mae and Freddie Mac, purveying failed stimulus bills, controlling student loans—and it is now in the process of socializing the country's health care industry. A rose by any other name is still a rose. In other words, if the above roster does not clearly illustrate the tenets of socialism, then I certainly don't know what does! As a nation, we simply do not have the means with which to pay the bills for all of this hogwash. The recent IMF bailout of Greece and Ireland in 2010 should be a stark reminder of this, yet America persists on following in the footsteps of these socialistic European utopians! Precisely who is going to come riding to the rescue of America like a proud European Knight in shining armor while mounted upon a stout white horse should we manage to collapse economically? Nobody really comes to mind! The only way this country can reverse the dangerous and suicidal course it has embarked upon is to politically replace secular-progressives currently serving in the halls of power in all of our states as well as the federal government!

Indeed, once many of these politicians of all stripes get entrenched in the inner-workings of the Beltway, they conveniently forget from whence they came. They become ensnared in the impregnable halls of bloated bureaucracies only to become arrogant lords of their own various fiefdoms. They are selfishly looking out for what is in their best interest and survival rather than what is truly in the best interest of the American people or our nation as a whole. By this time, many of our illustrious leaders view the American people as mere peasants whose sole job is to kowtow and bow before such lords who manage to remain entrenched in their fortified castles of state capitals and Washington, DC, at least until the next election cycle! No wonder the American people are fed-up with career politicians. No wonder we clamor for "change," or as I previously alluded to, a return to the virtues of our past. As such, it would be appropriate at this point to examine with greater detail the positive influence the Puritan "New England Way" once exerted upon American society. [7]

The Puritan attributes that constituted a very strong work ethic, education, Godliness, honesty, and strict discipline were prime examples of the "New England Way" that pastors would preach about from their pulpits, and these church leaders demanded absolute obedience to this covenant from their flocks.[8] These virtues would permeate American society and be passed down from generation to generation throughout the centuries. The Puritans would gather at their meeting houses not only to pray, but to establish laws for their communities and elect representatives to a lawmaking body called the General Court.[9] Such tasks appear somewhat similar to what is evident throughout modern America. We have cities with elected mayors and city councils that establish and enforce local ordinances. Our country is still known throughout the world for its American work ethic, and we value the importance of education, as evidenced by the positive results of both public and private education. The majority of Americans continue to value honesty and integrity as virtues in their daily lives as exemplified by their harmonious interaction with their fellow citizens. We are still considered to be one of the world's most devout nations of faith, although that particular virtue is undergoing serious assault today by the sinister forces of secular-progressives that are being unleashed upon our culture. There is an insidious war that is being waged upon the US Constitution with the weapons of mass destruction consisting of radical groups such as the ACLU, People For the American Way, and Americans United for Separation of Church and State, to name just a few. I will address my deep concerns with these reprehensible groups in chapter three of this book. For the time being, let us continue to examine with additional detail the various virtues of the Puritan "New England Way," such as the Puritan work ethic and its influence on both America and the world.

I read with great interest, an article that appeared in a local newspaper several years ago reporting that the former first woman finance minister of France, Christine Lagarde, and her former boss, President Nicolas Sarkozy, both desired to return France to a more capitalistic, pro-market economy as opposed to adhering to the current socialistic system that demands only a thirty-five-hour work week from its citizens. Lagarde basically told the French people that they needed to roll up their sleeves and embrace an American-style work ethic so they could create more businesses and reward hard work with more money and lower taxes.[10] Just imagine the government of France desiring to emulate anything that is American!

The Puritan work ethic that has been passed down to us from generation to generation has served America well economically. Gradually, over the passage of time, we have provided all Americans with the opportunity to succeed and profit from the labors of our blood, sweat, and tears. We even have the freedom to fail and resume our efforts to achieve success if we desire to do so. With enough hard work, education, and pure grit, any of us can achieve tremendous results if we are willing to take risks. Even those amongst us who are slovenly or, at times, down and out, still manage to live a lifestyle in America unlike the poor of third-world nations. Is it any wonder we are still a strong magnet that draws people from all over the world who strive to attend school here and attempt to latch onto a piece of the American Dream? Indeed, the Puritan Governor of Boston, John Winthrop, was proven correct with his bold, prophetic proclamation. As a nation, we continue to remain that "City upon a Hill" where all eyes are upon us. We continue to be that shining beacon of light, hope, and opportunity to the world.

The Puritans held education in high esteem. After all, they established Harvard College in Cambridge, Massachusetts, in 1636 to train and educate future ministers, and a number of our Founding Fathers were graduates of that exemplary college. Americans can take considerable pride in the fact that this institution of higher learning is still considered to be amongst the finest in the world academically. Nevertheless, Harvard's Puritan founders would be rolling over in their graves with grief and disgust if they were to actually observe the direction their university has embarked upon during the past fifty years. Over the course of time, all universities must adapt and make necessary changes in conjunction with society, but in this author's opinion, Harvard has not only strayed from its original purpose, but it has also lost its moral compass and intellectual honesty that once guided it throughout its esteemed history.

Ironically, Harvard University has succeeded in holding fast to one **negative** puritanical trait over the centuries, and that is the one that exhibits intolerance toward those outside of the fold. God forbid any true conservative be tolerated in Cambridge, Massachusetts, with the current atmosphere of political correctness being permitted to run amok, effectively eradicating any pretense of real political diversity. I am not talking about classic liberal diversity or multiculturalism, but diversity of thought and expression that offers significant balance between liberals and conservatives. If you doubt that, explore just how intolerant Harvard's disgusting policy was, for a period of time, toward our nation's armed forces with regard to the university's prohibition of the operation of any ROTC program on its campus because of the federal government's former policy of "Don't Ask, Don't Tell," which ran counter to the politically correct views of Harvard's administration, faculty, and student body. The military was compelled to pay heed to Harvard's equivalent puritanical message of "Get thee out for thou doth not belong!"[11]

Harvard and other New England Ivy League universities were rearing their ugly heads by behaving in true negative puritanical fashion while exhibiting their absolute contempt and intolerance of our military in this particular instance, just as the Puritans once banished political and religious dissenters from Old New England during the 1600s. What an abhorrent way for these universities to show gratitude and respect to the men and women who put their own lives on the line every day in order to sacrifice so much for the defense of our country so that the communities of Harvard and other fine universities can continue to enjoy the very security and benefits our nation has to offer these institutions of higher learning and all of their stakeholders. Furthermore, to my way of thinking, this shameful repudiation of our military's ROTC program on Harvard's campus should have unequivocally disqualified Elena Kagan from being given any serious consideration by our current president and the US Senate for service as an associate justice on the US Supreme Court. Elena Kagan once served as the dean of Harvard Law School, and she had a supportive role in agreeing with the university's outright hostility that was being perpetrated against our military. Kagan was seriously questioned about her views in this regard by Senator Sessions during her confirmation hearings with the Senate. Conservatives are still scratching their heads with consternation and shaking their heads in disbelief while attempting to figure this one out, especially given the fact that a number of RINO (Republican In Name Only) senators voted affirmatively with Democratic senators to confirm Kagan's appointment to the highest court in the land.

In addition, consider some of these sobering statistics. According to Greg Jackson, author of the book, *Conservative Comebacks To Liberal Lies*, a poll conducted by Luntz Research revealed that more than eighty percent of Ivy League professors who voted in 2000 voted for Al Gore while only nine percent voted for George W. Bush.[12] Now that really smacks of political diversity doesn't it? In addition, the poll also revealed that only three percent of those teachers polled affiliated themselves as Republicans! It is interesting to note that while more than seventy percent of the professors named a Democratic candidate as their pick for president, a mere eight percent named a Republican candidate as their choice to occupy America's highest office.[13] With statistics like these, one could seriously put forth the compelling argument that Harvard University, as well as the majority of the nation's other universities scattered about from coast-to-coast, are hardly bastions of diverse political thought in and out of the classrooms. This not only poses a serious threat to any significant, meaningful presence of political diversity within academe circles, but it also threatens the overall well-being of our republic as we are currently raising a generation of college students who are being brainwashed by leftist, radical professors and their political and social psycho-babble!

Perhaps it is about time conservative alumni of such institutions show some gumption by rethinking their blind loyalty to their progressive alma maters and seriously consider denying these institutions financial donations and contributions to their various endowments. While we are at it, conservatives might want to consider denying our left-leaning alma maters the blessing of enrolling our children and grandchildren in such narrow-minded institutions whose curricula often run counter to practically everything we believe in and hold dear. There are a number of conservative universities scattered about our nation that could better serve our children, teaching them a traditional, vigorous curriculum while upholding the values conservatives cherish. In the meantime, we might just do ourselves and our nation a huge favor by eradicating the ongoing fear that the vast majority of our children will one day return home to us advancing the twisted values and fallacious thinking of the likes of left-wing radicals and secular-progressive professors who are contributing to the decline of our country! One could only hope and pray!

In the spring of 2000, when one of my eighth-grade school groups and some of their parents toured Boston with me and a fellow educator and friend of mine, Shad Kirkland, we were treated to some very astute comments from our tour guide on the bus as we entered the vicinity of Harvard. He announced to all of us on the loudspeaker, "If there are any Republicans on our bus, hold onto your hats! You're in liberal country now where conservatives are definitely not welcomed!" These unsolicited, yet intriguing comments of a local Bostonian were sincerely expressed, and his observations contributed to my view that Harvard University lists sharply to the left, resembling anything but the conservative leanings and moral underpinnings of its founders—the Puritans of Old New England.

In addition to establishing Harvard College in 1636, the Puritans also saw to it that their children were literate so they would be able to read and comprehend the Bible for themselves. They established the first dame schools, which served as early prototypes of public primary education— using Puritan hornbooks with which to teach young children reading and writing. As a matter of interest, the Puritans established the first public school in America called the Boston Latin School.[14] It was established on April 23, 1635, by the town of Boston with a curriculum centered in the humanities, and the school is still in operation. The Puritan minister, Reverend John Cotton, was primarily responsible for supervising the establishment of this school. From its earliest years, Boston assigned public funds to support the school to the tune of fifty pounds for the master and his house, and thirty pounds for an usher who was the assistant teacher. Five of the fifty-six signers of the Declaration of Independence were students of the school and included the following: John Hancock, Samuel Adams, Benjamin Franklin, Robert Paine, and William Hooper.[15] This is certainly not a bad legacy to leave America, nor should it ever be forgotten.

To read some modern, revisionist historical accounts of the Puritans, one would come away with the impression that the primary legacy they left America was one fraught with nothing but intolerance, bigotry, religious fanaticism, and insensitivity. Americans of today often envision the Puritans as nothing but a bunch of overly religious, radical, dour sourpusses who walked about the towns of New England with nothing else on their minds but fulfilling the express purpose of tracking down suspected witches in order to satisfy their bloodthirsty desire to conduct public hangings on the village greens. While there is some element of truth to this, such as their infamous Salem witch hunts, their ill treatment of the Quakers in New England, and other embodiments of very strict punishment administered to adults and children alike for sinful or lazy behavior, the Puritans are overly maligned to the degree that we tend to forget their positive and constructive contributions to our society and culture, for which we should be eternally grateful.

While the Puritans were indeed quite strict in enforcing local civic and religious ordinances, they also had a great capacity to laugh at their vicarious quandaries, poke considerable fun at each other, and merrily engage in communal festivities such as holding huge banquets in order to dedicate new meeting houses and other important events. They did so dressed in colorful clothing, not just the formal black and white dresses, hats, and coats we stereo-typically ascribe to them.[16] They certainly were not as pure as the driven snow either as there are recorded instances of some children being taken away from their homes when their parents engaged in child abuse as a result of excessive drinking or where adultery was occasionally taking place. The children of such offending homes were then placed in homes of neighbors or relatives who would be more than willing to care for them.[17] I find it quite fascinating that they had their own version of Child Protective Services and foster homes. That pretty much puts to rest the argument that the Puritans had no sensitivity to the needs of others or that they were completely heartless. We all ought to chew on that fact for a while.

Let us explore the interesting "New England Way" somewhat further as we continue to compare and contrast that culture with America today. The Puritans were known to be submissive to authority, holy service, and communal service. They did believe in chastity before marriage, modesty in behavior and apparel, keeping shops closed on the Sabbath, and passing legislation

against immorality.[18] As discussed earlier, they were committed
to a covenanted relationship amongst themselves as well as with
Almighty God, and they zealously guarded this relationship most
carefully as they held everyone in their communities accountable
for their actions. They consistently frowned upon sinful behavior
because the Puritans steadfastly maintained that when members
of their communities sinned against one another or violated civic
and moral laws, the resulting effects would have devastating
consequences upon the well-being of their commonwealth. The
unforgettable lessons of the witch hysteria of both Salem and
Salem Village in 1692 bear this out. These two communities suffered dearly from their succumbing to wild superstition and false
accusations hurled against innocent citizens by others for reasons
of greed, envy, and politics—which led to the horrific deaths of
nineteen innocent villagers. The people of these two communities in Massachusetts paid an enormous price as a result of their
losing sight of their own "New England Way," and this is a topic
of great interest and fascination to this very day.

When I was a young boy growing up in Great Falls, Montana,
we weren't sissies in the way we went about holding our friends and
neighbors accountable to each other as well! My own community
certainly believed in—and for the most part—adhered to similar
puritanical values unlike the current dysfunctional Addams family
values that are being given license to proliferate in American society. This personal reflection of mine may appear to be somewhat
Pollyannaish, yet it is quite true. It mattered not whether you were
a Democrat or Republican back in the 1950s and 1960s when I was
a young boy as we all shared common values which were not at all
divisive or controversial. While some citizens of the country were
engaged in protesting the Vietnam War, conducting sit-ins on college
campuses, and participating in a variety of counterculture antics, my
community was still stuck in the quaint, if not somewhat naïve, time
period of the 1950s, a decade often referred to as "the happy decade."

I can just about imagine my detractors carrying on at this point while smirking and saying something like, "There goes that Stevens again with his bridge to the past!" Be that as it may, but am I one of the few Americans who nostalgically recalls a time in our great country when it wasn't controversial in the slightest bit to perform Christmas concerts and plays in the public schools without the obnoxious ACLU breathing down our necks, or a time when as citizens, we could take considerable delight and pride in enjoying the heartwarming sight of our communities festively decorated during the Christmas season with sacred nativities as well as beautifully illuminated Christmas trees? Remember when it was once scandalous behavior for a teenage girl to be caught pregnant while attending high school? Such an occurrence back then would surely have brought some level of shame and humiliation upon her family, at least in my community, and she would have immediately been removed from the local public high school and placed in an alternative educational environment. Not nowadays! Currently, even the slightest criticism of such behavior would be characterized by many as judgmental, out of step with reality, and simply nobody else's business. For goodness sake, we wouldn't want to be critical or judgmental in any manner now would we? After all, it may just ruin somebody's self-esteem for life and bring on a lawsuit by the ACLU, completely supported by the liberal Ninth Circuit Court of Appeals in San Francisco!

Fast forward only fifty short years from the 1960s and we now have the local school board of Portland, Maine, approving the distribution of contraceptives to the students in its middle schools without parental notification or approval. And this is apparently with a wink of the eye and nod to the affirmative by the majority of the parents living in Portland. To be sure, not all parents in Portland subscribe to this bizarre policy as there are still many who have some common sense, but unfortunately such parents are not in the majority.[19] Now, you must understand that aspirin cannot be administered to our young children in our public schools by school officials, yet it appears vital that we must now encourage middle school students to go ahead and have casual, premarital sex if they so desire by giving them contraceptives in school! Since when has it ever become the responsibility or purview of public schools to take on this type of parental responsibility? And why are parents so eager to wimp out and remain smugly content with abrogating their own responsibilities as legal guardians of their own children by rendering such responsibilities over to the local school board? I am sure the school board of Portland, Maine—together with the support of the majority of the city's parents—are proud about how enlightened and progressive they have become. Well, they truly deserve each other! They can also cope with the negative consequences that will ultimately be visited upon their community as a result of engaging in such irresponsible behavior! Ladies and gentlemen, behold the striking metamorphosis of New England as we witness before our very eyes the dimming of the lights of a "City upon a Hill."

Here is another recent embarrassing example for the nation! How about the drug and sex scandal at Boulder High School in Boulder, Colorado, that made national headlines when it authorized a highly controversial assembly for its student body without parental notification or approval on April 10th, 2007? According to Bill O'Reilly of *The O'Reilly Factor* on Fox News, four guest presenters discussed the virtues of participating in promiscuous sex, drug taking, and breaking the law by experimenting with the illegal drugs of marijuana and ecstacy.[20] Again, a significant number of parents in Boulder—a very secular-progressive community—in conjunction with the local school board, defended such an outrageous assembly! These recent examples are but the tip of an enormous, culturally debased iceberg floating about the country, ready to sink America! These two examples clearly illustrate how far we have come in our nation in just fifty years.

If that weren't bad enough, the nation has had to shamefully endure the spectacle of a vice-principal in a California public high school sending five students home for displaying the American flag on their clothing during the school's celebration of Cinco De Mayo in May of 2010! The administrator in question apparently deemed such a display of the American flag on the offending boys' clothing to be inappropriate and provocative. Fox News reported on another case where a high school student in Texas was suspended from school for removing a Mexican flag from a school corridor without authorization because he was deeply offended by the fact that the Mexican flag was being displayed higher than our own American flag! It is true that the young man should have approached the school administration first before taking it upon himself to commit such a minor act, but his action should really have been applauded, not criticized or condemned. Had I been the school district's superintendent, I would have either disciplined or terminated the high school administrator for permitting such an un-American display to occur in a public high school in the first place rather than disciplining the boy who removed the Mexican flag!

Another Fox News report featured a video clip of a talent show at some public high school student body assembly at which a male teenage student stripped down to his Speedo underwear and performed sexual gyrations on stage before all of the cheering students while the school administrators and teachers did absolutely nothing to halt the offensive spectacle. The school may just as well have arranged for a group of men from Chippendales to strip and perform before the students. What precisely is the difference other than the age of the performers? Evidently, we have now evolved to a point in public education where it is perfectly acceptable to permit burlesque entertainment to occur at high school talent shows. How progressively wonderful! I will address my views and perspective on public education and issues associated with it—especially from a conservative teacher's point of view—in much greater detail in chapters six and seven of this book.

Moral decadence and impassivity is not lost with the entertainment industry and the debilitating impact it is having upon our youth. This morally bereft industry is broadcasting vile shows that are robbing our children of their childhood innocence by glorifying casual premarital sex, and the use of drugs and alcohol. For Pete's sake, what is happening in America? As a nation, we are losing the very essence of our soul as well as the puritanical virtues that once made us the envy of the world.

Tragically, we are beginning to morph into a nation that many of us barely recognize anymore, and neither would the majority of our ancestors. Our Founding Fathers sacrificed much to establish a country we can all be proud of regardless of political party, race, religion, gender, etc., and we owe it to posterity to hand over a country to our children and grandchildren that is nothing other than the strong ship of state our generation inherited. As a society, we had better pause for just a few moments and conduct a serious reality check. Americans had better wake up and smell the coffee before our nation crumbles from within as the former Soviet Union once predicted we would. If we are not wiser and exceedingly careful as a society, all of us will be reading a book in the not-too-distant future with the title, A City upon a crumbling and fallen Hill. Even so, as this book will continue to reveal throughout its chapters, we are already observing some very substantial cracks in the foundation of our great "City upon a Hill."

Just like the Puritans of long ago, we certainly were not saints in Great Falls back when I was a young boy growing up in the 1950s and 1960s by any stretch of the imagination, and unlike the Puritans, it wasn't necessary for us to wear our religion on our sleeves. Lord knows we had our own fair share of faults, crime, brawls, community drudgeries, and family trials and tribulations just like any other town in America. But what we did possess was a universal grasp of common sense as well as a united commitment to achieve that which was generally good for the community and good for the country, regardless of political party or affiliation—unlike the very strident, divisive discourse and issues confronting us today. My community was far from perfect, yet it was on the right course by-and-large, and I don't think Great Falls was altogether that much different from most communities throughout America during that particular period. Old-fashioned puritanical values were manifested in my hometown in other ways as well.

As young children, we played outside with our neighborhood friends until dusk, and we had to be very careful with what we said or did as the adults in our neighborhood had an unspoken covenant with each other that implied it was perfectly acceptable to spank each other's kids when necessary. As precocious young boys, we had a profound respect and healthy fear of all of our friends' parents because we clearly understood that if we were to potentially commit any infraction contrary to acceptable standards of behavior of the day, we could very well be whipped by most any neighborhood adult and immediately sent home. During the 1950s and 1960s, parents of all stripes were not to be trifled with. Although my own mother and father were divorced when I was in the first grade, neither one of them tolerated inappropriate behavior from me or my sister Carol, and they certainly did not spare either the rod or the belt. Can you imagine such scenarios possibly occurring today? If a neighbor were to similarly punish another neighbor's child as was done when I was growing up, he would be arrested for assault and most assuredly hauled into court to face a civil lawsuit as well as some serious jail time for criminal felony conduct! Today, if parents were to administer old-fashioned butt whippings to their own children for misbehaving at home or in public, they would be charged with child abuse. Child Protective Services would be called in, and the long arm of today's oppressive and intrusive "nanny state" would remove the supposedly abused children from their own homes.

Look at the consequences our society is currently coping with on a daily basis as a result of implementing secular-progressive ideas and policies with regard to the rearing of our nation's children. We are raising a generation of youth that is, to a large degree, unruly, disrespectful, in-your-face, lacking in personal discipline and drive, and lazy both at home and in school. While this is certainly not the case with the majority of today's children, it is nevertheless a stark and undeniable reality with regard to a significant percentage of today's youth, and this is a clear and present danger to the future well-being of our nation. I will support these observations with sobering facts and statistics in chapter six of this book. At any rate, the Puritans of New England were absolutely correct when they steadfastly maintained that negative deportment exhibited by their citizens as well as raising their children with soft discipline would wreak havoc upon their respective communities. America has gradually forsaken these fundamental truths during the course of the past several decades and as a direct result, we really are transforming into a nation replete with sissies.

Growing up in Great Falls, Montana, during the 1950s and 1960s also meant that one would not dare sass or defy a public school teacher or principal all the way up to the level of high school as the board of correction would be administered to the seat of knowledge in the form of a very painful—yet most effective—attitude correction seminar. It is no coincidence that the nimble song often sung by American schoolchildren while frolicking on playgrounds of years past began with the following rhyme:

> School days, school days, good old-fashioned school days.
> Reading and writing and arithmetic, taught to the tune
> of the hickory stick....

Currently, only twenty-three states continue to permit the administering of corporal punishment in public schools, and most of them are located in the South. Is it any wonder that the children being reared in the South today are still required to address their parents, teachers, and other adults with "Yes, sir" and "Yes, ma'am?" It is by far the one region in the country that still exhibits some guise of respectable and proper manners with most adults and children. Bravo to American Southerners as this is more than likely a reflection of some of the lingering manners of the antebellum South, and God forbid it should ever lose those manners!

The judicious methods of old-fashioned discipline once utilized by parents, teachers, and neighbors of yesteryear would be considered draconian by today's standards, but here's the rub: There was once a time in our society when the vast majority of our children respected their parents, they respected their teachers, they respected their neighbors, and they had a healthy respect and fear of authority. There existed an American tradition whereby parents did not function in the role of being their children's best friends; on the contrary, they functioned in the proper and serious role of being parents—charged with the responsibility of raising their kids to be functional, well-disciplined, hard-working, and self-sufficient contributors to society. As a result, most of us—regardless of age—were civil to one another instead of behaving as we do today in an in-your-face manner. Just like the Puritans of centuries ago, we looked out for each other. We possessed a deep sense of societal responsibility and commitment that acknowledged the fact that terrible decorum, whether exhibited by children or adults, would have a negative impact with devastating consequences upon society. The majority of Americans are deeply concerned, as revealed in current opinion polls, that our nation is headed in the wrong direction, and they also believe America is in serious decline. Americans worry that the very fabric of our society is being torn asunder and for very good reason! Sadly, many of us feel practically powerless to do anything about it as our elected representatives as well as our appointed judges on the local, state, and federal levels have lost practically all sense of propriety and common sense, and the majority of such elected or appointed individuals continue to forsake us as they shamefully intrude upon our constitutional rights as parents, citizens, and educators. The American people must arise in the spirit of the old "New England Way" and seriously devise a realistic and sound solution as to how we can effectively unite together once again as a nation in order to battle this appalling and frightening trend lest we all turn into a cabal of sniveling and ineffectual twits.

As previously stated, the Puritans were realists who felt both sin and laziness could have far-reaching implications for their own families as well as the community at large. They took their sacred commitment of a covenanted life with God and each other very seriously. The laws passed by the General Court or by local villages were to be observed and enforced. When sin, laziness, and lawbreaking occurred in their communities, punishment was administered swiftly, and in most cases, quite harshly. The Puritans were intolerant of sin and slothfulness with adults just as much as they were with their children. Adults could be whipped and put in the stocks for both communal punishment and public humiliation as could children. Most Americans today would certainly not advocate a return to the stocks, and corporal punishment in and of itself is not always the answer to all problems, and it can certainly be abused. To believe otherwise would be foolish and naive. In addition, reasonable societal safeguards need to be in place and enforced in order to ensure the safety of our children. As I previously stated, even the Puritans had such safeguards in place within their own communities. However, the pendulum has definitely swung too far in the direction of both permissiveness and victimhood to the point of outright absurdity in our country.

Let us be completely honest and forthright with our current predicament as a society. We are permitting secular-progressive ideas and dogma to have too strong an influence on our culture, and we are witnessing on a daily basis the devastating havoc they are inflicting upon our families, our schools, our local communities, and our nation as a whole. Some earnest soul searching within America's hierarchal ranks needs to occur lest all of the pernicious secular-progressive rocks and pebbles be permanently encased in an impenetrable wall of oppression nobody will be able to penetrate or tear down.

I would like to conclude this chapter by recalling a fascinating event that occurred in 1994 with a young American male citizen while he was temporarily residing oversees. You might recall an eighteen-year-old American teenager at the time by the name of Michael Fay, who was temporarily living in Singapore with his mother and stepfather. Michael confessed to Singapore authorities that he had spray-painted and vandalized some cars, and he had also stolen road signs. Michael was sentenced by the local authorities to be put in their version of the stocks in order to be cane whipped by a martial-arts expert. There was a public outcry by some in America. The official position of the United States government was that it opposed the sentence. The American Embassy tried to intervene on Michael's behalf, and President Bill Clinton maintained that the sentence of caning was unjustified and extreme. He was unable to convince the Singapore authorities to grant Michael clemency from the caning, though the Singapore authorities did agree to reduce the number of swats from the initial six down to four, and Michael's sentence was ultimately administered to him.[21]

To the great credit of the Singapore authorities, they didn't wimp out to the demands of the American government. I can recall how the bleeding-heart bunch in America was indignant, of course, while the majority of Americans, according to public opinion polls taken at the time, believed Michael Fay's punishment was justified, and most felt the young man definitely had it coming. I even read with considerable interest articles in local newspapers reporting on sentiments being put forth by some Congressmen that perhaps we should carry out similar sentences publicly upon our own miscreants here at home. Many Americans, myself included, speculated that our nation might benefit immensely from returning to some old-fashioned forms of punishment. Alas, we allowed the issue to gradually fade away, but isn't it interesting to note that as of the year 1994, America still remained a tad-bit in touch with the Puritan "New England Way?"

2

We Mutually Pledge to Each Other Our Lives, Our Fortunes, and Our Sacred Honor

There are only two creatures of value on the face of this earth; those with a commitment and those who acquire the commitment of others.

— John Adams

The above quote attributed to the Founding Father John Adams is most appropriate as it pertains to the following unnerving scenario: Picture yourself sleeping quite comfortably in bed when suddenly, in the middle of a brisk, early spring night, you are aroused by the sounds and commotion emerging from nearby Buckman's Tavern next to the Lexington Green. Disquieted about what is occurring outside, you quickly get dressed and join the other men in the cold and dampness of night who are gathered around an anxious man sitting upon his horse. Paul Revere gives the unnerving news to all gathered that he has been riding his horse for some time now on the Menotomy Road, stopping briefly at various villages to warn all of the assembled Colonials that 700 British Regulars are on the march in the middle of the night—all the way from Boston. They are heading for Concord in order to seize the muskets, powder, and shot being stored there by the various local colonial militias. Before leaving Lexington, Revere stops at the house of the Reverend Jonas Clark, where the heroic figures of John Hancock and Samuel Adams, two leading agitators and members of the famous Sons of Liberty, are secretly hiding from British officials. The two Patriots hear the urgent news from Paul Revere about the approaching Redcoats and quickly flee in order to escape their impending arrest as well as the hangman's noose—just in the nick of time.

By now, the bell is being tolled from the bell tower on the Lexington Green. You and your friends are gathering at the nearby meeting house for the purpose of signing the muster book of the local militia as you receive detailed orders from Captain John Parker, the leader of the Lexington Militia. All Minutemen are to assemble together with their muskets, powder and shot—as well as some necessary provisions—in order to stand ready on the village green to confront the approaching Redcoats. Some of your friends choose to wait for the arrival of the British Regulars in their homes, giving comfort and words of encouragement to their frightened wives and children, while you and others choose to wait at Buckman's Tavern, drinking ale while apprehensively discussing the approaching tempest. Never before have you actually been called upon as a citizen to face the approaching army. Certainly the militiamen have drilled and trained together on the green in order to be prepared for such a possibility, but now the Minutemen are confronted with the inevitability of standing armed and face to face with British Regulars!

As dawn approaches, you hear the militia drumbeat, which is the call to muster on the green. The wives, sons, and daughters of the Minutemen are told to keep the windows of their homes shuttered and their doors closed for their own safekeeping. Meandering from their homes as well as from Buckman's Tavern, the seventy-seven brave Lexington Minutemen begin to assemble in several ranks of formation on the village green in order to face the formidable Redcoats. You and the other volunteers are on the green primarily to make the statement to the approaching soldiers that you are willing to defend your village if necessary. The time seems to drag on at a snail's pace. Gradually, you hear the sounds of the approaching Lobster backs as their drumbeats and marching become more pronounced.

Coming around the bend on the Menotomy Road is the approach of the army under the command of Colonel Francis Smith and Major John Pitcairn. You are praying to Almighty God that the soldiers will see the insignificant presence of only seventy-seven of your fellow Minutemen standing on the King's Green and hopefully decide to move on to Concord without incident. However, much to your fear and dismay, the Redcoats choose to stop and confront the militia standing in protest with their muskets! It is now shortly after 5:00 a.m. Your heart is pounding like a hammer in your chest, and you seriously wonder whether or not your wife is about to become a widow that morning, since the Minutemen are outnumbered ten to one! Captain Parker certainly does not anticipate that a battle is about to erupt, but he shouts out to the men, "Don't fire unless fired upon! But if they want a war, let it begin here!"[1] That is precisely what transpires as America's Revolutionary War is about to commence on April 19th, 1775.

The frightened men begin to scatter as Captain Parker orders the militia to disperse, but it is too late. A shot is fired, but no one is quite sure which side is responsible for it. By this time, muskets are being fired from both sides, and pandemonium breaks loose. Even Major Pitcairn temporarily loses control of his troops. One British officer later noted, "The men were so wild they could hear no orders."[2] You watch in terror as some of your friends fall down on the green, blown away with holes in their chests as a result of enemy musket fire while others are writhing in pain as they are being skewered with British bayonets. You and the rest of your surviving friends scatter like wild animals and hide in the nearby woods to escape certain slaughter. By the time the British Regulars are reassembling on the green to continue their march to Concord, eight Colonials lay dead and fourteen more are wounded. There are no British casualties.

The second battle at the North Bridge in Concord takes place the very same day. As the citizens of Concord learn the British Regulars are after the stored cannons, muskets, powder, and shot, they hasten to hide the munitions under plowed fields, under piles of manure, and within the homes of farmers. The Concord Militia, under the command of Colonel James Barrett, observes the Redcoats looting and burning some of the homes in town. During the second battle of the morning at Concord's North Bridge, three British soldiers and two American Minutemen are killed, and scores of men are wounded.[3]

By no means were the Minutemen of Lexington and Concord, Massachusetts—the sites of the first two battles of the American Revolution—indecisive wimps with regard to their actions. They clearly understood what their responsibilities as men were: to defend their homes from attack, take a brave stand for freedom, and protect their honor from the tyranny of Great Britain. As word spread like wildfire of the attacks on Lexington and Concord, thousands of men from all of the surrounding villages and farms took up their weapons to fight at a minute's notice. These brazen men rose to the occasion throughout that fateful spring day and ultimately defeated the British Regulars on their return march from Concord back to Boston. The Minutemen valiantly fought back in larger numbers and effectively leapfrogged the British all the way back to Boston. They used brilliant Indian-style tactics to gain the upper hand by firing behind stone walls along the Menotomy Road, by firing from the rooftops of nearby farmhouses, and by accurately targeting the British Redcoats from behind the cover of trees. The Minutemen would fire, then move on, fire, then move on, etc. These were not defiant acts of the faint of heart, but rather the acts of brave, driven men who displayed incredible courage, wisdom, and fortitude, and they truly exemplified the spirit of pledging to each other their lives, their fortunes, and their sacred honor—even before these immortal words would be put to quill and ink by Thomas Jefferson some fifteen months later in the Declaration of Independence.

In Deborah Kent's booklet, *Lexington and Concord*, she reports a British officer wrote the following in his diary: "The soldiers were so enraged at suffering from an unseen enemy that they forced open many of the houses from which the fire proceeded and put to death all those found in them. Those houses would certainly have been burnt had any fire been found in them, or had there been time to kindle any; but only three or four near where we first formed suffered in this way."[4] On April 19th, 1775, American Patriots ceased to be British citizens and became real Americans for the very first time. This would not be formally codified until July 4th, 1776, when the Second Continental Congress signed the Declaration of Independence at Independence Hall in Philadelphia, Pennsylvania. Nevertheless, the deed was done in 1775, and the shots American Minutemen fired across Great Britain's bow at Lexington and Concord were accurate and unmistakably clear with regard to their volition!

This particular fleeting segment of time is one of the most heroic and defining moments in American history. It significantly contributed to the shaping of the American character that John F. Kennedy referred to in his speech to the American people in 1946. The battles of Lexington and Concord also serve as a pertinent historical reminder to the American people as to the precise reason why our Founding Fathers enshrined the **individual's** right to bear arms in the Second Amendment to the United States Constitution. Our government in Colonial America, which was the British government during that particular time, attempted to disarm its citizens so that Americans would not be able to properly defend themselves, but the British soldiers were unsuccessful in their attempt to do so. In the meantime, with the bold and heroic actions of the Minutemen, coupled with our audacious declaration of total independence from Great Britain, our fledgling new nation embraced the implacable challenge of taking on the world's greatest and mightiest army—the British Army. During this tumultuous period in American history, the slight majority of American Colonials who considered themselves to be British Loyalists initially considered this rebellion to be an act of treason against England, which they felt would amount to nothing more than a devastating and humiliating defeat for America with tragic consequences to follow. How wrong these initial sentiments of Loyalists and cynics proved to be, as we were to finally defeat the British at Yorktown, Virginia, in 1781 and sign the Treaty of Paris in 1783, formally ending the war between America and England.

However, American Patriots were certainly not naive as to who and what they were up against. They were keenly aware that the military forces of England had earned a well-deserved reputation for being the best in the world. How could America possibly survive with a ragtag bunch of inexperienced, local militiamen fighting against the mightiest empire on earth? How could an initially untrained, unsophisticated, disorganized, poorly funded, and often ill-equipped Continental Army under the command of General George Washington possibly defeat the superior British Army? How could we win? How could we possibly survive? Would any other foreign nation risk coming to our aid and assistance at any point in time during the war? If we were to lose, what kind of punishment would England inflict upon us? These were very daunting questions being raised by the American people living through this cataclysmic period in American history. Yet, against all odds and with the blessing of Almighty God, we were victorious in the war against

England under the brilliant leadership of George Washington, the steadfast commitment of the Continental Army and various militias, and with the assistance of France at the Battle of Yorktown. As a matter of fact, the American Revolution would eventually inspire the French to conduct their own revolution in 1789 as all French eyes would turn to face the direction of the Atlantic Ocean and proceed to replicate the astounding, revolutionary success of "A City upon a Hill."

The events crisscrossing the American road to independence make up a captivating story of both intrigue and bravery, one that is probably unique in world history! During the first half of the 1700s, British-American Colonials and their mother country, England, lived together in relative peace, and both enjoyed success and prosperity. This changed dramatically after the conclusion of the French and Indian War in 1763. The war was quite costly to England, and she needed new revenue with which to finance not only her war debt, but to govern the vast North American territory she had acquired from France. As a result, Parliament in London levied new taxes on her colonies and appointed more stringent Royal Governors as well as customs officials to carry out the duties of enforcing its new policies. Britain also dispatched thousands of its soldiers to American shores to help protect British rights and enforce her authority over the colonies. Americans, who were still British citizens at the time, were used to administering their own political affairs through their duly elected local assemblies. The Colonials were also accustomed to relative financial independence, and they began to bitterly resent the interference of Parliament and King George III into colonial affairs.

From Britain's perspective, she felt she had a legitimate right to tax the American Colonials, since England had defended them from both the Indians and the French in the French and Indian War. Parliament maintained the Colonials had a responsibility to assist it in the paying off of the war debt as well as the costs incurred with the governance of the colonies. From their perspective, the Colonials argued that it was England's civic and moral responsibility to bear these costs because England was, after all, the mother country. The British-Americans maintained it should have been an obvious and natural affair for England to protect her colonies from competing imperialist interests. In the meantime, Southern Planters from the Southern Colonies became agitated with their indebtedness to British creditors. In the Middle Colonies, merchants resented British prohibitions on trade and restrictions on certain products, and frontier settlers bitterly resented tight restrictions with regard to not being allowed to settle west of the Appalachian Mountains as a result of the Proclamation of 1763.[5] In essence, American settlers were ordered by British authorities to stay put. The New England Colonies deeply resented British interference in the governance of their commonwealths as they were compelled to abrogate more of their own local political control over to corrupt Royal Governors.

The first direct tax levied upon the American Colonists by Parliament was the Sugar Act of 1764.[6] This tax was applied to any sugar, molasses, and other products shipped by England to her colonies. Of course, molasses was used to manufacture rum, a staple of American cuisine, and the American Colonials were furious with this heavy-handed act of England! Any intrusive governmental interference with Americans and their historical cultural love affair with the manufacture and consumption of alcoholic beverages runs the equivalent impetuous risk of challenging a mother grizzly bear while defending her cubs! An example of this point would be to recall the famous Whiskey Rebellion of Pennsylvania in 1794. Farmers violently protested against our newly established government when it foolishly levied a tax on whiskey. It took 13,000 of our own soldiers to quell this riot! You would think our own government in the early days of our republic would have learned its lesson from the Sugar Act of 1764 that England imposed on Colonial America, but it didn't. Nor did we learn our lesson when we passed the 18th Amendment of the US Constitution in 1919, better known as Prohibition, only to have it repealed by the 21st Amendment in 1933.

Nevertheless, in 1764 Colonial merchants often traded in smuggled goods, doing so at their own risk since being caught in this illegal act could result in the confiscation of offending American ships by British authorities. Founding Father John Hancock, who was the presiding president of the Second Continental Congress when the Declaration of Independence was debated and signed, amassed his great fortune in shipping and smuggling while defying tightfisted English policies and restrictions. Referring to England, Hancock once remarked, "No vessel hardly comes in or goes out but they find some pretense to seize and detain her."[7] A young Massachusetts farmer and Colonial leader, James Otis, first coined the words "taxation without representation" when he exclaimed the following: "Taxation without representation is tyranny!"[8]

To add insult to injury, Parliament then passed the Stamp Act of 1765. This new law required all legal and commercial documents to have an official stamp affixed to them to exhibit proof that the tax had been paid.[9] Any American Colonial walking the streets of Boston might be stopped by a British official demanding such proof be rendered. If the stamp, even on something so innocuous as a deck of playing cards, was not evident, the poor offender could be carted off to jail. Since these stamps on all diplomas, legal contracts, wills, and newspapers had to be paid for with silver coins, severe economic hardship took its toll on the Colonials. Benjamin Franklin traveled to London himself in order to try and reason with Parliament and petition the legislature to repeal the tax, saying it was unfair to the American people. Even though Franklin's sincere attempt was met with arrogant contempt and ridicule by British authorities, Parliament ultimately relented and repealed the Stamp Act in 1766.

Further seeds of discourse and animus were brewing throughout the thirteen colonies as tempers were flaring everywhere.

Samuel Adams, a leader in the Massachusetts legislature, addressed the unfair application of British taxation upon the colonies when he inquired, "Why not our lands? Why not the produce of our lands and, in short, everything we possess and make use of?" Patrick Henry of Virginia, a member of the House of Burgesses, which is America's oldest legislature, called for ignoring the Stamp Act. When he was chastised and accused of treason by a fellow member of the assembly, Henry forcefully replied, "If this be treason, make the most of it!"[10]

Recalling the sentiments of two of our famous Founding Fathers, Samuel Adams and Patrick Henry, as well as their wrath directed toward the unfair application of the British government's taxation and tyrannical policies being foisted upon British-Americans throughout the thirteen colonies of the 1700s, is remarkably akin to the current sentiments and indignation being expressed by the Tea Party movement. Millions of Americans from coast to coast are currently protesting the fiscal policies and bona-fide power-grab pageantry being exhibited by Team Obama. In addition, widespread anger and frustration by a large segment of the American people manifested itself in various town hall meetings across our nation during the summer of 2009. Such protestations were analogous to the reactions once exhibited by the Sons and Daughters of Liberty in Colonial Boston.

A very significant number of our current state and federal politicians, especially Democrats, were given the equivalent political treatment of a colonial-style tar-and-feathering at the polling booths by a massive, powerful, sleeping giant called the American people. When this sleeping giant was provoked, there was a palpable reaction very similar to what occurred in America during the 1760s and 1770s, albeit a nonviolent one. All politicians would do well to take heed of this fact in future elections. There is currently bitter anger and resentment brewing in the boiling pot of American discontent with the tyranny being exhibited by our federal government as well as some state governments. When one thinks about it, history does have a tendency to repeat itself. Our state and federal governments are not only out of touch with the average American, but they conveniently forget from whom or what they derive their authority to govern. They all need a basic refresher course in American history, civics, and economics, as well as a good swift kick in their posteriors—metaphorically speaking—for putting this nation at serious risk of insolvency.

My family and I currently reside in the state of California. According to our state constitution, the legislature and governor are required to enact a state budget on time each summer. Do they consistently accomplish the task? You might have guessed it—absolutely not! California is in the worst economic condition since the Great Depression, as is our federal government. The state legislature is made up of a very large majority of Democrats who have held that majority for quite some time now. During the Republican administration of former governor Arnold Schwarzenegger, with the Democrats in control of the state legislature, the state government was woefully dysfunctional and inept. To borrow a clever euphemism the former governor is fond of saying, "They were all acting like girly men." California has recently been forced to endure annual massive budget deficits year-after-year in the staggering amounts of billions of dollars, leaving infrastructure, schools, and various contractors, to name just a few, in utter disarray. The latest prognosis is there will not be any relief from this fiscal quagmire for a great many years to come.

The Democrats in California's state legislature stubbornly maintain the primary way out of our predicament is to increase taxes and other fees on the people of California. We currently have the honor of being one of the highest-taxed populations in the entire nation, yet that is not sufficient for our liberal political leaders. The problem is not one of a lack of sufficient taxation; the problem is bloated, wasteful, government spending on a plethora of public services this state can scarcely afford, and the obese government of California needs to be put on a very strict diet. Ironically, despite the dire condition the state finds itself in fiscally, it did not follow the national trend in the midterm elections of 2010. With the election of "moonbeam" Jerry Brown as governor—together with the sizable Democratic majority in the state legislature in Sacramento—California is now under complete control of the big-spending progressives just like the federal government was from 2008–2010. Consequently, only the wealthy will be able to afford to reside in this state by the time the middle-class is drawn and quartered with the torturous instruments of higher taxes and fees as well as intrusive regulations.

What is incessantly typical is the fact that the middle-class citizens of California are the unfortunate saps who will be given their marching orders as their salaries, properties, and investments are levied with additional burdensome taxes by liberal politicians with absolute impunity, especially since California is currently governed by progressive Democrats. The income and assets of most California citizens and businesses will continue to be redistributed in true fashion to those who are not deserving of any of it. Of course the liberals will see to it that the poorer citizens of California will benefit by every kind of cradle-to-grave welfare and social "redistribution of wealth" program conceivable. Such ever-expanding programs will make both FDR's New Deal alphabet soup programs and Lyndon B. Johnson's War on Poverty programs appear as slim pickings in comparison. In addition, some of California's lazy ne'er-do-wells who have managed to learn how to game the system will survive and prosper in their own right courtesy of the Robin Hoods who reside in the state's version of Sherwood Forest—none other than Sacramento! We are anything but the Golden State anymore; we have effectively managed to evolve into the Tarnished State! What precisely are the devastating consequences the people of California are going to be required to bear as a direct result of all of this inept, out-of-control, drunken-sailor spending our politicians are guilty of engaging in?

Well, here they are: Businesses both large and small that provide California with much needed jobs and tax revenue for essential state services are either going bankrupt, or they are fleeing the state in droves for other competing states because it is getting too costly for them to conduct business here. This is due in large part to the burdensome Workman's Compensation Insurance fees, the exorbitant cost of living expenses for its employees, out-of-sight housing costs, job-killing business regulations, undue restrictive and punitive environmental laws courtesy of California's version of cap-and-trade, and a myriad of other onerous laws that are so characteristic of a state that is not in the slightest bit friendly to either large corporations or small business concerns. When business is lured to other states that are more competitive and business friendly, it deprives our own state treasury of desperately needed funds, such as sales tax revenue, business tax revenue, and state income tax revenue from employees.

Indeed, our state politicians continue to behave in their usual pompous, contemptible manner and pass asinine legislation that compels businesses of all stripes to flee California because they can scarcely continue to operate profitably here. People then lose their jobs, placing a further burden on state services as well as the rest of employed California taxpayers who are left holding the bag. When citizens lose their jobs, many go bankrupt and lose their homes, which exacerbates the financial problem. Then the governor and state legislature, with their insatiable appetite for spending, determine that the most appropriate solution and quick fix to what ails the state is to levy additional taxes upon already financially strapped individuals, families, and businesses attempting to garner either decent livings or profits. Consumer spending and investment plummets, and the vicious cycle continues to spiral out of control. Now that makes a great deal of sense, doesn't it?

Have any of these politicians in Sacramento ever contemplated these facts? Do any of them have any business experience or have any of them ever been required to meet a payroll on time? When Arnold Schwarzenegger was governor, it was more than apparent to me that he and the state legislature were practicing a version of kindergarten economics, but then again, Schwarzenegger did star in the film, *Kindergarten Cop,* so he should know, shouldn't he? His kindergarten class was the state legislature in Sacramento, who appropriately completed the cast of cute but sappy characters. With our new governor, Jerry Brown, nothing has changed, nor will it because the eviscerated state economy continues to follow in the path of "Governor Moonbeam"—all the way to the moon and back. Many of us were hoping Jerry Brown might restore some common sense to Sacramento when he was elected governor; however, such is apparently not the case—at least as of the writing of this book. The hit song "California Dreamin" that the Mamas and the Papas made so famous in the 1960s could aptly be renamed "California Nightmare"!

Sacramento politicians don't have the guts or wherewithal to make the necessary tough decisions to either prioritize or outright eliminate their precious pet projects and programs that are having a huge noxious impact on the state budget. What about the billions of dollars the state spends annually on various welfare and social programs not only for California's citizens, but illegal aliens as well? Maybe, just maybe, we cannot afford them anymore! Perhaps we should emphatically apply some good old-fashioned tough love to the progressive citizens of California by saying "no more" to them as well as their various special-interest groups. Of course this implies we would actually be required to grow up and vote somewhat intelligently and elect responsible people to office who would be willing to return fiscal sanity and discipline to our state. The people of California must shoulder partial responsibility for the financial Armageddon we are currently facing because, after all, as long as we insist upon electing and reelecting many of these progressive ninnies to public office in Sacramento, we are going to continue to reap what we sow for years, if not decades to come. We would do well to remind all of the American people in every single state of the following quote by American entrepreneur Henry Ford:

> Thinking is the hardest work there is, which is probably why so few people engage in it.

Well, perhaps many politicians do very little thinking most of the time, but the midterm elections of 2010 proved beyond a shadow of a doubt that the majority of Americans were thinking quite clearly when they gave the Democrats in Congress a sound spanking. Team Obama pathetically attempted to portray the verdict of the American people as nothing other than a miscommunication problem, or they pompously boasted of and defended a number of Democratic Party accomplishments during the 111th Congress. Fortunately, the majority of Americans vehemently disagreed with such accomplishments, and they were no longer being duped. While other Democratic leaders and politicians such as John Kerry, Bill Clinton, and Jimmy Carter arrogantly called into question the motives and anger as well as the supposed lack of thinking on the part of the electorate during the campaigns of 2010, the American people did not fall for their duplicitous and patronizing rhetoric. On the contrary, they took Henry Ford's quote to heart and began to think!

The Tea Party movement arose very quickly throughout this country, much in the same manner as the Sons and Daughters of Liberty did in the 1760s, because the people of this contemporary grassroots movement are absolutely fed-up with the abuse of power and tyrannical policies of a government that is both deaf and indifferent with regard to their needs and their dignity as people. Yes, we exhibit righteous, nonviolent anger; we are filled with indignation, and just like the Sons and Daughters of Liberty of the 1760s and 1770s, we are not going to fade away until we are satisfied that we have once again restored sanity and common sense to our federal government. We are outraged that some corporations, financial firms, banks, government agencies such as Fannie Mae and Freddie Mac, etc., together with some of their greedy and inept CEOs, have been completely exonerated and let off the hook for their unsound financial chicanery by rewarding them with federal bailouts—courtesy of the American taxpayer. Let us not ignore the fact that our president and the bleeding-hearts in Congress also forgave, bailed out, defended, or looked the other way as some irresponsible Americans bought homes they could ill afford—some with no credit, some with bad credit, some with no stable jobs, and some with little chance of paying their mortgages off at all, much less on time. Collectively, these irresponsible, bloodsucking leeches were rewarded for their incomprehensible and vile behavior with huge bailouts by our federal government in Washington, DC.

Meanwhile, millions of responsible, honest, hardworking Americans and small business owners were left holding the bag! Now, we work very hard all of our adult lives to earn our money, contribute to our pension funds, play by all of the rules, save to buy our homes, and invest our money in what we assume to be credit-worthy stocks, bonds, mutual funds, banks, and retirement plans. We dutifully pay our state and federal taxes on time, and we withdraw funds from our retirement accounts to help pay for our children's opulent college expenses because the vast majority of us in the middle class do not qualify for federal student grants or federally subsidized student loans because we supposedly earn too much money. Just how are we rewarded? We are arrogantly ordered to suck it up as we find ourselves, our wealth, our estates, and our pensions and retirement accounts at serious risk because of the flagrant actions of both public- and private-sector derelicts and crooks! Where is the fairness in all of this? Where have some of the government oversight agencies such as the Securities Exchange

Commission been hiding out recently? Were they not supposedly established in the first place to monitor or serve as the public's "watch dog" so that crooked firms and devious governmental activity would not be permitted to run roughshod over innocent and unsuspecting Americans? An irreverent, yet very frank line from the film *The Shawshank Redemption* can best answer these questions because it is quite apparent to this author that such oversight agencies have "up and vanished just like a fart in the wind!"

My wife and I weren't able to purchase our first home until the late 1990s when we were both in our forties. We were told that in order to secure the house of our choice, we had to pony up 20 percent of the purchase price of the home and deposit it in an escrow account as a down payment. Next, we had to pass a stringent credit check, and then we had to prove that we had stable jobs by providing the lending institution with six months worth of payroll stubs in order to demonstrate that we would be able to comply with the payment of our monthly mortgage bill. We did not whine and bellyache about these rules because we clearly understood they existed not only for our protection, but the protection of financial institutions as well. How utterly naive we were as we erroneously assumed everybody had to play by the same rules. Well, here are some very pointed questions we would like to pose to President Obama as well as many of our wimpy senators and Congressmen of both political parties in Washington, DC.

God forbid, but should my wife and I, or millions of other Americans for that matter, lose our jobs or become disabled and unable to work, just who is going to bail us out and pay our mortgages and other creditors? Precisely who is going to repay us the pensions we have labored on for years should we lose them because of incompetent management of corporate funds, Wall Street firms, stocks, bonds, and the various insurance companies our retirement funds are invested in? Are all of you supposed compassionate federal politicians willing to forgo **all** of your generous salaries, investments, medical insurance policies, homes, and bloated pensions in order to set an example for the rest of the nation that we are all in this together? Call us Tea Party activists cynical if you must, but we seriously doubt it. Why don't you pathetic politicians put your money where your mouths are and place your own fortunes at serious risk before you are so eager to be generous with the spending and handling of our precious money? Do I sound somewhat angry and resentful? You bet I am, and I know I am not the only average "Joe the Plumber"—or in my case, "John the Public School Teacher"—who is! I am typical of the average member of the Tea Party movement many of the progressive elitists in both the government and mainstream media love to malign and marginalize. Well, we had the last laugh on election day in November of 2010, and it most assuredly will not be the final belly laugh progressives will hear emerging from our mouths in the very near future!

In the local community where I reside, I have over the span of thirty-four years seen numerous small businesses and restaurants come and go for reasons of lack of business, of having to pay greedy, unreasonably high rents, or because of being inadequately run by some managers and owners. I can't for the life of me recall the state of California or our federal government in Washington, DC coming to their rescue. These budding entrepreneurs took a risk by taking out loans and investing their life savings into businesses they hoped would succeed. Some did and some didn't. That is what we call capitalism, the bedrock of American society. Risk taking is the American way! Our Declaration of Independence guarantees the American people the right to **pursue** happiness, but nowhere in my reading of that sacred document does it say we are guaranteed the right to **possess** happiness, nor is that guarantee anywhere to be found in the American Constitution.

Now why, for the love of Pete, is our government even remotely in the business of either bailing out or becoming part owners of General Motors, Chrysler, and various banks, or deciding what kind of compensation packages business executives should or shouldn't be permitted to take? Why should our federal government be allowed to compete in the private marketplace of providing medical coverage for the American people when it can unfairly have access to unlimited taxpayers' funds and can determine all of the rules and regulations that competing private insurance firms must adhere to? When Tea Party activists examine the fraud, waste, and mess the federal government has made of the Postal Service, Social Security, Medicare, Prescription Drug Care, the national debt, etc., we have to say in all sincerity that the efficiency of the federal government somehow eludes us. As a nation, we are gradually transforming into a society whereby our economic foundation is beginning to list more and more socialistic. Should we fail in our efforts to keep the socialistic wolves at bay, almost every business and financial institution in America will wake up one morning only to find it owned and controlled, lock-stock-and-barrel, by the United States government! How quaint, how charming! Socialistic European countries would be so deeply proud of us as they enthusiastically embrace America with open arms and invite us to join their exclusive club, now wouldn't they? As a result, we could convert our currency to the Euro and cede our sovereignty over to the European Union and World Court as we all live happily ever after!

These are the reasons as to why the Tea Party movement is going to remain vigilant in its ultimate quest of **politically** purging this nation, to the greatest extent possible, of the vile influence and control of secular-progressive socialistic politicians, and we are gearing up for one hell of a long and protracted fight. The spunk of the Tea Party movement not only reminds me of the undying resolve once exhibited by the Sons and Daughters of Liberty of the eighteenth century, but it also reminds me of the pugnacity that was so characteristic of the tough, scrappy, and ethnically diverse copper miners of Butte, Montana, during the early 1900s when the brutal "War of the Copper Kings" was being waged. People who dared cross such colorful characters during that particular time period in Butte's history, while foolishly assuming the citizens were nothing other than bumpkins or simpletons simply because they were copper miners, did so at their own risk, and as a result, many outsiders came to regret the lessons they learned the hard way. So in the **true spirit** of the old scrappy copper mining camp which is Butte, Montana, Tea Party patriots across our great nation are not going to be intimidated and cowardly cajoled into silence or beat into submission by well-financed, leftist thugs and bullies, nor will we roll over, play dead, or give up the ghost, so to speak, as we prepare to engage in a **politically** charged, portentous, knockdown, drag-out, Butte-style Irish brawl against the very people who are dragging our country down into the gutter—namely, secular-progressives and socialistic politicians who truly desire to "transform America."

As I stated earlier, there are striking similarities of what is currently occurring in America to what transpired here in the 1700s. England repeatedly violated American Colonials' rights, which were enshrined at the time in the English Bill of Rights and the philosophy of John Locke. It was Locke, the English Enlightenment philosopher, who inspired Thomas Jefferson to include the immortal words of "life, liberty, and the pursuit of happiness" in our Declaration of Independence. These were not Jefferson's original words; he borrowed them from John Locke! The indignation currently being displayed by our citizens against our federal government is also reminiscent of Founding Father Patrick Henry of Virginia. His oratories delivered to the Virginia legislature were very succinct and emotionally charged. It was Patrick Henry who once said, "Give me liberty or give me death!" Before the British executed Colonial Patriot and schoolteacher, Nathan Hale, in 1776, the calm and dignified condemned schoolteacher said, "I only regret that I have but one life to lose for my country." The fighting spirits of Patrick Henry, Nathan Hale, and other Colonial Patriots are alive and well in contemporary America just as much as they were in the 1700s!

Let us now resume our treatise of this American spirit and character as it was displayed in the latter half of the 1700s with America's reaction to England's oppressive Stamp Act as well as other acts of tyranny. These events would gradually propel us down the path of open rebellion and revolution.

Before Great Britain revoked Parliament's Stamp Act on its colonies in 1766, the American Colonials began to protest it in very interesting and effective ways. Colonial merchants organized boycotts of British goods, which impacted business in London. Secret organizations emerged throughout the colonies to oppose not only the Stamp Act, but other oppressive British policies as well. Samuel Adams established the famous Sons of Liberty with 300 formidable dock workers from the harbors of Boston.[11] An elm tree called the Liberty Tree came to represent the symbol of this imposing organization. The area under its branches where the secret members would gather to discuss their rights and plot courses of action was referred to as Liberty Hall.[12] In addition to dock workers, membership of the Sons of Liberty gradually expanded to include lawyers, merchants, and craftsmen.[13] The Sons of Liberty were not always benign and peaceful. As a matter of fact, they were a vibrant and vivid early example of American-style vigilantism at work throughout the colonies. There are many recorded instances of the group planning and carrying out threats of intimidation against shop owners who continually conducted commerce with Great Britain. Some colonial stores were vandalized by having rocks and bricks tossed through store windows. British tax collecting officials, such as Andrew Oliver, were hung in effigy from the Liberty Tree, and rocks were chucked through Oliver's house.[14]

The Sons of Liberty were also responsible for conducting riots on the streets of Boston as well as setting fires to the various homes of judges and customs officials sympathetic to the British government. In addition, they occasionally engaged in the draconian act of tarring and feathering any British official whom they deemed it necessary to make a public spectacle of on the streets and public squares of Boston. First, the targeted British official would be stripped butt naked. Secondly, hot sticky tar would be poured over his entire body, causing third-degree burns. Finally, plucked goose feathers would be cast over his body head-to-toe, and the ghastly victim would be paraded about town to the wild and loud cheers of unsympathetic Colonials. Often the tarred-and-feathered victim would not survive the hellish incident, and if he were to live through this sadistic punishment, he would be severely scarred for life. It appears that some elements of rough and tough Puritan influence and justice were still evident at the time throughout New England. At any rate, the Sons of Liberty were certainly stout men and rabble-rousers who were not to be trifled with.

Colonial women who were the wives of the Sons of Liberty formed their equivalent secret society called the Daughters of Liberty. They would conduct boycotts of British goods and supported their husbands in the cause of protest—including the preservation of plucked fowl feathers their husbands would require for tarring and feathering. These scrappy, determined men and women of both secret societies were not sissies or wimps by any long shot as they bravely carried out various acts of protest while placing their own lives, property, and prosperity at serious risk when confronting the tyranny of Great Britain. Such men and women reasoned they were more than justified for taking the law into their own hands since the laws of Great Britain had failed them at every turn. Such historical decisions and actions should serve as a stirring reminder to the American people that this nation was forged, in large part, out of pure grit and steadfast determination.

This pure grit is not at all reflective of the romantic scenes we fondly recall while viewing Walt Disney's quaint film, *Johnny Tremain*. In this film, the Sons of Liberty are seen happily parading about the streets of Boston while singing a lovely little ditty in rhyme after successfully conducting the famous Boston Tea Party, as if they were impervious to British Redcoat retaliation. This makes for feel-good viewing, but the realities of Colonial Boston were a far cry from what that film portrays. The stark reality is this: Such acts of protest and violence perpetrated by the patriotic Sons and Daughters of Liberty were conceived in secret places out of desperation and often carried out in secrecy under the cover of dark nights. Why do you think the Sons of Liberty, who organized and participated in the Boston Tea Party of 1773, did so under the disguise of Native Americans? They didn't want to reveal their true identities to British officials and soldiers because they feared the hangman's noose!

Naturally, England determined these protests to be unfair, unjustified, and a direct challenge to her authority over her colonies. Parliament passed the Quartering Act in 1765 to help protect its officials, customs agents, and Royal Governors against all forms of protest and mob violence. The Quartering Act forced American Colonials to not only provide free housing for British Redcoats, but it also required the Colonials to provide soldiers with free food, clothing, and supplies.[15] General Thomas Gage was dispatched from England to command thousands of troops quartered in Boston and New York. Most of the British Lobster backs were gentlemen with regard to how they treated their American hosts, but there are instances in which some unscrupulous soldiers took advantage of the situation by pillaging and burning some American homes. One can imagine the outrage and indignation exhibited by American Colonials in response to being compelled to house, feed, and supply these troops at their own expense. Americans were busy enough trying to fend for themselves and their own families without having to fret about providing sustenance for British Redcoats who were not welcomed on American soil in the first place. Because the Quartering Act had such an indelible impact on the

American people, the Founding Fathers saw perfectly fit to include the Third Amendment in the Constitution, which stipulated that Americans would no longer be required to quarter soldiers in their homes.

As tensions between England and her colonies increased, Royal Governors began to dissolve some of the colonial assemblies. Samuel Adams of Boston was furious because he viewed these acts as further violations of their rights as English citizens—rights that were espoused by the English philosopher, John Locke. Samuel Adams and other Founding Fathers maintained England was holding us to a double standard whereby the citizens in England were being given rights under the law and held to one standard while the British-American citizens in the colonies were being denied these same rights and held to an entirely different standard.

On March 5, 1770, British soldiers fired upon American Colonials at the Boston Customs House on King Street, killing five Patriots. This became known as the Boston Massacre.[16] Samuel Adams wrote an article about the massacre, and the silversmith Paul Revere, who was also a member of the Sons of Liberty, published an exaggerated illustration of the event in the Boston Gazette. The illustration became an effective propaganda tool for whipping up anti-British fervor in newspaper articles, pamphlets, and posters throughout the thirteen colonies.[17]

To further spread news of important events in the colonies, Samuel Adams established a Committee of Correspondence in November of 1772 so that the other colonies could be kept informed as to how the rights of Americans in New England were continually being violated by British authorities.[18] As similar Committees of Correspondence were established throughout the thirteen colonies, the American Colonials were truly united for the first time in their cause against England. Of course, these Committees of Correspondence were quite illegal at the time, and they go directly to the core of why our Founding Fathers would eventually include freedoms of speech, the press, and assembly in the First Amendment to the American Constitution. American Colonials could not legally meet in public to protest England's taxation without representation. They could not legally publish articles in local newspapers criticizing the quartering of British soldiers in their homes. They could no longer possess duly elected legislative assemblies for the purpose of enacting policies on their own behalf, nor could they legally conduct political discussions and debates in public because Royal Governors suspended such privileges.

The final roots of independence and revolution occurred in 1774 when Parliament passed the infamous Intolerable Acts to punish Boston for the Boston Tea Party, which was conducted by the Sons of Liberty in December of 1773.[19] When these men dressed up as Indians and dumped over 300 chests of expensive tea overboard from three British ships docked in Boston Harbor to protest the Tea Act of 1773, Britain was absolutely furious. The Intolerable Acts of 1774 closed the port of Boston until the Colonials paid for the destroyed tea. The acts officially banned all Committees of Correspondence, and they put Boston under martial law with the stationing of 6,000 additional British Redcoats on the Boston Common. The Intolerable Acts also permitted British officials accused of committing crimes in the colonies to stand trial in London rather than in America. The punitive restrictions were absolutely devastating to the economy of Boston, and as a direct result, local merchants were going out of business as all trade was halted not only between Boston and England, but between Boston and the other colonies. People began to go hungry as imported food became scarce. To maintain martial law, thousands of British Lobster backs patrolled the streets of Boston enforcing curfews. Out of necessity, both the First and Second Continental Congresses met at Independence Hall in Philadelphia in order to decide how the colonies were going to respond to Britain's continual tyrannical acts.

All of the historical events chronicled in this chapter were not only a driving force down the path of American independence and revolution, but they were also a direct cause for the inclusion of the Bill of Rights in the American Constitution. Before clarifying in greater detail the importance of the Bill of Rights historically as well as its relevance to contemporary America in the next chapter of this book, I should acknowledge the sacrifices our Founding Fathers made when they signed the Declaration of Independence on July 4th, 1776. Who were these men? What were their backgrounds? What kind of risk did they assume by meeting secretly in Philadelphia in 1775 and 1776? When we explore the answers to these important questions and reflect briefly upon the profound contributions they made in American history, perhaps we can invoke a deeper appreciation and respect for the sacrifices these men and their families made in formally establishing our great republic. I would like to recommend a book that is a fascinating read as it illustrates in considerable depth and detail the biographies, accomplishments, and sacrifices of the signers of the Declaration of Independence in 1776. The book is called the *Signers of the Declaration of Independence,* written by Robert G. Ferris and Richard E. Morris, and it is published by Interpretive Publications, Inc. For the sake of brevity as well as for the purpose of making some compelling arguments shortly, some key facts from the *Signers of the Declaration of Independence* will be included in this chapter.

The fifty-six resolute men who were delegates to the Second Continental Congress met secretly in 1776 in what would later be dubbed Independence Hall in Philadelphia, Pennsylvania. These dauntless men were diverse in background, yet they possessed similarities in education, experience, and personal accomplishments.[20] Such illustrious delegates were indeed the "cream of the crop" of their respective colonies, and they were dispatched to Philadelphia by their legislative assemblies to devise a response to the tyrannical acts of Great Britain. Most of these men were wealthy, and most were American-born.[21]

More than half of the Southern delegates were members of the planter class and owned slaves. The signers of the Declaration of Independence varied in age. Edward Rutledge was the youngest at the age of twenty-six, while Benjamin Franklin was the oldest at the age of seventy.[22] Five of the men, including the famous agitators John Hancock and Samuel Adams, had attended the Boston Latin School. Half of the delegates obtained their higher education in colonial colleges or from abroad. The others studied at home, in local schools or private academies, and some studied with tutors, while several men were self-taught.[23] With regard to wealth, there was diversity within the ranks. One of the wealthiest was Charles Carroll of Maryland, yet Samuel Adams of Massachusetts was of very limited financial means; friends back home in Boston deemed it necessary to supply him with money and clothes in order for him to attend Congress.[24] A number of diverse professions were represented in Congress. More than half were educated in law; some earned their living as merchants and shippers, and twenty-five percent of them earned their subsistence from agriculture. Last, but certainly not least, four of the signers were trained as ministers, including William Hooper of North Carolina, Lyman Hall of Georgia, Robert Treat Paine of Massachusetts, and the acting clergyman of the Second Continental Congress, the Reverend John Witherspoon of New Jersey.[25]

Our Founding Fathers clearly understood the impending danger as well as all of the ramifications that are intrinsic to resisting any large tyrannical government because they had witnessed these firsthand. That is precisely why they declared independence from Great Britain and proceeded to forge a republic consisting of a federal government with limited power. The Constitution provides for limited government through the application of the principles of Separation of Powers, Checks and Balances, and balance of power not only between the states and the federal government, but between the federal government and the individual as stipulated in the Bill of Rights. What is truly remarkable about the delegates of the Second Continental Congress in 1776 is that they were not at all disingenuous with one another or with the people they represented. They were very open and transparent with their viewpoints, and the Founding Fathers believed continual personal contact between them and their constituents was equally important. Indeed, the arguments for or against independence were at times very heated, but they did not pretend they were above the law or had any less of a stake in what their Declaration of Independence would require of the new nation they were about to establish. Personal sacrifice would be required of every Patriot or Loyalist, of every class, of every occupation, of every race, of every man and woman, of every adult and child. As such, every reader of this book should seriously reflect upon the meaning of what the concluding sentence of the Declaration of Independence states:

> **And for the support of this Declaration, with a firm reliance on the protection of divine Providence, we mutually pledge to each other our Lives, our Fortunes and our sacred Honor.**

These concluding words are very profound, and they were not penned by Thomas Jefferson only for the purpose of serving as quaint and poetic thoughts to be affectionately reflected upon by future generations of Americans. Jefferson's concluding statement reflects the exact same seriousness of thought and bold aspiration once proclaimed by John Winthrop when he delineated the purpose of his "City upon a Hill." In *The Signers of the Declaration of Independence*, authors Ferris and Morris brilliantly illustrate for us just how **heroically** these closing words of the Declaration of Independence would be played out in the exciting drama of our illustrious history. Here are some of the authors' closing words to their introduction of part two of their book:

For their dedication to the cause of independence, the signers risked loss of fortune, imprisonment, and death for treason.... The homes of nearly one-third of the signers were destroyed or damaged, and the families of a few were scattered when the British pillaged or confiscated their estates.

Nearly all of the group emerged poorer for their years of public service and neglect of personal affairs. Although a couple of the merchants and shippers among them profited from the war, the businesses of most of them deteriorated as a result of embargoes on trade with Britain and heavy financial losses when their ships were confiscated or destroyed at sea. Several forfeited to the Government precious specie for virtually worthless Continental currency or made donations or loans, usually unrepaid, to their colonies or the Government. Some even sold their personal property to help finance the war. Certainly most of the signers had little or nothing to gain materially and practically all to lose when they subscribed to the Declaration of Independence. By doing so, they earned a niche of honor in the annals of the United States.[26]

The signers of the Declaration of Independence were not the only Patriots who sacrificed a great deal for the American Revolution by mutually pledging to each other their lives, fortunes, and sacred honor. As Americans, we can all be eternally grateful to Jewish financier and Patriot Haym Salomon, who opened a brokerage house in Philadelphia and became one of the wealthiest men in the colonies. Salomon contributed his **entire fortune** to our Continental Congress so that the Continental Army could be clothed, fed, and compensated for services rendered. His funds also paid the salaries of government officials and officers in the army. Salomon died a young hero's death at the age of forty-five, and his fortune was nearly depleted. His descendants were never repaid the debt owed by the United States government.[27]

What about the valiant sacrifices made by other common men and women? There were thousands of Patriots of all ages who sacrificed their lives and fortunes by serving in the Continental Army under George Washington as well as in the various volunteer militias throughout the newly established United States of America. African-American colonists, both free and enslaved, contributed heroically to their country during the Revolutionary War. More than 5,000 black soldiers volunteered for military service to defend America against the tyranny of Great Britain and fought valiantly in all of the major battles of the Revolution. More than 6,000 blacks who were slaves at the beginning of the war were free men and women when it ended. The African-American Patriot Crispus Attucks was one of the first of five men to die in the famous Boston Massacre in 1770. While defending a friend from British Redcoat attack, Attucks is reported to have said, "Don't be afraid. Knock 'em over. They dare not fire!"[28] As a matter of fact, the British did fire on the colonists on King Street, and Attucks and four others died. The talented African-American poet Phillis Wheatley wrote a stirring poem dedicated to General George Washington. Washington sent Wheatley an invitation to visit him at his headquarters in Cambridge, Massachusetts, to personally thank her, and they both enjoyed a thirty-minute private conversation. Sadly, America's first African-American poet died at the age of thirty-one. Peter Salem was another distinguished African-American Patriot whose career began at the Battles of Lexington and Concord. In June of 1775, Salem faced Major Pitcairn of Great Britain a final time. It was Salem's musket shot that felled Pitcairn at the Battle of Bunker Hill. Peter Salem continued to fight for America at the Battles of Saratoga and Stony Point.

More than 20,000 brave Daughters of Liberty assisted their soldier husbands during the Revolution in order to tend babies and injuries from camp to camp. Female Patriot Margaret Corbin is a remarkable character in American history. She was twenty-five when she accompanied her husband on the battlefield. When Corbin's husband was killed at Fort Washington, New York, she took-up arms and was wounded herself. Margaret transferred to the Invalid Corps where wounded soldiers recruited and trained cadets. She was discharged in April of 1783 and earned the nickname "Captain Molly." Sarah Fulton was known as the Mother of the Boston Tea Party. During the Revolutionary War, she led a group of women carrying baskets of bandages and liniment to the bloody scene of Bunker Hill in Boston. Sarah and other women Patriots created a temporary hospital in the rugged surrounding to tend to the wounded Americans, and it was reported that "she never left until every wound had been dressed and every sufferer cared for."[29] One of the most heroic figures of the Revolutionary War was Deborah Sampson, who disguised herself as a man in order to join the Continental Army. She took on the identity of "Timothy Thayer." When discovered, she was discharged, but she reenlisted in the Fourth Massachusetts Regiment in 1782 as "Private Robert Shurtleff." She fought in several battles and was wounded. Martha Bratton stored gunpowder for the American Continentals at her home in South Carolina, and when Loyalists informed the British what she was up to, they proceeded to march to her home to try and confiscate the contraband. Martha Bratton saw to it that the British would not succeed with their plan when she spread a line of gunpowder from where it was being stored all the way to the road. She patiently waited for the approach of the British. When they arrived at her home, she lit a match to ignite it, and the huge explosion effectively thwarted the mission of the British.

Now, compare the heroic activities of the more than 20,000 Daughters of Liberty during the Revolutionary War period in American history to those women whom I choose to refer to as America's Daughters of Shame—namely, members of the radical antiwar movement, CodePINK. I recently discovered this disgusting article on their Contra Costa Times website for Night Owl that appeared in October of 2007. The title of the article is "Little

Berkeley House of Horrors: Taking It to The Pink." Here are some excerpts from the ladies in Pink:

Dearest CodePINK Com Madres and allies:

CodePINK invites you to join us all day Halloween 7:30 a.m. until 5:00 p.m. at the Real House of Horrors: Marine Recruiting Station, 64 Shattuck Square, Berkeley. Bring your pumpkins to carve into heads of horror! We'll mount them on bamboo poles in front of the station. Bring Real Faces of War photos, dead babies, bloodied hands/limbs for the House of Horrors. Paint R.I.P. tombstones with our Bill of Rights. Come dressed as the Ghost of our Constitution, the cost of war, the horrors of war. Or, come dressed as the Witch of Peace who will cast a powerful spell over these horrors...... Together we WILL SHUT DOWN the Marine Recruiting Station.

Posted on Tuesday, October 30, 2007.[30]

Now isn't that just lovely and quite noble? The above posting is an example of CodePINK's interpretation of "**we mutually pledge to each other our lives, our fortunes, and our sacred honor.**" Look how far we have come in such a relatively short period of time! Imagine our brave Marines and their recruiting stations being compared to a Halloween horror house. Don't you just appreciate the manner in which these CodePINK women make a mockery of our brave men and women in uniform, our Bill of Rights, and our Constitution? Thank God the Daughters of Liberty during the 1700s did not behave so deplorably as CodePINK does today or we may never have won the American Revolution. We would still be British citizens to this very day. Here is another choice example.

The following excerpts are from an article called "Activists Talk Love, Not War, With Iranian President" by Jennifer Lawinsky, which appeared on the FOXNews.com website on Thursday, September 25, 2008. Ms Lawinsky reported, "Activists from the radical antiwar group CodePINK met with the president of Iran in New York on Wednesday, pitching a 'peace park' and investment in a bicycle maker as ways to patch relations between the United States and Islamic republic."[31] She continues to report, "Mahmoud Ahmadinejad, in New York to address the U.N. General Assembly, met with CodePINK co-founders Jodie Evans and Medea Benjamin and about 150 peace activists at the Grand Hyatt Hotel. During the two-hour meeting, members of CodePINK presented the Iranian president with a petition signed by 50 American mayors calling for diplomacy, not war, in dealing with Iran. CodePINK wants to take the mayors who signed the petition to Iran to create 'sister cities.' 'We're modeling diplomacy,' Evans said of her meeting with Ahmadinejad." Lawinsky continues, "Ahmadinejad told the group that he wants a million Americans to come to Iran, but members of CodePINK have had trouble getting visas to visit the country—including Benjamin who is Jewish....Evans said Ahmadinejad is really about peace and human rights and respecting justice."[32]

This entire mishmash of naiveté on the part of CodePink is nothing but a prime example of mindless, foolish hogwash, and as far as this author is concerned, CodePink's actions are at the very least unpatriotic, and at worst, border on acts of treason by consorting with the enemy. The words of hate we have all heard spewing forth from Ahmadinejad's evil mouth have reflected nothing other than blind hatred, bigotry, and violence—especially when targeted toward Israel and America. Now this is coming from a man who CodePINK believes promotes peace and human rights, correct? Ahmadinejad is about as sympathetic to the cause of peace, justice, and human rights as was Adolf Hitler! Ahmadinejad would love to see the Jewish people and the State of Israel wiped off the face of our planet, yet CodePINK and its radical leftist leaders take on the role of peacemaker. Their repugnant exploits are reminiscent of the exploits of Jane Fonda, or "Hanoi Jane" as she is aptly remembered, with the traitorous manner in which she cozied up to the Vietcong in North Vietnam during the Vietnam War of the 1960s and 1970s. Again, one would think individuals or special-interest groups would learn from history, but apparently there are still numerous fools amongst us who continue to ignore its lessons.

Shame on CodePINK and those fifty mayors! Perhaps our government should go right ahead and issue all of the necessary visas to members of CodePINK who desire to travel to Iran. Maybe we would actually be fortunate enough to find all of these schlemiels in the hands of radical Muslim terrorist groups who just might give them a lesson in extreme, radical Islamic justice! They could experience firsthand, without the protection of our brave US Marines whom they despise, the ghastly version of peace, justice, and human rights al-Qaeda or Ahmadinejad would be more than willing to dispense. In fact, CodePink members could really celebrate Halloween together Middle East-style, just as our innocent American hostages of the 1970s were forced to until they were finally released. However, in this particular case, CodePink could slowly saunter down the bloody halls of Iran's House of Horrors—courtesy perhaps of its Ayatollahs or al-Qaeda! Many of us back home would be quite curious as to whether or not CodePINK's Witch of Peace could cast an effective spell, thus thwarting the violent acts of al-Qaeda! Code-PINK certainly does have First Amendment rights to free speech, protest, and peaceful assembly here in America, just like the rest of us. However, there is a huge difference between engaging in those types of activities protected for all of us by the Constitution versus actually consorting with our enemies and their leaders. Communication and diplomacy with our enemies should best be left to our duly elected representatives and their appointed officials, such as those working in the State Department. None of us elected Code-PINK or any of our cities' mayors to fulfill that role, last I checked.

Wouldn't it be quite fascinating if we could somehow bring back the Daughters of Liberty of the 1700s from their graves? It would be most intriguing to witness how these tough ladies of our past would effectively deal with these CodePINK ladies of today, or the Daughters of Shame, as I prefer to call them. We would more than likely be treated to the resurrection of the use of tarring-and-feathering amongst other things. As was the case with the Sons of Liberty, the Daughters of Liberty were women not to be trifled with. They would have absolutely no patience or tolerance for the likes of CodePINK and other like-minded individuals!

In conclusion to this chapter, I would like to reiterate that we Americans are tragically witnessing before our very eyes the governmental takeover of our corporations, banks, and other financial institutions as well as the federal government's tyrannical power-grab being perpetrated against the fifty states and the American people. This is our current government's interpretation of **"we mutually pledge to each other our lives, our fortunes, and our sacred honor."** How many of our senators, Congressmen, and greedy Wall Street corporate thieves of the recent past are more than willing to set an example for the rest of the nation by mutually pledging their own lives, fortunes, and sacred honor for the good of the country? Are President Barack Obama and the members of his administration also willing to do the same for the nation? They are more than willing, however, to pledge on everyone's behalf, our own lives, fortunes, and sacred honor for the supposed good of the country. Just where are the contemporary counterparts to the heroes and heroines of our country's past to be found today? Where are the Minutemen and Sons and Daughters of Liberty of today?

I'll tell you where they are! They are the brave men and women serving in our armed forces, who are more than willing to pledge and sacrifice their own lives, fortunes, and sacred honor so that the very freedoms and rights our Founding Fathers fought and died for are preserved for posterity. They are also the average working men and women of this country who get up every morning in order to put in an honest day's work. They are the teachers, policemen, firefighters, doctors, nurses, farmers, ranchers, preachers, and businessmen and businesswomen who continually strive to make this country great. They are also the Americans who are volunteering their time in their local communities and donating some of their money to charity in order to assist their neighbors in need when tragedy strikes—whether it be hurricanes, earthquakes, oil spills, or hard financial times. On the other hand, where are the politicians who are willing to fight for the ideals expressed in our Declaration of Independence? As a nation, America is desperately searching for them, and perhaps we found many such individuals in the midterm elections of 2010. Only time will tell. There certainly isn't a shortage, however, of shameful or traitorous behavior out and about, now is there? Recall the outrageous MoveOn.org add that ran several years ago in the nation's newspapers that had a picture of General David Petraeus with the following caption under his profile stating in bold print:[33]

GENERAL PETRAEUS OR
GENERAL BETRAY US?

When General Petraeus once appeared to testify before Congress on our progress in Iraq, he was confronted by a bunch of whining, sniveling, childish wimps that accurately portrayed our Congress in Washington, DC, for what it truly is—a Congress that is undoubtedly the exact opposite of the intellectually driven and patriotic Second Continental Congress that met in secret at Independence Hall in Philadelphia, Pennsylvania, from 1775 to 1776. Had our Founding Fathers resembled our current Congress in any fashion, our great nation would never have had the wherewithal to sever its ties with Great Britain, to aggressively fight the Revolutionary War and prevail, and proceed to establish the greatest republic in the history of the world.

3

Common Sense
R.I.P.

How few there are who have courage enough to own
their faults, or resolution enough to mend them.

— Ben Franklin

The first chapter of this book alluded to the fact that an insidious war is being waged upon the Bill of Rights of the US Constitution by well-organized and well-funded secular-progressive organizations. Chapter two included a brief synopsis of pertinent historical events in American history which laid the foundation for the creation and inclusion of the Bill of Rights in our Constitution, and this was necessary in order to link the historical significance of the Bill of Rights to its relevance in today's society. This chapter will grapple with the current weapons of mass destruction being utilized by far-left advocacy groups as well as radical, liberal judges who are intent on twisting and manipulating the original meaning of our Constitution as a direct result of their legislating from the bench. Since the year 1961, the United States Supreme Court, often dominated by progressive, far-left judges, has tragically betrayed the American people, and our country has never been the same. As a nation currently in decline, we are reaping what we have sowed because of some of the vile decisions that have been handed down by the Supreme Court in the early 1960s. Consider the following:

We are presently at another defining moment in American history wherein Americans must determine once and for all whether we are going to be guided and governed by the US Constitution, which is the supreme law of the land, or whether we are going to continue to be governed by elected officials and judges who only pay quaint lip service to that remarkable contract. It is extraordinarily ironic that our elected officials must pledge allegiance to the Constitution when they are sworn into office with the vow that they will obey and defend it, yet when they assume office and govern, many either neglect the Constitution or they totally sidestep that very oath they promised to obey! Do words and oaths of allegiance continue to mean anything anymore in this country, or have such obligatory oaths recited by various elected officials every two years become nothing more than just benign, hackneyed ceremonies of frivolity? **The American Constitution says what it means and means what it says.** Should we fail to hearken back to that fundamental tenet, our republic—as we currently know it—is doomed, and America will become a nation that our Founding Fathers would not even recognize.

From time to time, I receive fascinating anecdotes of interest on my computer at home. When I stated earlier that we are reaping what we have sowed since 1961, here is one fascinating example that perfectly illustrates the very point that is the topic of this chapter. The following anecdote is written by Lori Borgman who graciously granted me permission to reprint it in its entirety. You can also find it on Ms Borgman's website, lori@loriborgman.com.[1]

The Death of Common Sense

Three yards of black fabric enshroud my computer terminal. I am mourning the passing of an old friend by the name of Common Sense. His obituary reads as follows: Common Sense, aka C.S., lived a long life, but died from heart failure at the brink of the millennium. No one really knows how old he was, his birth records were long ago entangled in miles and miles of bureaucratic red tape. Known affectionately to close friends as Horse Sense and Sound Thinking, he selflessly devoted himself to a life of service in homes, schools, hospitals and offices, helping folks get jobs done without a lot of fanfare, whooping and hollering.

Rules and regulations and petty, frivolous lawsuits held no power over C.S. A most reliable sage, he was credited with cultivating the ability to know when to come in out of the rain, the discovery that the early bird gets the worm and how to take the bitter with the sweet.

C.S. also developed sound financial policies (don't spend more than you earn), reliable parenting strategies (the adult is in charge, not the kid) and prudent dietary plans (offset eggs and bacon with a little fiber and orange juice).

A veteran of the Industrial Revolution, the Great Depression, the Technological Revolution and the Smoking Crusades, C.S. survived sundry cultural and educational trends including disco, the men's movement, body piercing, whole language and new math. C.S.'s health began declining in the late 1960's when he became infected with the If-It-Feels-Good, Do-It virus.

In the following decades, his waning strength proved no match for the ravages of overbearing federal and state rules and regulations and an oppressive tax code. C.S. was sapped of strength and the will to live as the Ten Commandments became contraband, criminals received better treatment than victims and judges stuck their noses in everything from Boy Scouts to professional baseball and golf.

This deterioration accelerated as schools implemented zero-tolerance policies. Reports of 6-year-old boys charged with sexual harassment for kissing class-mates, a teen suspended for taking a swig of Scope mouthwash after lunch, girls suspended for possess-ing Midol, and an honor student expelled for having a table knife in her school lunch were more than his heart could endure.

As the end neared, doctors say C.S. drifted in and out of logic but was kept informed of developments regarding regulations on low-flow toilets and mandatory air bags. Finally, upon hearing about a government plan to ban inhalers from 14 million asthmatics due to a trace of a pollutant that may be harmful to the environment, C.S. breathed his last.

Services will be at Whispering Pines Cemetery. C.S. was preceded in death by his wife, Discretion; one daughter, Responsibility; and one son, Reason. He is survived by two stepbrothers, Half-Wit and Dim-Wit.

Memorial contributions may be sent to the Institute for Rational Thought. Farewell, Common Sense. May you rest in peace.

Ms Borgman is absolutely correct. We really have come a long way since 1961 with the death of Common Sense, which will be further elaborated upon throughout this chapter. But first, let us reflect upon some additional germane historical facts.

Two very influential Virginians played important roles when crafting the US Constitution at the Federal Convention being held in Independence Hall, Philadelphia, in 1787. They were James Madison, the Father of the Constitution, and James Mason, author of the Virginia Declaration of Rights, and both men inspired the federal Bill of Rights.[2] Madison believed that the new federal government should be of limited powers and that power not delegated to it would be retained by the states or the people. Mason, on the other hand, believed the federal government could erode or intrude upon the powers of the states. Mason said, "there would be much difficulty in organizing a government upon this great scale and at the same time reserving to the state legislatures a sufficient portion of power for promoting and securing the prosperity and happiness of their respective citizens...."[3] Mason was wary of the enormous power of the federal government, and he and his followers called for guarantees of personal liberties. Because of their political stance, Mason and his followers were better known as Anti-Federalists, whereas James Madison and his followers were referred to as Federalists because they thought the Constitution, in its original form, already guaranteed personal liberties.[4] The political theory of the Federalists had its advocates with the Federalist Papers, written by John Jay (the nation's first chief justice), Alexander Hamilton (the first secretary of the treasury), and of course, James Madison (the fourth president). The Anti-Federalists had their eloquent advocates with Mason's essays called "Objections"; George Clinton of New York used the pen name "Cato" for his newspaper articles, and Melancton Smith wrote under the title of a "Federal Farmer."[5] During the heated debates at the Federal Convention, both sides argued as to whether the Constitution needed the inclusion of some form of statement of rights for American citizens. We should be eternally grateful that the Anti-Federalists won the argument, and posterity will forever be in debt to these men as they forced the Federalists to compromise. By December of 1791, the Bill of Rights was officially part of the US Constitution when Virginia was the last state to ratify it. Here is precisely what the First Amendment says:

> Congress shall make no law respecting an establishment of religion, or prohibiting the free exercise thereof; or abridging the freedom of speech, or of the press; or the right of the people peaceably to assemble, and petition the Government for a redress of grievances.

Of the five individual rights embedded in the First Amendment, the most controversial today is the one dealing with the "establishment clause," so that is the one I would like to address first.

Our Founding Fathers broke with the tradition other European countries had established over the centuries when such countries compelled their citizenry to worship in state-sponsored churches. As was pointed out in chapter one, when the Pilgrims and Puritans of England landed on our shores in the early 1600s, they did so because they sought religious freedom from the Church of England that they were forced to attend while residing there. They came to these shores to escape religious persecution so they could worship in the manner of their own choosing. Even when the Puritan Roger Williams was banished from the Commonwealth of Massachusetts in 1635 for his unorthodox beliefs, he secured a Royal Charter in 1644 for the colony of Rhode Island. As a result, Rhode Island became a tolerant safe haven for religious minorities such as Roman Catholics, Jews, and Quakers.[6] It was because of our ancestors fleeing religious persecution in England as well as in our own New England, that our Founding Fathers deemed it prudent not to have Congress fashion a law establishing a national church or religion. Having said that, however, a clarion call needs to ring forth.

Make no mistake about it; there is ample evidence which will be cited in this chapter that will substantiate how modern secular-progressives and other radicals are spinning an elaborate, sinister web of deceit with the intent to completely eradicate all religious practices and references to religion from our local, state, and federal governments as well as other public arenas in America. They are attempting to dupe all Americans into believing that the "establishment clause" in the First Amendment was designed by our Founding Fathers to do just that! Nothing could be further from the truth. Pay heed to this quote from George Washington in a reassuring letter he wrote to the Jewish Touro Synagogue of Newport, Rhode Island: "Happily, the Government of the United States, which gives to bigotry no sanction, to persecution no assistance, requires only that they who live under its protection should demean themselves as good citizens...."[7] James Madison, the architect of our Constitution also said, "There is not a shadow of right in the general (federal) government to intermeddle with religion. Its least interference would be a most flagrant usurpation."[8] Madison is referring, of course, to the "free exercise clause" of the First Amendment (which tends to be ignored by secular-progressives). With regard to religious diversity, Madison also stated more than 200 years ago, ".... America is the best and only security for religion...."[9] The following treatise will shed more light on the "establishment clause" of the First Amendment as well as America's religious heritage.

Joseph Loconte is the *William E. Simon Fellow in Religion and a Free Society* at the Heritage Foundation. The following excerpts of Mr. Loconte can be found within Heritage Lectures No.

899, published by The Heritage Foundation, and it was delivered on May 26, 2005. Mr. Loconte's lecture is titled, *Why Religious Values Support American Values,* and his remarks are adapted from a debate sponsored by the Oxford Union Society at Oxford, England. He argued against the proposition that "Christian Values Undermine American Values." Here are some highlights of Mr. Loconte's scholarly lecture that are quite illuminating:

> Consider this statement from James Madison: "We have staked the whole future of American civilization, not upon the power of government.... We have staked the future upon the capacity of each and all of us to govern ourselves, to sustain ourselves, according to the Ten Commandments of God." And this, from Thomas Jefferson: "No nation has ever yet existed or been governed without religion. Nor can be. The Christian religion is the best religion that has ever been given to man, and I as chief Magistrate of this nation am bound to give it the sanction of my example." Benjamin Rush observed: "I have always considered Christianity as the strong ground of republicanism." And John Jay (the first Chief Justice of the Supreme Court) declared: "No human society has ever been able to maintain both order and freedom, both cohesiveness and liberty apart from the moral precepts of the Christian religion....Should our Republic ever forget this fundamental precept of governance... this great experiment will then surely be doomed." That rugged English Quaker, William Penn, founded a "holy experiment" in religious liberty in Pennsylvania, a model that would inspire America's Founding generation....

Joseph Loconte continues:

> And so it was that James Madison, architect of the American Constitution, came to regard freedom of conscience as a

sacred right and a binding political obligation. It was Madison, a pupil under the evangelical minister John Witherspoon at Princeton, who enshrined the guarantee of religious liberty in our political imagination. "If this freedom be abused," he warned, "it is an offense against God, not against man."

Loconte continues:

But consider the fruit of this Christian virtue translated into the American experience: The United States is a nation of breathtaking ethnic and religious diversity, with thousands of different religious groups and traditions. And yet we have sustained a level of civic peace and social stability that is the envy of the world....

Loconte further states:

Consider another consequence of this biblical value of freedom of conscience, reinforced in American society. It is our great tradition of social protest, of social reform. Who led the decades-long fight to end slavery in the United States? It was Northern evangelicals, who petitioned lawmakers, rescued runaway slaves, and gave birth to the Republican Party. Who launched massive rescue missions for thousands of poor families during the economic upheaval of the early 20th century? It was that British import known as the Salvation Army. Who led the civil rights movement in the face of violent white supremacists and a hostile legal culture? A Baptist minister, the Reverend Martin Luther King, joined by brave foot soldiers from black churches throughout the country.

In each case, the Christian concept of religious freedom, embedded in our political system, made possible the great challenges to that same political system....Thus, the United

States is, and always has been, a nation of dissenters. Whether the cause is civic, political, or religious, we insist on the right to disagree....[10]

These excerpts from Joseph Loconte's lecture accentuate the point that our Founding Fathers never envisioned the "establishment clause" to be twisted and manipulated into something other than what it truly is. Up until the second half of the twentieth century, when we began to witness the demise of Common Sense, as Ms Borgman so aptly illustrated, religious elements and their practice in the public arena by both private citizens as well as public servants were never interpreted by our federal courts or Supreme Court to be a violation of the "establishment clause!" We have always had government paid chaplains in Congress leading our Congressmen and senators in prayer throughout the centuries. Our presidents have continually recited the oath of office before the chief justice of the Supreme Court as well as the American people, doing so with their hands resting on the Holy Bible while stating, "So help me God." The Ten Commandments are the foundation of America's jurisprudence, and that is precisely the reason why they are permanently enshrined upon the wall that is poised directly behind the seats where the nine justices of the United States Supreme Court sit. Isn't it ironic, not to mention hypocritical, how perfectly acceptable and constitutional it is for the US Supreme Court to publicly acknowledge the Ten Commandments, yet the judges who have served on that same court have illogically and arrogantly ruled that lower courts throughout our nation may not be permitted to do the very same thing? The Supreme Court has ruled similarly with regard to the posting of the Ten Commandments in America's public schools. This is absolute lunacy—as if somehow the lower courts and public schools in this nation are any more public than the United States Supreme Court, which is a branch of the federal government.

The New England Primer was a textbook used by public school students throughout New England and other English settlements from the 1700s to the 1800s.[11] It followed a tradition of combining the study of the alphabet with Bible reading. The primer also contained a catechism of religious questions and answers. Emphasis was placed on fear of sin, God's punishment, etc.[12] Take a look at examples of the 1777 edition of *The New England Primer*. Over five million copies of the book were sold.[13]

THE NEW ENGLAND PRIMER

1777 edition

A Lesson for Children.

Pray to God. Call no ill names. Love God. Use no ill words. Fear God. Tell no lies. Serve God. Hate Lies. Take not God's Speak the Truth. Name in vain. Spend your Time well. Do not Swear. Love your School. Do not Steal. Mind your Book. Cheat not in your play. Strive to learn. Play not with bad boys. Be not a Dunce.

Divine Song of Praise to GOD, for a Child,

by the Rev. Dr. Watts.

HOW glorious is our heavenly King,
Who reigns above tha Sky!
How shall a Child presume to sing
His dreadful Majesty!
How great his Power is none can tell,
Nor think how large his grace:
Nor men below, nor Saints that dwell,
On high before his Face.
Nor Angels that stand round the Lord,
Can search his secret will;
But they perform his heav'nly Word,
And sing his Praises still.
Then let me join this holy Train;
And my first Off'rings bring;
The eternal GOD will not disdain
To hear an Infant sing.
My Heart resolves, my Tongue obeys,
And Angels shall rejoice,
To hear their mighty Maker's Praise,
Sound from a feeble Voice.

A — In ADAM'S Fall / We sinned all.

B — Heaven to find; / The Bible Mind.

C — Christ crucify'd / For sinners dy'd.

D — The Deluge drown'd / The Earth around.

E — ELIJAH hid / By Ravens fed.

F — The judgment made / FELIX afraid.

G — As runs the Glass, / Our Life doth pass.

H — My Book and Heart / Must never part.

J — JOB feels the Rod,-- / Yet blesses GOD.

K — Proud Korah's troop / Was swallowed up

L — LOT fled to *Zoar*, / Saw fiery Shower / On *Sodom* pour.

Another well-known textbook series used in America's public schools throughout the nineteenth and twentieth centuries were the McGuffey Readers. At least 120 million copies of McGuffey Readers were sold for use in public schools between the years 1836 and 1960.[14] The following is a sample lesson:

ECLECTIC SECOND READER.   3

LESSON II.

Time to Get Up.

1. James, it is now morning. The sun is just peeping over the hills in the east. Get up, my boy, for the sun has just risen!

2. I hope you have said your prayers, and thanked your Father in Heaven for all His goodness. I hope you have thanked Him for your good health, and the blessing of a home, for kind parents, for tender friends, for pleasant books, and all your other enjoyments.

3. Never forget, before you leave your room, to thank God for His kindness. He is indeed kinder to us than an earthly parent.

4. Let us now go out of doors. How beautifully the sun shines upon the hills! How glorious a thing is the sun. How much like that Being who dwells in the Heavens, sending down His mercies upon mankind, as the sun sheds its light and its warmth upon the world!

Such textbook reading materials were once considered to be a part of the mainstream of America's public school curriculum for the majority of our republic's history. That being said, most of us would probably not advocate a return to Sunday School instruction in our nation's public school curriculum, as that is really the function of our local churches. On the other hand, isn't it quite telling how perfectly constitutional it once was for our nation's public school teachers to instruct various reading lessons from such textbooks to our nation's children or for our students to be guided by their teachers in brief nonsectarian prayer at the beginning of the school day for hundreds of years?

Now, ladies and gentlemen, entering "left" stage and taking a slick bow is one of the secular-progressives' early successful uses of the various weapons of mass destruction against the Bill of Rights. I am referring to the misguided misinterpretation of the "establishment clause" by the United States Supreme Court in the 1961 case of *Engel v. Vitale*. The board of Regents for the State of New York authorized a short, voluntary prayer for recitation at the beginning of each school day. The mildest of invocations read as follows: "Almighty God, we acknowledge our dependence upon Thee, and beg Thy blessings upon us, our teachers, and our country." The Supreme Court ruled that the reading of this nondenominational prayer at the start of the school day supposedly violated the "establishment clause," therefore rendering it unconstitutional.[15]

Not to be outdone, of course, is the 1963 case of *Abington School District v. Schempp*. The Abington case concerned Bible reading in Pennsylvania's public schools. At the beginning of the school day, students were allowed to read at least ten verses from the Bible. After completing these readings, school authorities permitted students to recite the Lord's Prayer. Now bear in mind, as was true of the Engel case, students could be excused from participating in such practices with written notes from their parents to the school if they objected to such practices for either personal or religious reasons. This included the atheists as well. Using the flawed "separation between church and state" reasoning, the Supreme Court ruled the practices unconstitutional because the activities supposedly encroached on both the "free exercise clause" and the "establishment clause" of the First Amendment.[16]

Isn't it quite tantalizing that for some peculiar reason, between the years 1791 and 1963, the American people as well as all three branches of the federal government completely missed the boat with regard to the proper legal interpretation of the First Amendment? Heavens to Betsy, what took all of us so long to reach such enlightened decisions by 1961 and 1963? Could it be we were more politically and religiously diverse by the 1960s? Perhaps, but various religions as well as no religion, enjoyed constitutional protection up to that point in time. Oh, maybe it was because we didn't have the intellectual capacity until the early 1960s to properly discern the true intentions of our Founding Fathers. On the contrary, many of these men who wrote the First Amendment lived well into the 1800s and never quibbled about prayer being recited in our public schools, nor did they object to the use of the McGuffey Readers or *The New England Primer* in our nation's classrooms while they were still alive. Perhaps our Founding Fathers were also unenlightened and really didn't know what they were doing with the Bill of Rights in the first place, right? Now I get it—the secular-progressives must be correct when they persist in maintaining that all references to God, religion, religious practices, or religious figures are only constitutional in the privacy of our own homes and places of worship. Well, tell that to the numerous generations of American people, judges, and politicians who preceded us and were perfectly content between the years 1791 and 1961 with the public display of Christmas Nativities and decorations in the village squares during the Christmas season, or giving their explicit blessing to the public performances of religious plays, concerts, and parades, etc., that acknowledge and celebrate America's major religious holidays such as Thanksgiving, Christmas, and Easter. I suppose the men and women in the Congress of the United States should also bow their heads in shame for the fact that our national legislature had the mitigating gall to violate liberal dogma when it supposedly showed disdain for the Constitution by declaring Christmas a national holiday on June 26, 1870!

The US Supreme Court opened up this Pandora's Box of flawed decisions with the cases of *Engel v. Vitale* and *Abington v. Schempp*, which emboldened the secular-progressives and other like-minded ninnies. Take a moment to seriously reflect upon the devastating consequences such fallacious court decisions have visited upon the culture of America during the course of the past fifty years. To borrow a clever line from the movie, *The Devil Wears Prada*, "All right everyone, gird your loins!"

We are gradually morphing into a nation of secular-humanism— just like the countries of Western Europe—and we are being treated to all of the wonderful goodies that accompany it. Pregnancy rates of girls between the ages of fifteen to nineteen have greatly increased.[17] We are witnessing an explosive growth of sexually transmitted diseases amongst teenagers.[18] We are also witnessing an alarming increase in premarital sex, violent crime, adolescent homicides, and adolescent suicides.[19] We see students of a variety of ages going on mass murder rampages, such as what occurred at Columbine High School in Colorado in 1999 and Virginia Tech State University in 2007—to cite just a couple of examples. An increasing number of our teenagers are being treated for newly diagnosed diseases such as ADD, ADHD, AIDS, Bipolar Disorder, Anorexia, etc. Our state and federal prison populations are at an all-time high, yet there are not sufficient prisons to adequately incarcerate all of the dangerous miscreants who need to be taken off the streets in order to protect innocent, law-abiding citizens.

In addition, many parents are abrogating their parental responsibilities by passing them on to schools, foster homes, grandparents, churches, the courts, and other governmental agencies. The "nanny state" is all too anxious to comply—at taxpayers' expense of course! We literally have children raising children. Some parents are shamefully exploiting their children by attempting to nab a spot on some prime-time television reality show in order to claim their brief moment in the spotlight, even if it means breaking the law. Many parents will no longer discipline their children and hold them accountable for their poor behavior and bad choices because they are either afraid that they will be turned into Child Protective Services if they were to do the unthinkable, such as spanking their children, or because some parents are disgracefully engaging in what I like to refer to as "children worship," whereby they feel their children can do absolutely no wrong, thus spoiling them rotten and turning them into future bleeding-heart wimps. This is evidenced by far too many parents doing everything possible to justify and defend their children's poor behavior in school, in public, or at home. I have been a public school teacher for over twenty-five years, and I have witnessed this spectacle first hand! Watch a few television episodes of *Judge Judy* that involve juvenile cases brought before her and you will see exactly what I mean. All of this degradation is being manifested right before our very eyes on a daily basis throughout all of our communities.

If this were not bad enough, every December the American people are subjected to the so-called "War on Christmas" whereby municipalities are routinely sued by leftist organizations for publicly displaying various religious decorations, both Christian and Jewish. Public school officials throughout the land are being hauled into court annually for daring to have their school choirs sing sacred Christmas Carols at school concerts as well as at various community events. Now remember, Christmas is a national holiday established by Congress, therefore, how could it possibly be unconstitutional for our public schools to acknowledge and celebrate our nation's holidays? Go figure!

Many of our nation's school district administrators and school boards are behaving like shameful cowards when they succumb to threats of litigation from the ACLU without standing up for their own rights guaranteed them under the Constitution. Many school districts are intimidated by the ACLU because they do not wish to appear as if they are somehow offending the sensibilities of a small minority of their stakeholders, or they do not wish to spend the necessary resources to fight intolerant, anti-religion bigots in court even though there are legal organizations out and about that are more than willing to step up to the plate and fight for the rights of school districts with absolutely no charge. Many of these school districts just simply give up because they do not wish to be bothered, so it is far more expedient for them to capitulate to the demands of the ACLU rather than confront these legal bullies, take a stand for what is right, and fight the good fight! Shame on such school district administrators and school boards throughout this nation who cower behind the skirts of the ACLU like a bunch of frightened children in the night as if they were hiding from the Wicked Witch of the West herself! The Wicked Witch of the West still resides in Oz rather than Kansas! When school districts receive threatening letters from the ACLU, they are easily duped into believing that if it is a memo coming from the ACLU, it must be legal and Gospel truth. Well it isn't! The ACLU has been defeated quite often in federal courts of appeals as well as the US Supreme Court; therefore, this is certainly not the time to wimp out and cave in to the demands of these legal bullies and bigots. It is about time school districts set a proper example for the nation's schoolchildren by displaying some fortitude with regard to challenging these radical schoolyard bullies such as the ACLU—who wish to continue to impose their own twisted and warped secular values upon the rest of the American people.

Most school districts no longer call the two-week holiday break in December the "Christmas Break"; it must now be referred to as the "Winter Break" in order to be politically correct. Student-led graduation prayers, if allowed at all, or even commencement speeches mentioning religious figures such as Jesus or Moses, are screened and eliminated by school officials. God forbid we should offend the sensibilities of a few atheistic children and their parents amongst us. Whatever became of the time-honored American tradition of engaging in polite civility as well as extending the genteel nod of deference toward the vast majority in this country? Apparently, it too has gone the way of the death of Common Sense; thus, we are being compelled to live under the tyranny of the radical minority in America. Perhaps whining and sniveling atheists and other intolerant bigots of all things religious would be pacified if our country's current motto of "In God We Trust" were to be changed to read something like "To Hell With the Rest of You." I am sure the ACLU would be more than willing to take up such a cause in federal court. On second thought, the ACLU might conclude that the word "Hell" comes from the Bible and is, therefore, a violation of the "establishment clause" of the First Amendment.

The ACLU will battle to the bitter end for the right of hateful, violent Neo-Nazis or even the Ku Klux Klan to march in a parade down some American community's main street spewing their vile, intolerant hate speech, yet God help you should your church group march down a public street promoting Christianity and biblical moral values, especially should such a parade occur during the Christmas season and feature a float displaying any sacred image such as a Nativity! "Why them's fighten words" would more than likely be the ACLU's reaction to such an unthinkable sacred display!

Since we are on the topic of the ACLU, just where were they hiding when the majority of Californians voted "yes" for Proposition 8 in November of 2008 to keep marriage legal only between a man and a woman? Conservative individuals, as well as religious institutions such as the Mormon Church and Catholic Church, were verbally assaulted and vilified beyond belief by left-wing zealots for practicing their First Amendment "free speech rights." Where were the protestations of the ACLU over the vitriol being hurled against conservatives? If the ACLU did object to the manner in which the civil rights of such churches and various individual supporters of Prop. 8 were being violated by radical leftist groups, I certainly did not see it on television nor did I read about it in any of our local newspapers. The hate speech and deplorable tactics utilized by leftist radicals against people of good will who happened to take an opposing viewpoint on the issue of gay marriage and voted accordingly were not only beyond the pale, but outright fascist in nature when all of this hullabaloo was occurring in California. Evidently some Americans are no longer permitted to partake in "free speech rights" or "free association rights" in this country, nor can they freely vote their own consciences and express their opposing political or moral beliefs anymore—especially if they are conservative beliefs that are connected in any way to conservative religious organizations. Here are some additional sordid examples fleeing posthaste from Pandora's Box since 1961 that are worth mentioning.

Where precisely were the feminist organizations, such as NOW, when Sarah Palin and her teenage daughter were excoriated and mocked by David Letterman when he made a crass joke on national television about the sexual exploitation of Mrs. Palin's daughter? This kind of crass behavior on national television was enthusiastically embraced by the far-left. What was even more appalling to me was the audience's laughter at David Letterman's joke at the expense of Sarah Palin's underage daughter—and all young American girls for that matter. There was once a time in American history when such boorish behavior by a celebrity would simply not have been tolerated by the majority of people in this country. In my way of thinking, this is not progress nor is it really doing our country any good. If anything, it is driving a deeper wedge between Americans, and as a nation, we are becoming increasingly polarized. Besides, when you get down to brass tacks, the reality remains that this was not the type of "free speech" our Founding Fathers had in mind when they crafted the First Amendment. When one examines our Founding Fathers' application of the right to "free speech" in the context of the historical time frame in which it was written, they were more concerned with Americans having "free speech" rights in the **political** realm that was once denied them under oppressive British rule prior to the American Revolution. Even the US Supreme Court has ruled that the right to "free speech" is not absolute. For example, one is not permitted to yell "Fire" in a theater, which could precipitate a stampede of people heading for the nearest exit, resulting in the possible deaths of innocent people. Here are some additional examples fleeing like bats out of Hell from Pandora's Box, and they are a real pistol!

Over the past several years, the Fox News Channel has documented certain reprehensible individuals protesting the various policies of the Roman Catholic Church by disrupting Mass services in San Francisco and desecrating Holy Communion while dressed in bizarre costumes. Such clowns have violated the sanctity of church services with absolute impunity. Antiwar protesters have entered the sanctuaries of evangelical Protestant churches and violently disrupted Sunday services. We have also been subjected to shocking news accounts about pastors being targeted and shot outside their own parishes. Some churches have been compelled to hire armed security guards to protect parishioners as they attend church on Sunday! My wife and I are disheartened by the fact that as we enter and exit our own church, we observe there is a security guard "packing heat" while standing guard over the church's entrance. While we are comforted by the fact that our own church is taking prudent measures in order to protect our pastor and congregation, it is truly sad that we have progressed to a point in our nation where it is necessary to hire armed security guards to protect us and our pastors during Sunday services. Fifty years ago, such things would have been utterly unthinkable!

We are witnessing wonderful mainstream groups, such as the Boy Scouts of America, being taken to court and sued because of its own private requirements it deems necessary to enforce in order for members to become Scout Masters as well as its insistence on requiring boys to continue to swear allegiance to God and country. Various municipalities are denying the Boy Scouts necessary public facilities with which to conduct meetings and activities because they do not necessarily conform to various politically correct codes of conduct and municipal ordinances. We are also witnessing legal challenges being brought before the courts by secular-progressive bigots who are suing over the words "under God" in the Pledge of Allegiance as well as the words "In God We Trust" on our currency. I wouldn't be surprised at all to see legal challenges being brought to bear in the near future against various municipalities participating in the public performances of traditional American patriotic songs and hymns such as "God Bless America," "The Battle Hymn of the Republic," and "America the Beautiful." Church and synagogue attendance is at an all-time low, both with the youth and the adults in our country. Pornography and sexual filth has gone viral with all forms of the media and Internet, at all hours of the day—even during prime-time viewing on television. Old-fashioned standards of morality and decency are evaporating right before our very eyes. Yes, the list goes on and on ad nauseam, now doesn't it?

We can all thank, in large part, the so-called enlightened judges who once sat on the Supreme Court in the early 1960s for setting the stage for all of this harrowing change in our culture. These men are all dead now, but I truly wish they could see what is currently transpiring in America. They left us an indelible legacy we can all be proud of now, right? I am going to repeat a quote of John Jay, our nation's first chief justice of the Supreme Court, when he soberly warned this nation,

> No human society has ever been able to maintain both
> order and freedom, both cohesiveness and liberty apart
> from the moral precepts of the Christian religion....
> Should our Republic ever forget this fundamental pre-
> cept of governance...this great experiment will then
> surely be doomed.

Tragically, the justices of the Supreme Court who handed down decisions in the early 1960s that pushed this nation down the slippery slope of secular-humanism were either woefully indifferent or ignorant of John Jay's advice. Jay's warning to all Americans may very well be occurring at this particular moment in time, and all for the sake of "separation between church and state." Precisely where and when did this so-called phrase "separation between church and state" really come into play?

To begin with, it has to be noted that nowhere does that phrase ever appear in the US Constitution, especially in the First Amendment. Here is where "separation between church and state" appeared. In 1802, Thomas Jefferson wrote a private letter to the Association of Danbury Baptists in Connecticut. He coined the phrase "a wall of separation between church and state" to metaphorically reassure the Danbury Baptists that the federal government would not establish a specific state church or religion.[20] It is worth pointing out the fact that Jefferson was attempting to reassure a particular **Christian** denomination—the Baptists—that the government would not establish a state Christian church as compared to what occurred in England when our mother country aligned itself with the Anglican Church, the official Church of England established by King Henry VIII in the 1500s.

The first time Jefferson's metaphor was referred to by the Supreme Court was in 1947 with the *Everson v. Board of Education* case. A New Jersey law allowed reimbursements of money to parents who sent their children to school on buses operated by the public transportation system. Children who attended Catholic schools also qualified for this transportation subsidy. The Supreme Court correctly ruled that the New Jersey law did not violate the Constitution. In the majority opinion, Justice Hugo Black stated, "The First Amendment has erected a wall between church and state. That wall must be kept high and unpregnable."[21] The legal travesty with this case lies not with the ultimate outcome. The legal travesty lies with the fact that to justify and defend the court's decision, Justice Black cited a phrase written by Thomas Jefferson in a private letter to the Association of Danbury Baptists in 1802, and he saw fit to use Jefferson's metaphor to reword part of the First Amendment rather than citing the specific language of the Constitution itself. Where did Justice Hugo Black receive his law degree, from a fly-by-night correspondence law school? I didn't realize legal precedence and constitutional law were to be derived from personal letters and metaphors. I naively thought the Constitution itself was supposed to guide the deliberations and decisions of the justices of the Supreme Court!

Stephen Mansfield is a best-selling author, and his book *Ten Tortured Words: How the Founding Fathers Tried to Protect Religion in America* was released in June of 2007. He wrote an opinion article for The Forum in *USA Today* on July 16, 2007, and here is some of what he had to say that will shed some additional light upon Jefferson's phrase, "separation between church and state":[22]

Two days after he wrote the famous words "separation between church and state" in an 1802 letter to Baptists in Connecticut, Thomas Jefferson began attending church on the floor of the House of Representatives. He would attend the makeshift church in the national Capitol nearly every Sunday morning for the rest of his presidency. Clearly, his understanding of the connection between religion and government is not the one we endure today....It was Jefferson, after all, who insisted upon the Bible as part of the curriculum at the University of Virginia, Jefferson who approved federal funding for a Catholic priest to serve the Kaskaski Indians, and Jefferson who once said, "I am a Christian in the only sense in which He (Jesus) wished anyone to be."....Jefferson envisioned a government that would encourage religion while neither submitting to nor erecting a religious tyranny....Now, the secularist storm troops of the American Civil Liberties Union and its like drive religion from the public square with the mandate of the Everson ruling in hand....Religious symbols are removed from cemeteries, student prayer groups are driven from public facilities, and religious leaders are threatened if they dare speak about political issues from their pulpits.[23]

It is really unfortunate that Justice Hugo Black as well as the particular judges serving on the Supreme Court during the early 1960s didn't have much of a grasp on American history. If they had, perhaps the outcome of the cases *Engel v. Vitale* and *Abington School District v. Schempp* might have been different. In the long run, however, I seriously doubt it. This is what ultimately occurs when radical, progressive judges legislate from the bench, usurp their authority, and rule on various cases before them with unchecked commiseration and emotions rather than with sound legal constitutional logic, a command of history, and common sense. All of these judges would have better served the American people had they recalled the following statement by Thomas Jefferson, not just his church and state metaphor in his letter to the Danbury Baptists:

> In matters of style, swim with current; In matters of principle, stand like a rock.

Because of the horrific decisions handed down to all of us by flawed legal reasoning on the part of the Supreme Court during

the early 1960s, we have been living with the hellish consequences that have been visited upon this nation over the course
of the past five decades and counting. The following passages
in this chapter will focus with greater detail on three sordid
weapons of mass destruction employed by the radical left and
secular-progressives that have contributed significantly to the
decline of America.

Perhaps there are no greater menacing, radical organizations
that have visited more harm on the Bill of Rights during the past
several decades than the American Civil Liberties Union, People
For the American Way, and Americans United for Separation of
Church and State. These three weapons of mass destruction are
very well-organized, are funded to the gist of millions of dollars,
and they—together with their contemptuous agendas—garner a
great deal of free publicity and support from the leftist loons in
Hollywood, the mainstream media, and of course, like-minded
political supporters and advocates in our state and federal governments. They love to present themselves as the benevolent
defenders and advocates of the Constitution, but in reality, they
are turning our sacred document upside down while making
an absolute mockery of it. You can be assured that whenever a
sundry of cases arise, dealing with the issues I have raised in
this chapter, these three organizations are right in the thick of
the witch's boiling pot, stirring up nothing but "bubble, bubble,
toil and trouble."

Their real agenda is to completely secularize this nation in the
public arena under the guise of protecting civil liberties. Well, as we
have seen, since 1961 they have really managed to cast quite a spell
on the American people haven't they? Any mainstream American
individual or conservative group who dares to disagree with their nefarious agenda while advocating for the opposing point of view might
very well be castigated with the following litany of names by advocates of the far-left: right-wingers, rednecks, hillbillies, uneducated

simpletons, gun-toting clingers to religion, unenlightened idiots, haters, intolerant bigots, racists, anti-public education, anti-immigrant, anti-choice, anti-environment, anti-African-American, anti-Hispanic, mobsters, Nazis, Brownshirts, theocratic Christian radicals, conservative radio talk-show lackeys, Tea Baggers, town hall thugs, Southerners—and the list of terms goes on and on. You get the picture. Well, in reality, they would actually be describing the following citizens: Americans who devoutly believe in God, Blue-Dog Democrats, Reagan Democrats, Conservatives, Independents, Republicans of all stripes, Libertarians, Moderates, Fly-Over Countrymen, and Red-state Southerners. In other words, they are describing the vast majority of Americans who call the United States "home." Welcome to the club!

The ACLU's function is primarily legal. The organization provides legal counsel or files "friend of the court" briefs that analyze constitutional points for the court.[24] The ACLU was established in 1920 (a dark year in American history, in my humble opinion). A couple of high-profile cases in history the organization handled or participated in were the Sacco-Vanzetti murder trial in 1921 and the Scopes "monkey" trial in 1925, which challenged the Tennessee law barring the right of a teacher to instruct his students about the principles of evolution.[25] Isn't it ironic how we have come full circle? I think it would be quite safe to speculate that today's ACLU would not defend the right of any public school teacher to instruct creationism in school since it would argue that such instruction violates the "establishment clause" of the First Amendment. In later years, the ACLU played a key role in Supreme Court decisions holding, amongst other things, that Bible reading and recitation of prayer in public schools violate the principle of "separation between church and state."[26] Does this ring a familiar bell? The following are a few excerpts from the ACLU's own website. I have added my own response to each excerpt.

Issues the ACLU Champions:[27]

What is the PATRIOT Act? The PATRIOT Act was passed by the U.S. Congress in response to the Sept. 11, 2001 terrorist attacks. It ushered in an overnight revision of the nation's surveillance laws that vastly expands the government's authority to spy on its citizens, while reducing checks and balances on those powers. The ACLU is pushing for Congress to reexamine provisions of the PATRIOT Act to ensure that it is in alignment with key constitutional protections and prevent any further intrusions like the creation of a PATRIOT II.

My response: I guess the ACLU would rather risk further devastating terrorist acts being planned against our country, even if some Americans are conversing with known terrorist organizations oversees or with sleeper cells within our country. How dare our government attempt to protect its own citizens, which, by the way, is a primary constitutional function of the federal government. Why, the very nerve! Folks, you might want to purchase a gas mask or build a bomb shelter for protection. With friends and protectors like the ACLU, who needs enemies?

Is the ACLU against religion? The ACLU believes in the right of each and every American to practice his or her own religion, or no religion at all, is among the most fundamental of the freedoms guaranteed by the Bill of Rights. The ACLU works to ensure religious liberty is protected by keeping the government out of the realm of all religions.

My response: In other words, let's be sure we do everything possible—using every means at our disposal, to be sure and transform America into a secular-humanistic society, even if we have to totally ignore the "free exercise clause" of the First Amendment as well as 400 years of American history and precedent dating all the way back to the Pilgrims and Puritans. After all, The Mayflower Compact and Fundamental Orders of Connecticut are totally irrelevant influences on the Declaration of Independence and the US Constitution!

> What is the ACLU's position on gun control? The national ACLU is neutral on the issue of gun control. We believe the Second Amendment does not confer an unlimited right upon individuals to own guns or other weapons, nor does it prohibit reasonable regulation of gun ownership, such as licensing and registration.

My response: In other words, we do not believe the Second Amendment protects the individual's right to gun ownership, yet we remain neutral on the issue. I will address this idiocy in greater detail in chapter four of this book.

People For the American Way has existed for more than twenty-five years. It was established by Hollywood producer Norman Lear who produced such 1970s television hits as *All in The Family, The Jeffersons,* and *Goodtimes.* I personally enjoyed watching all of these shows, so I guess Norman Lear can't be all bad. His organization, however, certainly is. Here is PFAW's mission statement as it appears on its own website:

> People For the American Way is an energetic advocate for the values and institutions that sustain a diverse democratic society. Many of these are now threatened by the influence of the radical right and its allies who have risen to positions of political power. Our most fundamental rights and freedoms—and even our basic constitutional framework—are at risk. People For the American Way works in close collaboration with other leading national and state progressive organizations to mobilize Americans at this defining moment in our history.[28]

My response: Well, I certainly agree with PFAW that we are at a defining moment in our history. However, many of us conservatives simply do not agree one iota with this organization's vision for our nation's defining moment in history. Its mission statement extols the values and institutions that sustain a diverse democratic society. Oh really? PFAW's diversity is limited only to far-left institutions like themselves. I just love it when liberals attempt to extol the virtue of diversity, because what they really mean is progressive diversity only. Conservatives need not attempt to be participants on their huge plantations of thought and discourse, not that we really desire to do so, because conservatives would be relegated and confined only to the cotton fields of these particular leftist, secular-humanistic plantations. In reality, these narrow-minded people can be some of the most intolerant bigots around. Don't you just feel terribly sorry for the fact that PFAW's mission statement bemoans the influence of the far-right and its allies in positions of political power? Now let me see, we currently have a very liberal president residing in the White House together with a Democrat-controlled Senate in Washington, DC, effectively controlling the agenda of two of the three branches of the federal government. So what precisely are they bellyaching about? Ralph G. Neas is PFAW's president. Here is what he has to say:

> We're fighting to maintain and expand 50 years of legal and social justice progress that right-wing leaders are trying to dismantle. We won't let them turn back the clock on our rights and freedoms.[29]

My response: Oh, I see! Earlier in this chapter, I cited court cases from the early 1960s that PFAW has enthusiastically embraced as well as the achievements secular-humanism has championed in America. From my perspective, PFAW and other radical organizations have pretty much had it their way for five decades, so they should be happy campers, correct? At least Mr. Neas has the timetable accurate. However, the type of progress during the past fifty years he and his organization champion is not exactly the kind of legal and social justice most mainstream Americans would like to continue to see for our nation, I would wager! Obviously, I am not referring to the important and excellent strides we have gained in America with regard to civil rights. I am referring to the long litany of devastating consequences cited earlier in this chapter that have been visited upon the culture of our nation as a result of the negative influence of secular-humanism that is championed by far-left progressives. The nation's liberals had better take heed, for their fears may soon come to fruition! **Ooooooooooooh—you wascally, wepublican wabbits,** as Elmer Fudd might say, are indeed going to attempt to dismantle the progress secular-pro-gressives have accomplished thus far in order that we may once again restore some semblance of sanity and common sense back into the equation. Mr. Neas wants to even expand on this secular-progressive agenda. To make matters worse, here is what Norman Lear, PFAW's founder, has to say:

> When we see anxiety and alienation manipulated for political gain, and people of all ages losing enthusiasm for democracy, we are moved to do whatever we can to make sure that our children and grandchildren grow and live in a society shaped by the American promise. People For the American Way gives us a way to help realize that promise.[30]

My response: Is the American promise and legacy Mr. Lear longs to leave his children and grandchildren the desired outcomes secular-humanism has dumped upon America's doorstep with all of its accompanying flotsam and jetsam specifically cited in this chapter? Apparently so, since good old-fashioned morals and values once trumpeted by liberals and conservatives alike do not seem to fit into his equation or that of his organization as I see it. Perhaps Mr. Lear should revisit some episodes of his hit television show *Goodtimes* in order to reacquaint PFAW with some of the lessons and virtues promoted by old-fashioned family values that were the cornerstone of the fictional African-American family, the Evans, who were the inspiring protagonists of that wonderful show. In addition, Mr. Lear might do well to remember the fact that during the fall elections of 2008, seventy percent of the African-Americans in the state of California who participated in the election process voted "yes" on Proposition 8 to keep marriage legal only between a man and a woman. The majority of California's Hispanics also voted similarly, yet both of these groups remain large constituents of the Democratic Party—not exactly right-wingers, last I observed. Perhaps this reveals an underlying fact that secular-progressives do not necessarily hold an absolute monopoly on the hearts and minds of these two constituencies, and this should definitely inspire conservatives to aggressively persuade various minority groups that the Democrats ultimately do not have their best interests at heart. I see a huge opportunity here for conservatives to pursue with future elections! We simply need to do a much better job of reaching out to these voters in order to point out to them that they have a great deal more in common with conservative family values and principles than they do with the values trumpeted by progressives.

Americans United for Separation of Church and State is a third weapon of mass destruction being positioned by the far left on the battlefield—pitting secular-progressives against mainstream America and the Constitution. It is a radical, leftist, watchdog group founded in 1947 and based in Washington, DC. Its current executive director is the Rev. Barry W. Lynn.[31] According to the Americans United website, the following is a description of its purpose:

Americans United is a religious liberty watchdog group based in Washington, D.C. Founded in 1947, the organization educates Americans about the importance of church-state separation in safeguarding religious freedom.[32]

The following excerpts are from an article that appeared on the Americans United website in May of 2007 after the death of Jerry Falwell, the former senior pastor of Thomas Road Baptist Church and founder of Liberty University in Virginia.[33] I will offer my response to each excerpt:

> The Christian Coalition emphasized working within the Republican Party to achieve its goals. While the Coalition has followed the Moral Majority into eclipse, the fundamentalist voting bloc in the GOP ensures that its theocratic agenda still has enormous power.

My response: Now let me see. As a proud, lifelong conservative, I have watched many Republican conventions over the years, and I have listened to countless speeches of various conservative candidates running for political office; never have I heard anybody in the GOP advocate for a Christian theocracy to be imposed upon America. I suppose if Republicans dare to defend political and moral views that have been a part of the American mainstream for hundreds of years yet may be contrary to the agenda of Americans United, they are now pushing a theocracy down everyone's throats. How interesting!

> Religious Right groups are better organized and often operate from multi-million-dollar, tax-exempt broadcasting or denominational empires.

My response: Harrumph! And Religious Left groups do not, I suppose.

> Dr. James Dobson's Focus on the Family radio/publishing outfit brought in $137 million in fiscal year 2005. Dobson sat in the

front row at the White House May 3 and was personally welcomed by President George W. Bush during a National Day of Prayer observance.

My response: What precisely did President George W. Bush do that could be considered either unconstitutional or not very presidential? At least he publicly acknowledged the importance of the National Day of Prayer unlike President Barack Obama in May of 2009. Who should President Bush have invited to sit in the front row at the White House on this particular occasion? Should the invited guest have been an avowed atheist in order to demonstrate diversity and tolerance before the American people? Perhaps President Bush would have been seen in a much better light in the eyes of Americans United had he done so.

The Rev. Pat Robertson's Christian Broadcasting Network took in $236 million in contributions in fiscal year 2005. It claims nearly a million daily viewers. Robertson uses CBN to spread his often shrill religious-political message nationwide, and right-wing politicians and Republican political candidates are often showcased on his "700 Club" program.

My response: Robertson's so-called shrill message obviously appears shrill primarily to far-left and religious-left organizations such as Americans United, otherwise CBN would not have millions of members and contributors—much to the consternation of Americans United. I might be jumping to a wild conclusion here, but it appears to me that the moaning and groaning of Americans United smacks of sour grapes. Robertson and CBN must be reaching the hearts and minds of many Americans with their "shrill" message, otherwise they would not have been able to remain on television for more years than I can recall. Besides, I was under the distinct impression that First Amendment rights were still in vogue, even with regard to firebrand conservatives. Has participation in the free marketplace of ideas also gone the way of the dodo bird in our country? If not, America may be dangerously close, therefore, beware of the resurrection of the Fairness Doctrine or any other federal policy akin to it!

> The Southern Baptist Convention (SBC) is firmly in the grip of far-right fundamentalists, and its leadership pushes a Religious Right agenda. The SBC is the largest Protestant denomination in America with some 16 million members. SBC top lobbyist, Dr. Richard Land, acts as a power broker in the Republican Party, declaring which presidential candidates are acceptable to evangelical Christian voters. Land's office works alongside Religious Right groups to lobby on "moral" concerns in Washington, and its attorneys often file court briefs on the side of the Religious Right in court cases.

My response: If this isn't the pot calling the kettle black, I certainly don't know what is! It appears to me that the far left and Religious Left have more than their fair share of advocates such as the Rev. Jackson and his Rainbow Coalition, the Rev. Al Sharpton, Louis Farrakan of the Nation of Islam, and the Southern Christian Leadership Conference. During the presidential election of 2008, the Rev. Jeremiah Wright in Chicago certainly did not hold back his support for the people he and his church supported politically—or did not support—as the case may be. In addition, the Rev. Wright certainly saw fit to pontificate publicly on the issues he and his church fellowship held most sacrosanct! As far as attorneys filing court briefs, Americans United can always count on its partner in crime, the ACLU, to come riding to the rescue like a shining knight in armor on his horse. What exactly is the point the sanctimonious Americans United is attempting to raise here? Is it perhaps arguing that the Religious Right should not be allowed to practice its First Amendment rights as well as empower its organizations and attorneys to advocate and battle on behalf of its constituents? In any event, the outlandish hypocrisy of Americans United is truly astounding! One may find this next choice tidbit quite amusing!

> The Alliance Defense Fund, an Arizona-based legal group founded by Dobson, Wildmon and other Religious Right figures, has an annual budget of $18 million. Pat Robertson's American Center for Law and Justice (ACLJ) is so powerful it has helped vet the Bush administration's Supreme Court nominees.

My response: Perhaps if the Religious Right's legal defense firms were as well-funded and as powerful as the far-left's ACLU, the conservative movement would be in a much stronger position to better relay its message to the American people. Doesn't your heart just clamor for far-left groups such as Americans United, the ACLU, and People For the American Way? After all, they are so abused, they lack financial support, they receive scant political and judicial support, and they all receive such minimal national news coverage and moral support from the media and Hollywood elites! In my opinion, these whining whelps and namby-pamby cretins are, in reality, nothing other than frauds and charlatans of the highest order!

> Recognizing the movement's power, even some Democrats have sought to court the evangelical Christian bloc. Democratic advisers increasingly stress the importance of reaching out to "people of faith." In 2006, one top party adviser even told candidates not to use the phrase "separation of church and state" because it might turn off churchgoers.

My response: As I see it, this revealing avowal really gets to the heart of the Democratic Party's subterfuge. Indeed, many evangelical Christians were beguiled by such Democratic drivel during the recent elections of 2008. It very much reminds me of the old adage, "Fool me once, shame on you; fool me twice, shame on me." Evangelical Christians, as well as Conservative and Orthodox Jews, had better take considerable heed during the elections of 2012—both on the state and federal levels. Far too much is at stake, including the very survival of both America and our close ally, the state of Israel. In my opinion, President Obama is no friend of Israel, which is another reason why he should not be reelected in 2012! The radical left-wing and Religious Left elements of the Democratic Party are definitely not our friends or advocates by any stretch of the imagination and to believe otherwise would not only be incredibly naive, but outright foolish. They truly loathe everything we conservatives stand for. Nevertheless, they realize they need many of our votes to either get elected or to remain in power. What is equally troublesome to me is the fact that these left-wingers exert far too much control and influence over the Democratic Party at this particular point in American history. John F. Kennedy would be rolling over in his grave if he were to actually observe what has become of his own political party. I am also reminded of a conversation I recently had with my father in Great Falls, Montana, before he passed away in 2010. He told me that today's Republicans are, in reality, yesterday's Democrats. I think there is a great deal of truth inherent with Dad's observation.

The following brief excerpts are from an open letter written to Jerry Falwell when he was still alive in December of 2005. The letter was written by the Rev. Barry W. Lynn, the Executive Director of Americans United for Separation of Church and State and is quoted directly from its own website. Here are a couple of examples:[34]

Dear Jerry:

Here's some news: There is no "war on Christmas!" I've seen you on various television news shows claiming that there is but, in fact, there simply isn't....

Contrary to your wild allegations, Jerry, neither Americans United, nor any other civil liberties organization that I know, is waging any kind of war on Christmas....

My response: Well there it is, ladies and gentlemen, disingenuous statements that are front and center for all to see! Mr. Lynn, the Wizard of Delusion, would prefer that all of us pay no attention to that man behind the curtain. The great Oz has spoken! He truly does occupy the Land of Oz now doesn't he? Any seriously informed individual cannot help but acknowledge the fact that controversies surrounding Christmas or Hanukkah arise throughout the nation every December, no matter what side of the issue one happens to cling to. In short order, I would like to reveal the "man behind the curtain" for who he really is in order to illustrate precisely just how disingenuous Mr. Lynn's remarks truly are. I will cite specific court cases involving the various civil liberties organizations the Wizard maintains are not attacking Christmas! But before I do, I would like to introduce the readers of this book to the ACLJ and the wonderful, vital work this legal organization performs on America's behalf.

The American Center for Law and Justice specializes in constitutional law and is at the forefront in defending the rights of religious liberty, especially as it applies to the "establishment clause" of the First Amendment. The following excerpts can be found on the ACLJ's website, and they explain both the mission and history of the ACLJ:[35]

The American Center for Law and Justice is committed to insuring the ongoing viability of constitutional freedoms.

By specializing in constitutional law, the ACLJ is dedicated to the concept that freedom and democracy are God-given inalienable rights that must be protected.

The ACLJ engages in litigation, provides legal services, renders advice, counsels clients, provides education, and supports attorneys who are involved in defending the religious civil liberties of Americans.

History of ACLJ:[36]

The American Center for Law and Justice was formed in 1990 with the mandate to protect your religious and constitutional freedoms. From the beginning, the ACLJ has been committed to working to protect the American family.

As Jay Sekulow, Chief Council of the ACLJ, continued to build his legal and legislative team, the ACLJ achieved tremendous success in litigating cases at all levels of the judiciary—from the federal district court level to the Supreme Court of the United States.

In fact, during our short history, Sekulow has appeared before the high court on numerous occasions—successfully arguing several precedent-setting cases before the Supreme Court:

- Protecting the free speech rights of pro-life demonstrators.
- Safeguarding the constitutional rights of religious groups to have equal access to public facilities.
- Ensuring that public school students could form and participate in religious organizations, including Bible clubs on campus.
- Guaranteeing that minors could participate in the political process by protecting their free speech rights in the political setting.

The great Wizard, Mr. Lynn of Americans United, may have spoken, but he will not have the last word! His curtain is about to be torn asunder as promised. The following excerpts are from a letter that appears on the ACLJ's website dated Tuesday, July 03, 2007, under the section, In the News. The title is "Religious Holiday Displays Information Letter": [37]

Dear Concerned Citizen:

...This letter addresses the constitutionality of privately-erected holiday displays, and will assist you in defending the rights of citizens in your community who desire to erect such displays during the holiday season. This letter will specifically address your questions regarding the placement of religious Christmas displays in public parks....

The First Amendment to the United States Constitution protects the rights of citizens, civic groups, and churches to erect private religious displays in public forums.

The Constitution protects the rights of private citizens to engage in religious speech in a "public forum." In a leading First Amendment case, the Supreme Court held that a private group could erect a cross in a public park during the holiday season, *Capitol Square Review and Advisory Board v. Pinette.* The Court explained:

"Respondents' religious display in Capitol Square was private expression. Our precedent establishes that private religious speech, far from being a First Amendment orphan, is fully protected under the Free Speech Clause as secular private expression. Indeed, in Anglo-American history, at least, government suppression of speech has so commonly been directed precisely at religious speech that a free-speech clause without religion would be Hamlet without the prince."

...Before *Pinette*, the Supreme Court decided two other cases involving the constitutionality of holiday displays. *Lynch v. Donnelly,* 465 U.S. 668 (1984); County of Allegheny v. ACLU, 492 U.S. 573 (1989). Although they involved holiday displays erected either by the government itself on private property, *Lynch,* or on government property that was not a public forum, *Allegheny,* those two cases establish that religious displays on other types of government property (other than a public forum) may also be constitutional if they are accompanied by other secular symbols of the holiday. For example, the holiday display upheld in *Lynch* contained a creche as well as a Santa Claus house, reindeer, candy canes, a Christmas tree, carolers, and toys, 465 U.S. at 671. The display upheld in *Allegheny* contained a menorah and a Christmas tree, 492 U.S. at 582.

Thus, *Pinette*, *Lynch* and *Allegheny* teach that private citizens may erect religious displays on public property if: 1) the property is a public forum on which the government has permitted a wide variety of expressive conduct; and 2) there is a sign informing the public that the display is sponsored by private citizens and the government is not endorsing the message of the display; or 3) the display is accompanied by a variety of secular holiday symbols such that the overall message of the display is not exclusively or primarily religious.

Most lower federal courts have upheld the rights of private citizens to erect holiday displays in public parks. Any cases where the courts have denied private citizens such a right predate *Pinette* and are therefore no longer good law. Following is a summary of the decisions from various courts of appeals around the country. Even in the absence of a case from your jurisdiction, it is imperative to understand that the Supreme Court's decision in *Pinette* is binding upon every state.

The Court of Appeals for the Sixth Circuit—governing the States of Kentucky, Ohio, Michigan and Tennessee.

In Americans United for Separation of Church and State v. City of Grand Rapids, 980 F.2d 1538, 6th Cir. 1992), the Sixth Circuit has also held that a privately funded menorah display erected during Chanukah in a traditional public forum does not violate the Establishment Clause. The Court stated: "What the members of Chabad House seek in this court is fully consistent with, and does not violate, our traditional division between church and state.... They merely ask that they not be spurned because they choose to praise God. Instead of forcing them to remain on our sidelines, our Constitution offers them platform from which to proclaim their message. In a traditional public forum, as at the ballot box, all citizens are insiders as they seek to influence our civic life," Id. at 1555.

Conclusion:

There is virtual unanimity among the federal courts that private religious displays in public fora are constitutional. In parks, town squares, plazas, and even government buildings which have been opened up for public expression, citizens, civic groups, and churches can erect private religious displays without violating the "separation of church and state." Arguments that such displays cause an Establishment Clause problem are completely devoid of merit.

...Some officials mistakenly believe that the Constitution mandates that no religious activity can take place on public property—even when private citizens are involved. The Supreme Court has consistently ruled that the Establishment Clause does not require a state entity to exclude private religious speech from a public forum. It is, in fact, "peculiar to say that government 'promotes' or 'favors' a religious display by giving it the same access to a public forum that all other displays enjoy. And as a matter of Establishment Clause jurisprudence, we have consistently held that it is no violation for government to enact neutral policies that happen to benefit religion." *Pinette, 515 U.S. at 763-64.*

In one of the most powerful proclamations upholding the rights of private religious speech in a public forum, the Supreme Court stated: (emphasis mine)

"The contrary view...exiles private religious speech to a realm of less-protected expression heretofore inhabited only by sexually explicit displays and commercial speech. It will be a sad day when this Court casts piety in with pornography, and finds the First Amendment more hospitable to private expletives, than to private prayers. This would be merely bizarre were religious speech simply as protected by the Constitution as other forms of private speech; but it is outright perverse when one considers that private religious expression receives preferential treatment under the Free Exercise Clause. It is no answer to say that the Establishment Clause tempers religious speech. By its terms that Clause applies only to the words and acts of government. It was never meant, and has never been read by this Court, to serve as an impediment to purely private religious speech connected to the State only through its occurrence in a public forum." (emphasis mine) *Pinette, 515 U.S. at 766-67.*

Together, with the various federal court cases just cited, the following article should serve as the final nail in the peevish coffin of progressive civil liberties groups such as the ACLU and Americans United for Separation of Church and State. This article is from the American Center for Law and Justice website dated Tuesday, July 03, 2007 and is titled "Family News in Focus—The Christmas Battle."[38]

December 2, 2006
by Josh Montez, Family News in Focus

It's been said that the battle for religious liberty goes on all year, but it seems to be amplified during the Christmas season.

An Ohio school won't let teachers say "Merry Christmas," the ACLU has attacked a children's program in Tennessee because the kids sang "Away in a Manger," and the city of Chicago pulled the plug on the new movie "The Nativity" at a public festival.

Jay Sekulow with the American Center for Law and Justice says ACLU-types have been perpetuating ignorance about America's religious rights during Christmas for a long time.

Erik Stanley with the Liberty Counsel says the war against Christmas is reflective of what's happening in society.

We have seen the pendulum of political correctness swing radically to the opposite side where anything Christian at Christmastime is not allowed and is simply censored and sanitized under misinformation and mis-education.

Mike Johnson with the Alliance Defense Fund says celebrating Christmas is a protected religious right, and groups like his are successful at defending your expressions of the holiday.

Christmas is not just a meaningless, commercialized, "sparkle season" as the ACLU is recommending it be referred to now. The last time I checked, Christmas was about a child born in a manger, and I think we'd do well to remember that.

According to a new Rasmussen Report survey, 69-percent of Americans prefer the traditional greeting "Merry Christmas" over the generic "Happy Holidays."

No doubt, reading excerpts of numerous federal court cases can be quite tedious, but they are included in this book in order to document the fact that the "war on Christmas" is indeed occurring not only in the court of public opinion, but the federal courts as well. If there was no "war on Christmas," as the Rev. Barry W. Lynn of Americans United asserts, then why did these recent federal court cases and subsequent decisions occur in the first place? Is it any wonder that the Rev. Lynn would like us to pay no attention to that man behind the curtain? After all, we wouldn't want to confuse the American people with the facts, now would we? I believe the American Civil Liberties Union, People For the American Way, and Americans United for Separation of Church and State would prefer that mainstream Americans continue to naively sing "We're Off To See The Wizard" while merrily skipping down the yellow brick road toward the farcical, progressive Emerald City in the Land of Oz rather than returning to Kansas—the land of reality, common sense, and constitutional truth!

Speaking of constitutional truth, I am going to tread on a very touchy issue that may get me in some hot water with some of my fellow Christians in the conservative evangelical church community. This happens to be a controversial issue that deals specifically with "free speech" rights also guaranteed church pastors in the First Amendment that many of our nation's clergymen are tragically ignoring. Far too many of our pastors are simply dodging this thorny issue by refusing to stand up to the tyranny of the federal government.

Many Americans are troubled by the fact that our federal government is currently trampling underfoot the "free speech" rights of pastors in our nation's churches by treating them as second-class citizens. In order for churches to keep their tax-exempt status, they are being coerced into accepting unconstitutional ordinances that forbid them from discussing matters of politics from the pulpits as well as publicly endorsing political candidates for elected office while conducting church services—at least in conservative churches. This is not only blatantly un-American and unconstitutional, but it also flies in the face of American historical tradition and precedent. We need to have another reality check with regard to some pertinent historical facts that correlate directly with this current controversial issue.

During the 1730s and 1740s, America experienced the first Great Awakening throughout the colonies. This religious movement came about because many colonists feared they had lost their religious passion and fervor that had once driven their Puritan ancestors of the 1600s.[39] The Great Awakening lasted for several decades and altered colonial culture as congregations debated religious practices and politics of the day. Some churches in New England began to welcome women, African-Americans, and Native Americans into church membership.[40] In order to train future ministers, religious groups established colleges such as Princeton and Brown. From a moral standpoint, preachers lectured Americans about the injustices of slavery, they inspired colonists to provide assistance to orphans and the poor, and they encouraged ideas of equality.[41] From a political standpoint, the Great Awakening stressed the importance of the individual over the authority of the church. As a result, this movement encouraged the colonists to begin to question the authority of the British government in the 1760s and 1770s, and it was a huge contributor to the revolutionary fervor displayed by the colonists when they declared their independence from England in 1776.[42] The Sons of Liberty would deliver inflammatory speeches against the tyrannical acts of Great Britain from the Old South Church in Boston, which is where their secret signal was given to fellow Patriots who initiated the Boston Tea Party. In addition, it was from the steeple of the Old North Church where two lamps were lit and mounted in order to alert Paul Revere that the British Redcoats were arriving by sea.[43]

America's second religious revival, the Second Great Awakening of the early 1800s, would also greatly impact the nation's politics and social morals for more than sixty years.[44] At the tender age of sixteen, Peter Cartwright abandoned a life of gambling and became a minister who spent more than sixty years preaching on the American frontier.[45] In Eastern cities, former lawyer Charles

Grandison Finney conducted large revival meetings and preached "all sin consists in selfishness," and such sermons contributed to the awakening of a spirit of reform.[46] In the early 1800s, a temperance movement was initiated by American women to stem the negative influence of alcohol on families and businesses. Temperance workers handed out pamphlets pleading for people to stop drinking; dramas such as *The Drunkard* that illustrated the evils of alcohol were staged.[47] The Second Great Awakening inspired the organization of labor unions in the 1830s in order to seek better working conditions for factory workers that were deemed unsafe at the time. The religious movement inspired Americans to demand better schools. The first state board of education was established in Massachusetts in 1837 under the direction of Horace Mann, who called public education "the great equalizer."[48] In other words, education was made available to children of all social classes, not just the affluent who had the means to pay for expensive private education for their children. Churches founded hundreds of colleges that included Antioch and Oberlin Colleges in Ohio, the University of Notre Dame in Indiana, and Northwestern University in Illinois.[49] The Second Great Awakening also influenced other individuals such as Dorothea Dix from Boston who taught Sunday school to women prisoners. She discovered that some women were incarcerated in cold, unsanitary cells because they were mentally ill. She also discovered that the mentally ill were often neglected, chained, and beaten. Dorothea Dix made it her mission in life to travel all over the United States on behalf of such citizens, and her efforts led to the construction of thirty-two new hospitals.[50]

In the mid-1800s, northern evangelicals were the primary movers and shakers within the Abolitionist Movement. Former slaves Frederick Douglass and Sojourner Truth were excellent examples of brave Americans who were not afraid to take a moral and political stance during perilous times. They put their very lives and freedom at serious risk as they traveled throughout the North and spoke about their own experiences of slavery.[51] Christian sects such as the Quakers were actively involved with the secret Underground Railroad that assisted many runaway slaves with their escape to freedom in Canada. Sojourner Truth was a devout Christian who fled from her owners to live with the Quakers who set her free. They also assisted Truth with a court battle that reunited her with her son. Sojourner Truth would travel throughout the North and "declare the truth to the people."[52]

The late civil rights leader, the Rev. Martin Luther King Jr., was an inspiring religious leader of the twentieth century. He was co-pastor of Ebenezer Baptist Church in Atlanta and the pastor of the Dexter Avenue Baptist Church in Montgomery, Alabama. Dr. King spoke eloquently from the church pulpit concerning the issues of politics and civil rights. During the 1950s, he was arrested, his home was bombed, he was subjected to personal abuse, and he emerged as a hero and dynamic leader not only for the people of his own race and the Civil Rights Movement, but for all Americans.[53] Dr. King was also elected president of the Southern Christian Leadership Conference, an organization formed to provide new leadership for the Civil Rights Movement whose ideals King took from Christianity.[54] The following are some of my favorite excerpts from Dr. King's stirring speech, "I Have a Dream," delivered on August 28th, 1963 at the Lincoln Memorial in Washington, DC:[55]

...I have a dream that my four little children will one day live in a nation where they will not be judged by the color of their skin but by the content of their character....

...I have a dream that one day every valley shall be exalted, and every hill and mountain shall be made low, the rough places will be made plain, and the crooked places will be made straight; and the glory of the Lord shall be revealed and all flesh shall see it together....

...From every mountainside, let freedom ring. And when this happens, when we allow freedom ring, when we let it ring from every village and every hamlet, from every state and every city, we will be able to speed up that day when all of God's children, black men and white men, Jews and Gentiles, Protestants and Catholics, will be able to join hands and sing in the words of the old Negro spiritual:

Free at last! Free at last!

Thank God Almighty, we are free at last!

Since Dr. King delivered his profound and inspiring speech on government property at the Lincoln Memorial in Washington, DC, I wonder whether or not the ACLU and Americans United for Separation of Church and State ever filed a lawsuit in federal court against Dr. King—supposedly accusing him of violating the "establishment clause" of the First Amendment? After all, Dr. King quoted Isaiah 40: verses 4-5 from the King James Version of the Holy Bible. He also spoke repeatedly about God, and he advocated that Americans should join hands while singing an old Negro spiritual. It is a good thing, I reckon, that no public high school choir was present at the time to sing an old Negro spiritual on government property lest it be accused by the ACLU and Americans United of violating the "establishment clause" of the First Amendment. Somehow, I seriously doubt that these reprehensible civil liberties organizations would have filed a federal lawsuit, and we can all be most appreciative of the fact that they didn't. However, if Dr. King were alive today, he might actually run afoul of these anti-American organizations!

We should also pose this hypothetical question: Did the federal government ever dare threaten to revoke the tax-exempt status of the various churches throughout the South as well as the Southern Christian Leadership Conference when Dr. King addressed both the political and social mores of his day from various church pulpits? Again, I seriously doubt it. So why should any of our current pastors and churches, especially those that represent conservative political and social mores, be silenced throughout America and be faced with such intimidating threats from our federal government for engaging in the very same routine that Dr. Martin Luther King Jr. practiced some forty-seven years ago? **The hypocrisy and double standard currently being permitted to run amok in this nation is truly astounding to say the least!**

The point is this: Throughout our nation's history, church pastors and leaders, as well as their sacred facilities, have always been at the forefront of American political discourse, political debate, biblical preaching, etc., yet in today's society, churches risk being taken to the cleaners by our federal government if they dare speak out on similar issues of our time. How absolutely absurd! What is even more tragic about all of this tomfoolery is that most churches are willing to acquiesce to this tyranny. We may just as well be living under the oppressive tyranny of Great Britain during Colonial America of the 1760s and 1770s for all of the good this is doing us!

I can clearly recall a time in the not-too-distant past when my wife and I would be handed pamphlets courtesy of our church leadership at Sunday services. Such tracts took a conservative stance on abortion, taxes, traditional family values, etc., and they featured political candidates' positions on such controversial issues from both major political parties. I can also recall a time when the pastor of my own church once addressed these issues from his pulpit during election time, but not anymore! Too many of our pastors, both liberal and conservative, have been cajoled into remaining silent on political issues during elections in the fear that they may have their tax-exempt status revoked by the federal government. This is shameful behavior not only on the part of our federal government, but on the part of many of our nation's pastors as well. I realize church ministries have scant resources with which to fight the federal government in court, but it must be done. That is why they have the American Center for Law and Justice and the Alliance Defense Fund at their disposal. Why are these conservative legal organizations not being utilized to the greatest extent possible by our various church pastors and congregations?

The current tyrannical policy of our federal government concerning this travesty and injustice being perpetrated against our churches is unconstitutional, and it must be challenged at all cost. Our pastors have First Amendment rights as well, and they don't cease to exist at the church door! Furthermore, the American people certainly have the patience as well as the constitutional right to listen to various viewpoints from our pastors, both political and biblical, and if they disagree with their own pastors for whatever reason, they have the perfect freedom to not only vote their own consciences, but to leave their churches in order to attend others if they so desire. Mark my words ladies and gentlemen. If our churches continue to wimp out on this very critical issue of our time, the next thing the federal government is going to do is dictate exactly what our churches may or may not preach—regardless of what the Holy Bible and God teach! If that should ever occur, the pastors and congregations of our churches in America will have no one to blame but themselves!

This conservative author took some level of comfort and hope in an article I had read that was written by Dinesh Ramde of the Associated Press during the presidential election of 2008. It is titled "Protesting Pastors Endorse Candidates." According to Ramde, Pastor Luke Emrick of West Bend, Wisconsin, had delivered a sermon to his congregation of about 100 worshippers at New Life Church in which he politically endorsed the team of McCain-Palin for President and Vice-President of the United States. Here is a snippet from his sermon, as quoted in the article:[56]

"I'm telling you straight up, I would choose life. I would cast a vote for John McCain and Sarah Palin," he said. "But friends, it's your choice to make, it's not my choice."

According to the reporter, Pastor Emrick purposely violated the rules of the federal government in the hopes of inviting an investigation by the Internal Revenue Service. Ramde further reported that thirty-three pastors in twenty-two states were making similar recommendations about political candidates at Sunday services as encouraged by the Arizona-based Alliance Defense Fund. The pastors were hoping the sermons would initiate a legal fight that might lead to abolishing restrictions on church involvement in politics. Of course, critics were calling the protest of these pastors divisive and not likely to succeed.

I personally applaud such a challenge being put forth by these scrappy pastors against our federal government. Such religious leaders have had enough of this nonsense, and they are fighting back in the true spirit of American tradition—rebellion and protest! Good for them! They are anything but sissies as they are willing to stand up for what is right—both morally and politically—despite the fact that their actions may very well place their churches at risk. Such pastors are stalwart examples for the entire nation, and the rest of our nation's pastors should sit up and take notice. It is about time mainstream America reprise the old hymn "Onward Christian Soldiers," get some backbone once again, and reclaim our land once and for all for the sake of our children and grandchildren before it is too late! A Third Great Awakening is desperately needed in America!

The following humorous anecdote has been circulating on the Internet for some time now. While it is entirely fictitious, it nevertheless goes to the heart of the various issues that have been raised throughout this chapter. I do not know who the author is, yet it is quite amusing and definitely worth bringing to everyone's attention because it pokes fun of atheists, as well as some of their absurd positions that haunt this nation repeatedly.

FLORIDA COURT SETS ATHEIST HOLY DAY

In Florida, an atheist created a case against the upcoming Easter and Passover holy days. He hired an attorney to bring a discrimination case against Christians and Jews and obser-vances of their holy days. The argument was that it was unfair that atheists had no such recognized days.

The case was brought before a judge. After listening to the passionate presentation by the lawyer, the judge banged his gavel declaring, "Case dismissed!"

The lawyer immediately stood, objected to the ruling by saying, "Your Honor, how can you possibly dismiss this case? The Christians have Christmas, Easter and others. The Jews have Passover, Yom Kippur, and Hanukkah, yet my client and all other atheists have no such holidays."

The judge leaned forward in his chair saying, "But you do. Your client, counsel, is woefully ignorant."

The lawyer said, "Your Honor, we are unaware of any special observance or holiday for atheists."

The judge said, "The calendar says April 1st is April Fools' Day. Psalm 14:1 states, 'The fool says in his heart, there is no God.' Thus, it is the opinion of this court, that if your client says there is no God, then he is a fool. Therefore, April 1st is his day. Court is adjourned."

— Author Unknown

Common Sense would have been exceedingly proud of this magis-trate. May he rest in peace.

4

Concord Hymn

By the rude bridge that arched the flood,
Their flag to April's breeze unfurled,
Here once the embattled farmers stood,
And fired the shot heard round the world.

The foe long since in silence slept;
Alike the conqueror silent sleeps;
And Time the ruined bridge has swept
Down the dark stream which seaward creeps.

On this green bank, by this soft stream,
We set today a votive stone;
That memory may their deed redeem,
When, like our sires, our sons are gone.

Spirit, that made those heroes dare
To die, and leave their children free,
Bid Time and Nature gently spare
The shaft we raise to them and thee.[1]

— Ralph Waldo Emerson

Ralph Waldo Emerson, a distinguished American poet and writer, lived from 1803-1882. He was known for his love of American individualism and self-reliance. Emerson wrote *Concord Hymn,* a poem that was sung as a hymn on July 4, 1837 at a ceremony commemorating the completion of the Concord Monument at Concord, Massachusetts. His hymn was performed at this solemn occasion in order to pay tribute to the heroic resistance of American Minutemen against the British Redcoats on April 19, 1775. The poem's immortal phrase "shot heard round the world" serves as an endearing kinship to the American Revolution and the Second Amendment to the American Constitution.

The dawn of the American Revolution at Lexington and Concord was addressed at the beginning of chapter two of this book for a very important reason. During the past several decades, the Second Amendment has had to weather considerable assault as well as twisted misinterpretation by the far-left weapons of mass destruction. Gun-control advocates continually put forth the fallacious argument that the Second Amendment does not confer upon the American individual the right to bear arms, but promotes instead a collective right of the states to bear arms through its own militias—better known today as the National Guard. Nothing could be further from the truth. This chapter will effectively confront and challenge this dangerous argument with persuasive facts, not creative fiction as promoted by the opposing side. Here is precisely what the Second Amendment states:

A well regulated Militia, being necessary to the security of a free State, the right of the people to keep and bear Arms, shall not be infringed.

Founding Father Thomas Jefferson was a strict constructionist of the Constitution because he believed that particular approach to interpreting the Constitution is the only legitimate one America should adhere to in order to remain true and faithful to the original principles, text, and intentions of the Founding Fathers who crafted the Bill of Rights. If Americans are going to truly obey and defend the Constitution as written, we must no longer permit radical leftists to manipulate the genuine meaning of the words our Founding Fathers used when writing these amendments. As was divulged in chapter three, the Anti-Federalists insisted on the inclusion of a Bill of Rights in the original draft of the Constitution in order to guarantee that our **individual** rights would be protected from generation to generation. Gun ownership in our country is as uniquely American as apple pie. So why did our Founding Fathers deem the American individual's right to bear arms to be so vital that they assigned it priority number **two** amongst the first ten amendments? The answer is quite obvious—it lies with what occurred at Lexington and Concord in 1775.

In order to discern the actual meaning of words such as "a well regulated militia" and "a free state" as they were used in the late 1700s, we must once again reflect upon some pertinent American historical facts. A well-regulated militia, as defined by Americans in 1775, consisted of a volunteer force of armed male civilians of average everyday farmers and tradesmen from the various local villages throughout the thirteen British Colonies. These intrepid men were not a part of any standing army, they were not paid any salary as a result of serving in the local militias, and they were not professional soldiers by any means. In addition, they were not under the command and authority of professional military officers, they were not serving under any official terms of enlistment with the British government whatsoever, nor were they provided any uniforms or arms and ammunition by the same government. The militia, or Minutemen as they were often referred to, were volunteers who were ready, if need be, to fight the British Army at a "minute's" notice.[2] This is precisely what came to pass at both Lexington and Concord.

Of course, the British officers had their spies in place, and they were attempting to confiscate the stored muskets, cannons, and powder and shot that were being hidden by the local militias at Concord. In other words, the British government wanted to disarm the Colonial Americans in order to thwart any potential armed resistance. Fortunately, the Redcoats failed to seize the militias' supplies as the precious munitions were whisked away and secretly hidden by American Patriots prior to the arrival of the British Army.

When the First Continental Congress convened at Independence Hall in Philadelphia in 1774 prior to the outbreak of hostilities between the Colonials and Great Britain, one of the first acts of the Congress was to encourage all thirteen colonies to begin forming their volunteer militias in order to prepare for possible confrontation with the British Army. This is precisely the reason why our Founding Fathers considered the American individual's right to bear arms to be of such cardinal importance that they proceeded to place it as second in order of priority within the Bill of Rights. When the Bill of Rights was added to the Constitution and ratified by all of the states in 1791, only a mere sixteen years had transpired since Lexington and Concord, and our Founding Fathers were keenly aware of the dangers inherent with any government's potential tyranny, power, and abuse of its citizens' rights as well as its seductive tendency to want to disarm its own people. It is worth reemphasizing the fact that the Bill of Rights was spawned because of Britain's tyrannical abuse of power being leveled against its own citizens, the American people, during the 1760s and 1770s.

I would like to recommend an excellent primer that every American should take the time to read. It is *The Second Amendment Primer, A Citizen's Guidebook to the History, Sources, and Authorities for the Constitutional Guarantee of the Right to Keep and Bear Arms*. The primer can be made available by the National Rifle Association upon request. It is written by Les Adams, and it is published by Palladium Press of Birmingham, Alabama. This remarkable primer is a thorough source of compiled examples of primary source documents of early state constitutions as well as an excellent collection of direct quotes of our Founding Fathers, who clearly articulate their views on the Second Amendment. I will cite specific examples from chapter four of Mr. Adams's primer that support my historical analysis of the Second Amendment. From the perspective of this American history educator serving in one of America's public schools, the aforementioned primer should be required reading in all of our nation's high schools, and it should also be read by every sitting federal circuit court judge as well as every United States Supreme Court Justice.

Chapter four of Mr. Adams's primer is titled "The Development and Declaration of the Right in America; A Drafting and Ratification of the Bill of Rights in the Colonial Period."[3] Les Adams brilliantly reflects on our Founding Fathers' knowledge and reverence for English law and customs. He points out that Chief Justice Howard Taft once observed:

> The Framers of our Constitution were born and brought up in the atmosphere of the common law, and thought and spoke its vocabulary;...but, when they came to put their conclusions into the form of fundamental law in a compact draft, they ex-pressed themselves in terms of the common law, confident that they could be shortly and easily understood.[4]

Mr. Adams continues:

> The meaning of such words as "militia," "keep arms," "bear arms," "discipline," "well regulated," and "the people" was the meaning of these words as they were used in the English common law of the sixteenth through the eighteenth centuries—not as they are used today.[5]

Les Adams further quotes Chief Justice Taft:

> The language of the Constitution cannot be interpreted safely except by reference to the common law and to British institutions as they were when the instrument was framed and adopted.[6]

As was clarified at the beginning of this chapter, Thomas Jefferson was quite explicit as to how the Constitution was to be interpreted. In his primer, Adams quotes Jefferson:

> On every question of construction let us carry ourselves back to the time when the Constitution was adopted, recollect the spirit manifested in the debates, and instead of trying what meaning can be squeezed out of the text, or invented against it, conform to the probable one which was passed.[7]

These are very compelling arguments that lend credence to the strict constructionist approach to interpreting the Constitution. Thomas Jefferson was obviously admonishing all of us to guard against playing fast and loose with the Constitution, yet far too many of our elected officials and appointed judges during the past fifty years have lost sight of this important fact. In addition, Thomas Jefferson's statement proves beyond a shadow of doubt that he would be troubled with the manner in which his frequently quoted metaphorical phrase, "separation between church and state," has been misused and misinterpreted by a mob of misguided misfits. How is that for an effective use of alliteration?

Generally speaking, conservatives are strict constructionists of the Constitution who desire to remain faithful to our Founding

Fathers' original intent as well as their precise wording used in the Constitution as written in the eighteenth century. Progressives are loose constructionists who are guided by the principle that the Constitution is supposedly a "living document" that should be loosely interpreted and adapted at will in order to reflect our changing society. This is a very significant difference between these two competing political philosophies. Our Founding Fathers were intelligent and exceedingly wise men. They did provide a mechanism with which to either alter or add to the Constitution from time to time in order to meet the needs of a changing society, and that is called the **amending process**. However, they did not make this process an easy one to accomplish because they certainly did not want future generations to make a mockery of their Constitution by enacting numerous changes based upon the fanciful whims and desires of politicians. That is precisely why America has been successful in adding only seventeen amendments to the Constitution beyond the original ten that make up the Bill of Rights, since the year 1791.

Our Founding Fathers had a healthy fear of standing armies as a result of what had occurred at Lexington and Concord. According to Les Adams's research, this is what Founding Father and Anti-Federalist Richard Henry Lee, writing under the pseudonym "The Federal Farmer," had to say:

> A militia when properly formed, are in fact the people themselves, and render regular troops in great measure unnecessary...by providing that the militia shall always be kept well organized, armed, and disciplined, and include, according to the past and general usage of the states, all men capable of bearing arms....[T]o preserve liberty, it is essential that the whole body of the people always possess arms, and be taught alike, especially when young, how to use them...."[8]

Richard Henry Lee's statement does not, in any way, imply that our nation should never raise its own standing army. In fact, the Second Continental Congress in Philadelphia, of which Richard Henry Lee was a delegate from Virginia, established the Continental Army in May of 1775 and appointed George Washington as its commanding general.[9] Richard Henry Lee would also propose a resolution on American independence to the same Congress on June 7th, 1776.[10] At any rate, Lee's statement does give credibility to the fact that the Second Amendment allows the right of the individual to bear arms, not just a "collective right of the states" consisting of one component of our contemporary military—namely, the National Guard.

Our Founding Fathers were also deeply concerned with protecting our inalienable right to self-protection, not just for service in the local militia. Les Adams quotes from David Young:

> Most Americans were accustomed to having their individual rights protected from violation from the government because approximately two thirds of the population of the United States lived in states with constitutional bills of rights. In most of the other states some individual rights were protected in the state constitutions....An armed populace was guaranteed in one way or another in every bill of rights of the original states [of those seven states—Virginia, Maryland, Delaware, New Hampshire, Pennsylvania, North Carolina, Massachusetts (and later Vermont, after it was recognized as a separate state in 1791)—that chose to draft one]. These provisions were the early progenitors of the Second Amendment, since it was the state bills of rights which were cited when the necessity of adding a bill of rights limiting the federal government was discussed later during the controversy over ratification of the United States Constitution.[11]

Mr. Adams continues to make his own point concerning self-protection:

> Whether for frontier engagements with hostiles, for hunting, or for duty in the militia, practically the entire adult male population was armed. We know that many of the Founding Fathers, including George Washington, Thomas Jefferson, and George Mason, were gun collectors....a large number, of course, were hunters; and some were even marksmen. James Madison, for example, boasted that he could hit a small target at 100 yards, but he admitted that he was far from the best marksman.[12]

Here are some excerpts from the early state constitutions that appeared either directly before or some period after the adoption of the Declaration of Independence. They further document the thinking of our Founding Fathers with regard to the Second Amendment. You will discover many of them are worded quite similarly to the Second Amendment:

> Virginia (June 12, 1776) "That a well-regulated militia, composed of the body of the people, trained to arms, is the proper, natural, and safe defence of a free state..."
> Delaware (September 11, 1776) "That a well-regulated militia is the proper, natural and safe defence of a free government."
> Pennsylvania (September 28, 1776) "XIII. That the people have a right to bear arms for the defence of themselves and the state..."
> Massachusetts (October 25, 1780) "XVII. The people have a right to keep and bear arms for the common defence."
> New Hampshire Ratification Convention (June 21, 1788) "Congress shall never disarm any citizen, unless such as are or have been in actual rebellion."[13]

The precise language contained within the original thirteen state constitutions clearly influenced the thinking of our Founding Fathers when they drafted the Second Amendment, and why shouldn't it? After all, the authors of the Bill of Rights resided in these states and served in their state legislatures. The final excerpts I would like to illustrate from Les Adams's *Second Amendment Primer* are ones that quote the Founding Fathers directly.[14] Many Americans will find these statements quite illuminating, and I will contribute my own response to each of them.

> Thomas Paine: "The peaceable part of mankind will be continually overrun by the vile and abandoned while they neglect the means of self-defence...."

My response: In other words, woe to those who believe in the fallacy that peace will be achieved without an armed citizenry. Just the opposite would occur. Paine's supposition also rebuffs the arguments put forth by pacifists. My personal favorite is this next bombshell.

> Thomas Jefferson: "A strong body makes a strong mind. As to the species of exercises, I advise the gun. While this gives moderate exercise to the body, it gives boldness, enterprise and independence to the mind....Let your gun therefore be the constant companion of your walks. No Free man shall ever be debarred the use of arms. What country can preserve its liberties if their rulers are not warned from time to time that their people preserve the spirit of resistance? Let them take arms, the remedy is to set them right as to facts, pardon and pacify them. What signify a few lives lost in a century or two? The tree of liberty must be refreshed from time to time with the blood of patriots and tyrants. It is nature's manure."

My response: Now I would personally relish the opportunity to witness the possible reaction of the vast legions of the far left and bleeding-heart sissies of America concerning this one. I would imagine that they just might break down on television in a torrent of wailing and gnashing of teeth if they were to discover what Thomas Jefferson was really implying in a letter that bluntly reveals his reaction to Shay's Rebellion in Massachusetts in 1787. More than likely, today's progressives might not even be aware of the fact that Jefferson meant very serious business when he put these powerful words to pen and paper. If such contemporary poltroons were actually knowledgeable about this aspect of Jefferson's beliefs, they might not ever desire to step foot in the Jefferson Memorial in Washington, DC, once again. With regard to the issue of gun ownership, Thomas Jefferson is conceivably way too radical and over-the-top for their liking. After all, how could the left's supposed "apostle" of "separation between church and state" remotely commit such treason and blasphemy against their own proclamation that the Second Amendment does not confer an individual's right to bear arms! Indeed, Jefferson has more than likely burst their proverbial bubble with his quote equating the blood of American patriots and tyrants to that of nature's manure.

> Patrick Henry: "The militia, sir, is our ultimate safety. We can have no security without it....The great object is, that every man be armed....Everyone who is able may have a gun."

My response: As I just stated, according to the far left, the Second Amendment supposedly does not confer an individual's right to bear arms. Patrick Henry must have been speaking hypothetically or in figurative language, right? That would then justify, in the eyes of leftist radicals, the application of their loose interpretation to the "living Constitution." In other words, progressives will most assuredly divine out of thin air whatever twisted interpretation and manipulation they see fit in order that they may ultimately achieve their maniacal goal of forever disarming the American people. This is not only un-American and unconstitutional, but it is fascist in nature. The British Redcoats occupying America in the late 1700s would have relished the thought of having this bunch on board with them, now wouldn't they? So would contemporary American gangs, thugs, thieves, and murderers, leaving the rest of us utterly defenseless and vulnerable.

> John Adams: "Arms in the hands of citizens [may] be used at individual discretion....in private self-defence."

My response: I suppose progressives might reason that John Adams was really having a "senior moment" with this statement since he once defended the British Redcoats on trial in Boston after they killed five Americans during the Boston Massacre of 1770. Otherwise, how could he make such a brash statement that would appear to contradict one of his earlier actions as a prominent Boston attorney?

> Samuel Adams: "...and that the said Constitution be never construed to infringe the just liberty of the press or the rights of conscience; or to prevent the people of the United States who are peaceable citizens from keeping their own arms; or to raise standing armies, unless when necessary for the defence of the United States or of some one or more of them; or to prevent the people from petitioning, in a peaceful and orderly manner, the Federal Legislature for a redress of grievances; or to subject the people to unreasonable searches and seizure of their persons, papers, or possessions."

My response: Well, this brazen statement which is attributed to the founder of the Sons of Liberty in Boston pretty much says it all, now doesn't it? Samuel Adams's discourse contains elements of

Amendments 1, 2, and 4 all wrapped up together in one big neat and tidy individual package. Merry Christmas! On the other hand, could it be remotely true that adherents of the loony left are somehow noble and looking out for what is in the best interest of all Americans when they seek to cherry-pick certain rights and freedoms out of the Bill of Rights and target them for elimination because they do not happen to meet with their approval or agenda? I think not. On the other hand, if the ACLU claims to be neutral on the issue of gun control, yet interprets the Second Amendment to be one that does not necessarily guarantee the individual the right to bear arms, it must be Gospel truth, correct? For goodness sake, I am beginning to sound a bit like Tevye from *Fiddler on the Roof.* So in the spirit of Tevye—when he wrestled with and finally rejected the marriage of one of his Jewish daughters to a Russian Gentile—I am going to adamantly declare, "No—there are no other hands!" According to the secular-progressives who like to pretend that they are paragons of enlightened thought, tolerant political discourse, and sound legal reasoning, Amendments 1 and 4 of the Bill of Rights definitely confer individual rights upon all Americans, but Amendment 2 conveniently does not. I see how it works! I mean, where have I been all of these years? Apparently some individual rights are more important than others according to these liberal dunderheads! Oh, by the way, I think I may have just offended the sensibilities of certain progressive individuals by supposedly violating the "establishment clause" of the First Amendment. I carelessly and foolishly wished everyone Merry Christmas, and since I am a public school teacher by profession, I should certainly know better. Sorry!

George Mason: "To disarm the people is the best and most effectual way to enslave them....Who are the militia? They consist now of the whole people, except a few public officers."

My response: This Anti-Federalist Founding Father and strong advocate of the Bill of Rights certainly did not have any confusion or ambiguity with the definition and interpretation of "militia" of his generation. The Founding Fathers' intent with the wording of the Second Amendment was quite clear and unequivocal: it was to be sure that all law abiding and peaceful Americans were to be guaranteed the right to bear arms, except a few public officers. Was George Mason making a possible reference to politicians? Hmmmmmmmmmm!

> James Madison: "...Notwithstanding the military establishments in the several kingdoms of Europe, which are carried as far as the public resources will bear, the governments are afraid to trust the people with arms. And it is not certain that with this aid alone mere quiet private possession of ordinary personal firearms, they would not be able to shake off their yokes."

My response: James Madison was certainly comfortable with the people possessing personal firearms, and if that is good enough for the "Father of the Constitution," it should be good enough for all Americans, including our federal judges and elected politicians.

A few years ago, I was utterly dumbfounded as I was listening with considerable interest to a talk show host of a local radio program while driving to school one day. The host of the talk show was commenting on the fact that the Supreme Court was going to decide a case originating out of Chicago as to whether or not cities in the various states have the right to prevent their citizens from owning handguns in their homes for defensive purposes. The talk show host's basic assertion was that our Founding Fathers had done a piss-poor job of wording the Second Amendment because of what he considered to be the supposed contradictions between "state militias" and the right of "the people" to bear arms. He proceeded to ramble on as to the absurdity and confusion he maintained was inherent with our Founding Fathers' precise wording of the Second Amendment.

Normally, I find the radio talk show host in question to be well-informed on the issues of the day, but I believe he had missed the mark entirely on this one, if you will pardon the pun. The host's difficulty with the precise wording of the Second Amendment is only confusing to those individuals or special-interest groups who are ignorant of the history of the Constitution, ignorant of our Founding Fathers' original intent when writing it, and ignorant of the meaning of the terminology used during the era when the Constitution was written. The fact that this talk show host possesses a degree in law is proof positive, in my own mind, that lawyers do not always make the most lucid arguments with regard to the meaning of the Constitution. The fact that all three branches of the federal government are dominated and run by people of the legal profession is probably indicative as to why America is currently mired in the foul swamp of both corruption and tomfoolery. Attorneys may distinguish themselves as professionals who possess extensive vocabularies, who often demonstrate a proclivity toward the gift of the gab, and who have the ability to explicate a written flair with the English language, but, with rare exceptions, they are really filled with nothing but minds full of sentimental drivel.

Many conservatives seriously wonder whether or not highly educated Americans of other professions might actually do a better job of interpreting the Constitution by simply applying common sense rather than the flawed reasoning and hogwash being applied by a number of radical, progressive screwballs currently serving on the United States Supreme Court and federal circuit courts of appeals. Perhaps the author of this book missed his calling and should have become a constitutional lawyer and federal judge rather than a public school teacher, although in my humble opinion, serving as a teacher in this nation is a far more noble and higher calling than serving as some pompous, know-it-all, screwball magistrate. That being said, the American people are standing at the threshold of another turning point in American history. As a nation, we need to become emboldened and begin to hold all of our federal magistrates accountable for their decisions and behavior. Throughout the past fifty years, numerous progressive federal judges have been permitted to get away with murder as they have successfully managed to manipulate the Constitution for their own petty purposes and political ideologies with absolute impunity. For the well-being and protection of our nation and its citizens, this must cease once and for all.

One possible recourse of action that could be implemented by the American people, through their elected representatives in Congress of course, is to publicly conduct impeachment proceedings against any Supreme Court Justice or any other federal circuit court judge for that matter, who is guilty of a lack of the display of "good behavior." The wording of "good behavior" is stipulated in Article III of the Constitution. This is one of the important Checks and Balances the Legislative Branch has on the Judicial Branch, and it was placed there by the Founding Fathers in order to control or "check" the power of the Supreme Court. Some would argue that this is potentially dangerous and might actually infringe upon the impartiality of the nation's judicial system, and this would be a cogent dissenting argument put forth by people of good will and intent. However, I would counter that argument with the following rebuttal: our federal judiciary is already politically compromised ergo, judicial impeachment is but one legal remedy at our disposal that would permit the American people to put our federal judges on notice that we intend to hold their feet to the fire should they continue to practice judicial activism.

As is quite often the case, smarmy elitist federal judges are usurping their proper constitutional role by illegally infringing upon the delegated function of the Legislative Branch in their practice of legislating from the bench through the process of judicial activism. When this travesty occurs, there no longer exists any semblance of judicial impartiality or restraint whatsoever because, in effect, what these judges are doing is serving in the capacity as both legislators and judges who, for all practical purposes, end up ruling in favor of their own laws that are nowhere to be found in the Constitution. A cheeky quote by an intellectually brilliant Supreme Court Justice, Antonin Scalia, lends credence to this pertinent fact when he forthrightly opined in the 1990 decision, *Cruzan v. Director, MDH, 497 U.S. 261,* that the Justices of the Supreme Court are no more qualified to resolve such issues as the "right to die" than "nine people picked at random from the Kansas City telephone directory."[15] He also stated: "the Constitution has nothing to say about the subject." Some additional prime examples of progressive judicial activism that illustrate similar abuse of power by the Supreme Court are the specious decisions rendered in the 1973 landmark case of *Roe v. Wade,* the 1961 case of *Engel v. Vitale,* and the 1963 case of *Abington School District v. Schempp,* as discussed in chapter three of this book.

The stark reality is, however, that the potential impeachment of federal judges might be acts of futility because the Senate would rarely find itself in a position politically to muster the super-majority of votes necessary to remove offending judges from the bench, especially given the partisan atmosphere that currently permeates the Senate. For example, the only two presidents in American history to face impeachment were Andrew Johnson and Bill Clinton, and neither of these two men was found guilty by the Senate, so they remained in office to complete their terms. We can surmise, therefore, that the potential impeachment of Supreme Court Justices and other judges serving on the federal circuit courts of appeals would largely serve as nothing other than symbolic acts of Congress. This is most unfortunate because as a constitutional purist, I believe the impeachment process is a viable and legal path for the American people to embark upon by way of the Legislative Branch as clearly stipulated by the Constitution.

So what is another legal remedy available to the American people? We could propose and lobby for the adoption of a constitutional amendment whereby all US Supreme Court Justices and all judges of the federal courts of appeals would be required to be elected directly by the American people when vacancies occur and require such judges to run for reelection every four years as is required of the president of the United States. As part of such a new amendment, we might also desire to limit the number of terms any judge could serve in the Judicial Branch in order to protect the integrity of the Judiciary, especially given the fact that many of the judges within the Judicial Branch are no longer willing or capable of policing their own ranks on behalf of the American people by insisting that they engage in judicial restraint and serve according to the dictates demanded of them by the Constitution!

This is by no means a radical suggestion because it once took a constitutional amendment to alter the manner in which our senators are elected to the Senate. Perhaps it is time for federal judges to be elected directly by the American people as well because, unfortunately, too many of our federal judges have demonstrated that they can no longer be trusted to adjudicate with judicial restraint as they have repeatedly taken on the role of serving as legislators during the course of the past fifty years—thereby abusing the trust of the people. Think about it: when the American people become weary with the manner in which various representatives of the Legislative and Executive Branches discharge their respective duties, we do not hesitate to replace them by electing new representatives when necessary, and as a nation, we have come to the point where we should seriously consider doing the exact same thing with judges serving on the Supreme Court as well as the federal courts of appeals.

Some might argue that a "check" on the Judicial Branch by the Legislative Branch occurs sufficiently when the members of the Senate Judiciary Committee query various judicial appointees that are put before them by presidents of both political parties, and the committee subsequently reaches a decision as to whether or not to recommend such appointees for an up-or-down vote before the entire Senate. However, the truth of the matter is this: How often have the American people been subjected to the ugly spectacle of a game of political, partisan dodge ball being played out publicly on television? For example, in the recent past, various senators have obligingly acquiesced to some of the most vague responses spewed forth by judicial nominees—thereby giving such nominees a convenient excuse to claim they cannot answer frank hypothetical questions being elicited by senators of both political parties because such responses might serve as potential conflicts of interest when judicial appointees have to rule on future cases that come before them while serving on the Supreme Court. When these judicial appointees respond to senators' queries in such fashion, they are attempting to hide their judicial philosophy in order to gain unfettered access to the most powerful court in the nation. When they comport themselves in such a nontransparent manner, they too are acting like sissies, and they ought to be ashamed of themselves!

On the other hand, when senators do aggressively solicit honest answers and opinions from judicial appointees, their manners are most appalling as they often cross over the line by engaging in disgusting partisan grandstanding. For example, political hacks on the Senate Judiciary Committee, especially Democratic Senators, have repeatedly subjected conservative judicial appointees to a type of inquisition that would rival that of the Spanish Inquisition! For example, recall the overt drubbings both Robert Bork and Clarence Thomas were subjected to by Democratic Grand Inquisitors during their confirmation hearings that were a humiliating embarrassment to the entire nation! As such, both hearings were perfect examples of nothing other than the equivalent of drumhead trials—providing empirical proof that there is no longer any sense of fair play with regard to the proper application of Checks and

Balances supposedly being exhibited by the Senate. As a direct result of senators engaging in such shameful chicanery, no potential judicial nominees to the Supreme Court—be they progressive or conservative—are willing to go out on a limb any longer in order to be completely forthright with regard to revealing their judicial temperaments before the Senate Judiciary Committee, lest they fear being subjected to a "high-tech lynching," as Justice Clarence Thomas so aptly put it during his own drumhead trial by the Senate Judiciary Committee! In my opinion, this clearly supports my supposition that federal judges should now be elected directly by the American people rather than being left to the devices of the US Senate!

The United States Supreme Court was never designed by the Founding Fathers to function as an oligarchy, but that is precisely what we have permitted it to become. As a result, the Supreme Court has evolved over the years as an institution wielding the greatest power of the three branches of the federal government. The Supreme Court was created for the purpose of ruling on the constitutionality of laws passed by Congress, to adjudicate disputes between the states, and to settle disputes between citizens and the states as well as the federal government. Justices of the Supreme Court as well as judges of the lower federal circuit courts of appeals, were never given the authority in the Constitution to bypass the Congress and the states in order to conjure up new laws and rights out of thin air, such as the supposed right of a woman to have an abortion to cite just one example, and squeeze such meanings out of the text of the Constitution. As stated earlier in this chapter, Thomas Jefferson warned this nation not to travel down this perilous road.

In addition, the purpose of the constitutional principles of Separation of Powers and Checks and Balances is to assure the American people that the balance of power would remain **equal** among all three branches of the federal government so that no single branch would become more powerful than the other two. Likewise, the constitutional principle of Federalism exists to guarantee the American people that power is to be shared between the federal government and the respective states so that this nation would have limited government. All of these basic principles have been turned topsy-turvy over the course of the last five decades, and as a result, our nation currently has a federal government that is anything but limited. The underlying framework of the Constitution is tragically being ignored and forsaken by many of our elected officials and judges. The Founding Fathers would be absolutely appalled to witness all of these shenanigans currently taking place in America as well as the atrocious manner in which the Judicial Branch of the federal government sometimes exhibits "odious" rather than "good" behavior by engaging in the high jinks of judicial activism that is analogous to Greek gods and goddesses passing judgment down upon all of their subjects from Mount Olympus.

So precisely how do the American people, the fifty states, and the other two branches of the federal government respond to all of this folly? We collectively turn the other cheek and acquiesce to this unconstitutional power-grab by the US Supreme Court! As law-abiding Americans, we only need acquire the necessary backbone to respond accordingly, to cease wandering aimlessly about like a bunch of scaredy-cats or frightened children of the night, and take up the cause of passing a constitutional amendment limiting both the scope and the power of the US Supreme Court. If Supreme Court justices were compelled to make their cases before the American people just like representatives of the Legislative and Executive Branches are required to do, we could force them to reveal their judicial temperaments and as a direct result, should we determine from time to time that they are betraying the trust forged between the Founding Fathers and the American people, we could give them the boot just as we do our elected leaders serving in Congress and the White House rather than granting these judicial oligarchs lifetime tenure! There is absolutely nothing radical about this proposal. What is radical, however, is the manner in which federal judges have abused their positions in the federal judiciary by trampling on the civil rights of the American people, ignoring the will of the people, ignoring states' rights, throwing their weight around and bullying the nation as if they were dictators, and making an absolute mockery of the Constitution!

Speaking of power-grabs, in a recent related development that occurred during the winter of 2011, President Obama took it upon himself to declare he is now deciding for himself which federal laws are or are not constitutional and precisely which federal laws his administration will or will not defend in court. In 1996, President Clinton signed into law the Defense of Marriage Act that was passed by Congress. Since our most recent Justice-In-Chief, President Obama, has declared that such federal legislation is supposedly unconstitutional, he and his corrupt Attorney General, Eric Holder, are no longer going to defend the federal legislation in court because they both personally disagree with it—despite the fact that the primary function of the president of the United States is to enforce the nation's laws! Well, if the president maintains he has the supposed legal authority to throw his weight around and bully both the Legislative and Judicial Branches of the federal government as well as the rest of the American people, then perhaps conservative Americans should be permitted to equally violate **the rule of law** by boldly proclaiming: If federal judges, Congress, and presidents are going to continue to undermine our very sacred liberties and violate the contract our Founding Fathers made with the American people, then just who the hell are they to arrogantly and surreptitiously dictate to the rest of us what is or isn't constitutional?

The majority of the American people do clamor, however, for a return to constitutional democracy whereby our elected representatives are obligated to fulfill their weighty duties of governing the American people responsibly and according to the rule of law.

Likewise, our federal courts should be compelled to adjudicate various cases that come before them with proper judicial restraint according to the dictates of our Constitution. Our current state of affairs in America certainly prods me to reflect upon the wise words once spoken by the late conservative scholar William F. Buckley Jr.: "I'd rather entrust the government of the United States to the first 400 people listed in the Boston telephone directory than to the faculty of Harvard University." Buckley must have been an ideological soul mate to Supreme Court Justice Antonin Scalia!

As a side note of related interest, Tea Party activists are already encouraged by the fact that twenty-six states are challenging the constitutionality of ObamaCare in the federal courts. Such audacious action by the states is long overdue as they begin to reassert their states' rights once again against the ever-intrusive tyranny of the federal government! It is about time, and bully for them! Once this case appears before the US Supreme Court, there is but one correct decision the court could arrive at which would help to redeem itself before the eyes of millions of Americans who are constitutional conservatives. The Supreme Court has to incontestably rule that ObamaCare is brazenly unconstitutional. Nowhere in the Constitution, including the Commerce Clause in Article I, does it remotely stipulate or imply that Congress has the legal authority to compel Americans to purchase any specific product such as health insurance and then levy fines against the people should they fail to comply. This is clearly a contemptible abuse of both legislative and executive powers, and the Supreme Court should immediately rule that such parlor-tricks are unconstitutional, lest we find ourselves in an inconceivable position whereby the Legislative and Executive Branches have been given the blessing of the Judicial Branch to establish an onerous precedent to further engage in such unlawful behavior. Both the American people and the various states have simply had enough of this unscrupulous and bizarre overreach being exhibited by the federal government.

The majority of Americans are sincerely angry and absolutely fed up with the manner in which our sacred Constitution has been plundered, misquoted, and misinterpreted by an assemblage of leftist ninnies who are hell-bent on eroding the very foundation of our "City upon a Hill." As clarified in chapter two of this book, our Founding Fathers sacrificed a great deal in order to provide us with both the Declaration of Independence and the US Constitution. They didn't write these precious documents just for the benefit and welfare of their own generation, but for posterity as well. We owe it to them and all future generations to preserve these contracts intact and with the exact spirit in which they were written if our republic is to ultimately survive. As a strict constructionist, Thomas Jefferson had it perfectly right! He admonished this nation not to read anything into the text of the Constitution that is clearly not there or which would run counter to the spirit and original intent of the Founding Fathers when they wrote it.

Should conservatives ultimately fail in our quest to safeguard the original intent of our Founding Fathers as clearly expressed in the Constitution, then the American people had better be prepared to face the following hair-raising scenario: The Constitution will continually be chipped away by the chisel of the liberal elite, piece by piece, article by article, amendment by amendment, much like a building's foundation is gradually eroded by the continual lambasting of one virulent storm after another! The unique virtues that have distinguished and set America apart from any other nation on this planet, past or present, will evaporate expeditiously, and as a direct result, our nation will be destined to go down in the annals of history as nothing other than a grand failed experiment that had the most noble of intentions for its people—yet despite all of its efforts, succumbed to the exact same seductions and exploits typical of all other nations throughout world history. We will lose our national identity and abiding American spirit. We will cede our national sovereignty over to the United Nations. We will forfeit our military strength and dominance and be at the mercy of our enemies. We will bow to the authority of the World Court. We will no longer have national borders. We will cease to operate under the free enterprise system of economics and prosperity. We will no longer resemble the country our Founding Fathers established, nor will we continue to function in the manner in which we were created.

Is that what our Founding Fathers sacrificed a great deal for or worked so diligently to achieve? Is that the legacy we desire to leave our children and grandchildren? Is that ultimately how we want to be remembered? Most Americans, I reckon, would shun such a fate. Then again, if we continue to permit this travesty to occur, the American Constitution will one day not be worth the paper it is written on. America, as we know it, will cease to exist. We are already heading dangerously in that mercurial direction, as this book has painstakingly revealed. The following recent decision by the US Supreme Court will shed some additional light on the very point I am making, not because of the ultimate positive and correct outcome, but because of the fact that the following decision was a result of a very divided court that could have gone the opposite way. To think that a fundamental right guaranteed the American people in the Bill of Rights could possibly be left hanging in the balance between safety and jeopardy or left standing upon the shaky precipice of destruction by a sharply divided court is frightening beyond all imagination!

In a recent US Supreme Court case, *The District of Columbia v. Heller,* the court considered "whether a District of Columbia prohibition on the possession of usable handguns in the home violates the Second Amendment to the Constitution."[16] In Washington, DC, handgun ownership was outlawed while rifles and shotguns had to be registered and kept "unloaded and disassembled or bound by a trigger lock or similar device." The case involved Dick Heller, a federal police officer who was denied a registration certificate to keep a handgun at home. He brought suit under the violation of his Second Amendment right to bear arms.

At the time the case was adjudicated, the four conservative justices (Antonin Scalia, Clarence Thomas, John Roberts, and Samuel Alito) together with the moderately conservative swing judge, Anthony Kennedy, correctly sided with the individual right interpretation. Writing for the majority, Justice Scalia argued that "the right of the people [the amendment's key phrase] always and unambiguously refers throughout the Constitution to individual rather than collective rights,"[17] and that interpretation was correctly applied by the majority of the court. In addition, Scalia wrote, "The inherent right of self-defense has been central to the Second Amendment right. The handgun ban amounts to a prohibition of an entire class of 'arms' that is overwhelmingly chosen by American society for that lawful purpose."[18] Thank God these five justices prevailed and managed to preserve the Second Amendment for the American people!

On the other hand, we have the four progressive justices—Ruth Bader Ginsburg, Stephen Breyer, John Paul Stevens, and David Souter (two of whom have since retired)—who, in my opinion, utterly failed the American people and betrayed the Constitution. This is what former Justice John Paul Stevens had to say in his dissent: "The court would have us believe that over 200 years ago, the framers made a choice to limit the tools available to elected officials wishing to regulate civilian uses of weapons...."[19] Justice Stevens's statement is not only absurd at face value, but it is also an absolute insult to our intelligence! Of course our Founding Fathers designed a plan that would **precisely** limit governmental tools of power over the people. What could these radical, progressive, dissenting justices have possibly been thinking? Were they completely naive and ignorant of American history? Have they conveniently forsaken the lessons Lexington and Concord taught our Founding Fathers and their generation who helped shape the Second Amendment in the first place? Have they deliberately chosen to disregard the very reasons as to why America declared its independence from England, fought a revolution against a tyrannical king and government, and established a new constitutional republic that embodied everything they held so dear and sacred? Do they believe the Second Amendment has nothing in common whatsoever with the rest of the individual rights enumerated in the Bill of Rights? Could they possibly believe these historical facts should be relegated only to the history books while our Declaration of Independence and US Constitution serve as nothing but quaint, symbolic guidelines of governance to be displayed and affectionately viewed by schoolchildren while attending field trips to the National Archives in Washington, DC? Do they fundamentally grasp the ramifications of what they are saying in their collective dissent in *District of Columbia v. Heller?*

Simply put, the Heller case was of such paramount legal importance with regard to all Americans and the Bill of Rights, it should have been a unanimous vote on the part of all nine justices to affirm that Heller's suit against the nation's capital was—beyond question—a case where the city of Washington, DC, was engaging in a clear violation of Heller's Second Amendment right. Honest to God, we are not talking about some insignificant legal case of a lower superior court involving two opposing parties wherein opposite viewpoints are up for grabs, and the decision of the court only impacts the two parties bringing suit! We are talking about a fundamental liberty enumerated in the Bill of Rights of the Constitution that applies to every adult individual in the United States! There is a huge difference! This is a perfect example that clearly illustrates why we must eventually pass a new amendment to the Constitution that will enable the American people to fire liberal or conservative justices who exhibit this type of judicial activism if the people should so desire. These four ignoble magistrates, while ultimately failing to prevail in the Heller case, are unquestionably guilty of displaying judicial activism by making a mockery of the Bill of Rights. These progressive justices have betrayed the sacred trust forged between our Founding Fathers and the American people, and they have absolutely no honorable right to serve as sitting judges on the highest court of the land because they have clearly violated "good behavior" that is stipulated in Article III of the Constitution!

The Bill of Rights is a contract with the American people that guarantees **individual** rights and freedoms, and the Second Amendment is no different. Our individual right to bear arms is just as important as the other following individual freedoms: freedom of religion, speech, the press, peaceful assembly, to petition the government for a redress of grievances; not to be forced to quarter soldiers in one's home; the right to be secure in our persons, houses, papers, and effects; against unreasonable searches and seizures; the right not to be compelled to testify against oneself in court; not to have one's property seized without due process of law or without just compensation; the right to a speedy, public jury trial and legal representation; trial by jury in civil cases; limits of fines and no cruel and unusual punishment; or other rights reserved to the people. These are all individual rights, not collective rights belonging to the federal government.

Elections have consequences, and all Americans are compelled to live with these consequences—for good or for ill—and for many years to come. They set the course America will sail upon for generations. Currently, all presidents have the constitutional authority to appoint judicial vacancies to the Supreme Court as well as the federal courts of appeals, and the US Senate has the authority to either approve or reject such appointments to the bench. Therefore, before casting critical votes during presidential and senatorial elections, all voters need to be astutely educated and thoroughly informed as to the political and judicial philosophies such federal candidates espouse, especially since the opposing philosophies of conservatives and progressives profoundly impact the appointments of judicial nominees. After all, we must abide by the decisions handed down to us by the US Supreme Court regardless of whether we agree or disagree with such decisions. Therefore, when casting your votes for presidents and senators, be wise as owls and cunning as serpents. Constitutional conservatives who are not RINOS (Republican In Name Only) adhere faithfully to Thomas Jefferson's "strict constructionist" approach to interpreting the Constitution because we steadfastly strive to uphold, amongst other things, the ideals so eloquently expressed in Ralph Waldo Emerson's *Concord Hymn*:

> *By the rude bridge that arched the flood,*
> *Their flag to April's breeze unfurled,*
> *Here once the embattled farmers stood,*
> *And fired the shot heard round the world.*

May the "shot heard round the world" expressed in this hymn forever echo loud and clear throughout America! Amen.

5

Rendezvous

I defy the annals of chivalry to furnish the record of a life more wild and perilous than that of a Rocky Mountain trapper.

— Francis Parkman

A group of rugged men of the 1800s who are widely admired and considered by many Americans to be heroes are the famous mountain men of the American West. Personally, I would love to have traveled for at least one season with the great mountain man and trailblazer Jedediah Smith, who lived from 1799 to 1831. Although his life was cut short at a very young age, he accomplished a great deal for future American pioneers. Enjoy reading this bona fide, lionhearted account of one of Smith's early adventures during his second expedition out West.

When Jedediah Smith was leading an expedition to find a route through the Rocky Mountains, he was attacked by a grizzly bear. The grizzly came out of the trees and mauled Smith violently—thrusting him to the ground and damaging his ribs. The bear proceeded to seize Smith's head in its mouth, shredded part of his face, and his scalp was hanging on to his head by an ear.[1] Smith ordered Jim Clyman, a fellow trapper, to sew it back on. Clyman recalled:

> I asked Smith what was best. He said, "One or two go for water and if you have a needle and thread get it out and sew up my wounds around my head."...I told him I could do nothing for his ear. "Oh, you must try to stitch it up some way or other," said he. Then I put in my needle and stitched it through and through and over and over laying the lacerated parts together as nice as I could with my hands.[2]

Smith miraculously survived his encounter with the grizzly, and it took him approximately two weeks to recover before his expedition could continue exploring.

Jedediah Smith began trapping beaver at the age of twenty-two. He said, "I wanted to be the first to view a country on which the eyes of a white man had never gazed and to follow the course of rivers that run through a new land."[3] Throughout his journeys, Smith would travel more extensively than any other single mountain man. His expeditions took him through the central Rockies, Arizona, across the Mojave Desert, and into California—thus earning him the distinction of being the first American to travel overland to California through the Southwest. During his journey across the desert of the Great Basin, Smith and his fellow mountain men had to bury themselves in sand to keep cool because the heat was so unbearable and life threatening.

Smith was a very devout Christian. He never drank hard spirits, never used tobacco, never boasted, and faithfully prayed and read his Bible on a daily basis. When a fellow trapper, John Gardner, passed away, Smith gave this eulogy as recorded by Hugh Glass: "Mr. Smith, a young man of our company made a powerful prayer which moved us all greatly and I am persuaded John died in peace."[4] In 1831, Jedediah Smith was killed by Comanche warriors while looking for water on the Santa Fe Trail. He died an American hero, and he was quite satisfied with his career as a mountain man and trailblazer. Before he expired, Smith concluded, "I started into the mountains, with the determination of becoming a first-rate hunter, of making myself thoroughly acquainted with the character and habits of the Indians, of tracing out the sources of the Columbia River and following it to its mouth; and of making the whole profitable to me, and I have perfectly succeeded."[5]

The life of the mountain man was rugged and fraught with danger. He had to confront, on a regular basis, the possibility of starvation, dehydration, searing heat, freezing cold, diseases, and attacks of wild animals and hostile Indians. The mountain man's life was dictated by the seasons, so he would trap furs during the fall and spring. The pelts were more profitable in the spring because that is when they still had their winter thickness. Beaver hats were in high demand on the East Coast as well as London and Paris; hence, the fur trapping business could be quite profitable. Every July from 1825 to 1840, the mountain men and the fur company suppliers would gather at the summer Rendezvous which was an important event the men would eagerly look forward to attending every year.

The mountain men Rendezvous was a raucous event that was initiated by General William Ashley of the Rocky Mountain Fur Company. Initially, the gathering was held to exchange pelts for supplies, but over time it grew into a month-long party or fanciful, wild carnival which eventually attracted women, children, Indians, French Canadians, eastern businessmen, and other travelers. A prominent African-American mountain man, James Beckwourth, described it this way: "a festivity of mirth, songs, dancing, shouting, trading, running, jumping, singing, racing, target-shooting, yarns, frolic, with all sorts of extravagances that white men or Indians could invent."[6] An eastern businessman gave his view: "mountain companies are all assembled on this season and make as crazy a set of men I ever saw."[7] In addition to the competitive shooting activities, there was a considerable amount of gambling, drinking of whiskey, drunken escapades, and prostitution—as one might imagine.

When the Rendezvous was concluded, the men would return to their fall trapping territories. They usually traveled in groups of forty to sixty men and would set up brigade base camps throughout the wilderness for protection against hostile Indian attacks. The Blackfeet of Montana were feared the most, while the Shoshone, Crow, and Mandans were the friendliest. Once the beaver were trapped, the animals were immediately skinned, the pelts were given sufficient time to dry, and they were then folded in half with the fur to the inside for protection in order to be traded for supplies and money. Mountain man Osbourne Russell gave this physical description of the typical fur trapper of the time:

> A Trapper's equipment in such cases is generally one Animal upon which is placed...a riding Saddle and bridle, a sack containing six Beaver traps, a blanket with an extra pair of Moccasins, his powder horn and bullet pouch with a belt to which is attached a butcher Knife, a small wooden box containing bait for Beaver, a Tobacco sack with a pipe, and implements for making fire with sometimes a hatchet fastened to the Pommel of his saddle, his personal dress is a flannel or cotton shirt (if he is fortunate to obtain one, if not Antelope skin answers the purpose of over and under shirt), a pair of leather breeches with Blanket or smoked Buffalo skin, leggings, a coat made of Blanket or Buffalo robe, a hat or Cap of wool, Buffalo or Otter skin, his hose are pieces of Blanket lapped round his feet which are covered with a pair of Moccasins made of Dressed Deer Elk, or Buffalo skins with his long hair falling loosely over his shoulders complete the uniform. [8]

Approximately 1,000 trappers roamed the West from 1820 to 1840, which was the time period when the Rocky Mountain fur trade was at its peak. By 1840, the fur trade began to die out as silk hats replaced beaver hats as the fashion. After this decline in the beaver fur trade and demise of the annual Rendezvous in 1840, the mountain men had to look for other means with which to make a living. Some joined the US Army and interpreted various Indian languages for military officers, while others became land surveyors, and many became invaluable guides on wagon trains heading west on the Oregon, Mormon, California, and Santa Fe Trails during Manifest Destiny of the 1800s.

Their legacy was of vital importance to our nation's history. The trails these mountain men blazed made it possible for American pioneers to move west. The pioneers were able to cross rugged Rocky Mountain passes such as South Pass in present day Wyoming and Beckwourth Pass in present day northern California. Concerning his desire to assist people in need, Jedediah Smith once wrote to his brother, "It is for this that I go for days without eating, and am pretty well satisfied if I can gather a few roots, a few snails,…a piece of horseflesh, or a fine roasted dog."[9] Their self-sacrifice put others before their own needs. The mountain men's early explorations also provided Americans with some of the earliest firsthand knowledge of the West—similar to what the Lewis and Clark expedition accomplished from 1804 to 1806. Their personal experiences, which included trading with various Indian tribes, came in quite handy as they assisted both military and emigrant parties in communicating with the Indians, since most of the mountain men could not only speak one or more Indian languages, but they could also communicate using sign language. During the Indian Wars of the latter half of the 1800s, some mountain men utilized their skills acting as agents for the federal government. Without their wisdom, skills, experience, and guidance, Manifest Destiny would have taken much longer for our nation to accomplish.

I grew up as a young whippersnapper myself in the Big Sky Country of Montana during the 1960s, so hunting, fishing, and target shooting were all natural rites of passage into adulthood. During the summer months, when my cousins and I would visit my Uncle Bill and Aunt Francis on their ranch—which was located in a serene valley nearly an hour's drive from the capital city of Helena—my aunt would tell us to go to the trout-laden creek running through her property and catch some fish, and we would proceed to clean the catch-of-the-day on the porch before bringing them into the house to be cooked for supper. The current politically correct concept of "catch-and-release" would not only have been completely alien to my Aunt Francis and her generation, but she would have laughed herself silly at the notion of us kids catching trout and releasing them back into the creek. The only time we would remotely engage in that type of ritual was in the event that we should snag a "small fry." The code of proper fishing dictated that a small fish needed to be returned to the creek in order that it might survive that day to eventually grow larger for some future catch. In my day, going fishing served two purposes: to participate in a relaxing sport as well as to seek delicious nourishment. In addition, my Uncle Bill would temporarily furnish rifles for my cousins and me so we could attempt to pick off pesky gophers on the ranch when they occasionally emerged from their underground habitats. This was great fun and sport, and I still harbor very fond memories of the various adventures I participated in when I was a young boy. After completing daily chores, my cousins and I would run about the ranch for hours on end while pretending to be mountain men of the Wild West!

My best friend's dad took us on hunting trips when we were only in the first and second grades, and our mothers never cared a lick nor whined about the possibility of us shooting wild deer. As young scrappers, neither did we. My father and his best friend would take our families target shooting in the countryside outside of Great Falls, Montana, and we would have contests and place monetary bets on who we speculated could shoot the bull's-eye the most accurately and from the greatest distance. At the old Paris Gibson Jr. High School in Great Falls, hunter's safety courses were as commonplace as reading, writing, and arithmetic. Our elementary schoolteachers took great pride in teaching us about the wild adventures of America's mountain men—especially if they were Montana mountain men of the likes of John Colter. My fifth grade teacher believed these heroic and adventuresome men were worthy of attention and adulation because of their influential impact on American history.

Women in Montana would frequently dress fashionably, and they would proudly parade about downtown Great Falls wearing the most beautiful fur coats purchased from Beckman's Furs while shopping in stores and eating in downtown cafes. Montana women were not ashamed in the slightest bit to wear coats made of genuine animal fur, unlike most women of today. In fact, there was a time in America when most men and women took tremendous pride in the manner in which we dressed publicly as compared to the overly casual manner in which we parade about town today.

When my family would drive to the local forests on the weekends during berry season to pick chokecherries and huckleberries with which to make jams, pancake syrup, and mouthwatering milkshakes, we would have to be sure we were well armed in the event that brown bears or grizzly bears might be on the other side of the bushes gorging themselves with the exact same berries we were seeking. We did not want to foolishly risk any unpleasant life-threatening encounters with wild animals. While hiking in the forests of Lincoln and Monarch in Montana, one would be foolish not to take a rifle for self-protection in the event of a possible altercation with a bear or mountain lion. We had to take similar precautions when camping in the woods or staying in a vacation cabin in the Bob Marshall Wilderness of Montana. This was the environment I grew up in during the decade of the 1960s.

Ever since the Walt Disney Company released its 1942 hit film *Bambi*, negative attitudes toward hunting have gradually progressed to a point where freedoms once enjoyed by hunters since the founding of our nation have become intolerable to a bunch of sissies belonging to various animal rights organizations who maintain they have the moral authority to dictate to the rest of us what we can or can't eat, what we can or can't wear, or what we can or can't enjoy by way of recreation and entertainment. Many Americans of various political persuasions deeply resent this intrusion upon our liberties and rights, as well as the smug, holier-than-thou attitude that permeates the liberal elite, especially on the East Coast and Left Coast of America! Once attributes of personification were given to cute and darling animals of the forest like Bambi, Thumper, and Flower, all bets were off. After all, who would seriously desire to participate in the demise of a wild animal that talks, sings, and frolics about the forest like an innocent child?

As I recall, the Preamble to the American Constitution clearly states,

> We the people of the United States, in order to form a more perfect Union, establish justice, insure domestic tranquility, provide for the common defense, promote the general welfare, and secure the blessings of liberty to ourselves and our posterity, do ordain and establish this Constitution for the United States of America.

I would like someone to point out to me precisely where the Preamble declares or even remotely implies, "We the people **and the animal kingdom** of the United States, in order to form a more perfect Union...." Am I missing something here? Evidently so, because according to the radical Animal Liberation Front, a supposed "Bill of Rights for Animals" needs to be established for their protection. The following statements are the supposed rights of animals as provided on the ALF's website.[10] I will add my own response to each right they deem all animals are entitled to:

1. All animals are born with an equal claim on life and the same rights to existence.

My response: Tell that to the lions and tigers and bears—oh my! I was under the assumption that God provided human beings with animals, in part so that people could use some of them for food as well as array themselves with pelts for both warmth and fashionable beauty. As I recall from the Bible, the Lord Jesus was a Jew, and I never read anywhere in the Good Book where He objected to animal sacrifice in the Jewish Temple in Jerusalem. He also ate meat and drank wine with His disciples. Are we now to presume that Jesus as well as His disciples would presently come under politically correct scrutiny and condemnation by the Animal Liberation Front for their supposed mistreatment of the animal kingdom during biblical times?

2. All animals are entitled to respect. Humanity as an animal species shall not arrogate to itself the right to exterminate or exploit other species. It is humanity's duty to use its knowledge for the welfare of animals. All animals have the right to the attention, care, and protection of humanity.

My response: How utterly ridiculous! Can you imagine what our ancestors over the past several centuries would have thought about such mindless drivel? The mountain men would have responded to such gibberish by inventing a new competition to be held at their annual Rendezvous. They might have called it "Who Can Skin the Impish Animal Worshipper the Fastest?" Even the Native American nomadic tribes—as much as they revered the buffalo—relied upon such wild bovine mammals for their sustenance. We are foolish as a society if we elevate the animal kingdom to be on the equivalent level as the human race. Furthermore, the law of the jungle is "eat or be eaten." Even the wild animals instinctively adhere to that rule. According to the ALF, animals may enjoy the right of being predators for survival, yet human beings should somehow take the higher moral ground and ignore the law of the jungle.

3. No animal shall be ill-treated or be subject to cruel acts.

My response: I will concede that even I have a bit of a soft spot with regard to this statement. I love my own dog very much, and I hate it when I see pets being mistreated, cruelly neglected, or abandoned. My wife and I rescued our dog Ashling from an animal shelter as she was just about to be put to sleep. She is the kindest, most loving dog you can imagine. When we first rescued her, we spent $2,000 to bring her health back to normal, and we do not regret, for one moment, the money or time we spent on her recovery. She is a true love and brings pure joy to our family. I also do not like to see animals exploited in the inhumane and despicable manner that American football quarterback Michael Vick once engaged in with his reprehensible dog fighting ring. In my opinion, society does have a responsibility to protect animals from such abuse and cruelty. Having said that, however, I differ with the ALF with regard to its basic premise. Killing animals is not necessarily ill-treatment unless it is done in an inhumane manner. I have absolutely no objection to the killing of animals for either food or their furs for clothing so long as it is done quickly and in a humane manner and does not create any pain for the animals. I feel the same way about hunting, whether it is done for sport or for acquiring food. Furthermore, it does not bother me in the slightest bit to enter some western lodge and actually see a stuffed deer's head or moose's head mounted on a lobby wall for decoration. This is a longstanding American tradition, so ALF members and other like-minded saps need to get a life and get over it!

4. All wild animals have the right to liberty in their natural environment, whether land, air, or water, and should be allowed to procreate. Deprivation of freedom, even for educational purposes, is an infringement of this right.

My response: What a crock of bull, if you will pardon the pun! According to this asinine statement, zoos, circuses, wild animal parks as well as animal water parks, would no longer be permitted to exist. I have found the San Diego Wild Animal Park, the San Diego Zoo, and Sea World to not only be educational, but the animals appear to be quite content as they are allowed to reproduce, they are fed quite well, their habitats are clean and resemble their natural habitats in appearance, the animals are well cared for, and they are humanely treated by professional caretakers who have an abiding love and respect for the animals under their supervision. When I travel to Sea World in San Diego with my family, the killer whales and dolphins respond respectfully to their caretakers during the shows. The American people have enjoyed circuses for centuries, and most circus operators treat their animals with love and care as well. If they didn't, they would not be able to continue to operate as attendance would decline, and they would be forced out of business.

5. Animals of species living traditionally in a human environment have the right to live and grow at the rhythm and under the conditions of life and freedom peculiar to their species. Any interference by humanity with this rhythm or these conditions for purposes of gain is an infringement of this right.

My response: Why, shame on all of you zoos, circuses, and wild animal parks! Think how selfish and greedy all of you are, what with all of the research, money, love, and care you impart on behalf of all of the animals under your care and supervision! I just might have to reconsider attending your parks in the future. You should also quit encouraging your patrons to be involved with the animal adoption programs you promote in your parks, since you really do not care for the animal kingdom in the first place. You and your patrons are real animal haters and abusers! Didn't you know that?

6. All companion animals have the right to complete their natural life span. Abandonment of an animal is a cruel and degrading act.

My response: While I do not consider this to fall under the category of being a "right" per se, I really can't take issue with the premise of this statement.

7. Animal experimentation involving physical or psychological suffering is incompatible with the rights of animals, whether it be for scientific, medical, commercial, or any other form of research. Replacement methods must be used and developed.

My response: This is absolutely idiotic. There have been a number of advancements made in the areas of science and medicine that have benefited all of us because of specific animal experimentation. I wonder if the members of the Animal Liberation Front would be willing to decline the use of any medication that might save their lives or the lives of their own children as a result of medicines that may have been derived through the use of animal experimentation? Would they remain true to their convictions under such circumstances?

8. No animal shall be exploited for the amusement of humanity. Exhibitions and spectacles involving animals are incompatible with their dignity.

My response: The animal rights activists should interview the animals confined to the San Diego Zoo or San Diego Wild Animal Park to determine whether or not their dignity is being violated. I would like to see their collective response. I think these animal rights activists have been watching too much of *Planet of the Apes*.

9. Any act involving the wanton killing of the animals is biocide, that is, a crime against life.

My response: Oh, I see. If someone hunts a wild animal for food or sport, he is now guilty of a crime! Is this the direction our government desires to take our country? You may be quite surprised and alarmed to find out as I address this question shortly. In the meantime, I wonder if these radical screwballs are just as passionate about the taking of innocent human life through the act of abortion? My guess is probably not. They are more than likely pro-choice, and I seriously doubt any of us would find many of these folks attending a pro-life rally. In other words, it is perfectly acceptable and moral in this nation for an innocent human fetus to be killed while growing in his mother's womb, yet God help you should you shoot an innocent deer to make delicious, nutritious jerky and have the remainder of such an animal be stuffed by a taxidermist in order that the deer's head may be mounted on some wall. In today's politically correct climate, you would be guilty of a crime against life, deserving to become nothing other than the equivalent of an extinct Neanderthal—thus serving as an inconvenient and embarrassing remembrance of things past. But remember, according to animal rights activists, animals supposedly have a "right" to complete their natural life spans while a human fetus can be deprived of that same "right." In fact, human babies can still be deprived of life through a gruesome process called partial-birth abortion!

10. Any act involving the mass killing of wild animals is genocide, that is, a crime against the species. Pollution or destruction of the natural environment leads to genocide.

My response: I absolutely loathe the manner in which radical progressives pervert the meaning of the English language in order to advance their nefarious agenda. The Webster Dictionary defines genocide as "the deliberate and systematic destruction of a racial, political, or cultural group." This term has always been used to describe people, not animals, yet animal rights activists would have us all believe that the killing of animals is now genocide and the moral equivalent to what Adolf Hitler and Nazi Germany almost accomplished with their insidious plot to exterminate all European Jews during World War II. It is a human atrocity that six million Jews were murdered by Hitler's Gestapo, and the Nazis almost succeeded in committing total genocide against the Jewish race in Europe. In my opinion, the ALF's attempt to trivialize the meaning of the word genocide is truly demeaning not only to the Jewish people, but the rest of humanity as well. This is about as radical as one can get in this particular arena. What is more, if I were Jewish, I would really take these numskulls to task big time! This is what ultimately happens when various groups weaken and trivialize the meanings of important words and apply them in such a callous and fallacious manner to various political agendas.

This entire affair would be laughable—as if it were some kind of wild hilarious prank being thrust upon the American people— were it not for the fact that these people are quite serious with their agenda. Can you possibly fathom what some of our ancestors such as the American mountain men would think about all of this asinine nonsense? This type of "Bill of Rights for Animals" is so demeaning to our sacred Constitution and American tradition, our Founding Fathers would be rolling over in their graves if they knew just how sincere these animal rights advocates are with perverting the Constitution! Our Founding Fathers might conclude America is going to Hell in a hand basket, and I would agree with them! To add insult to injury, these loony animal rights activists have more than a sympathetic ear with the media, Hollywood entertainers, and leftist radicals in the political arena, especially in the Obama administration! I told you previously that I would address the question shortly as to whether or not our government could possibly make it a crime to kill or hunt animals in the near future. Well—fasten your seat belts, ladies and gentlemen, because here it comes! The following comments and beliefs of a member of President Barack Obama's administration might possibly alarm you just as much as it does me!

Cass Sunstein was appointed by Barack Obama to be the director of the Office of Information and Regulatory Affairs (OIRA). He is often referred to as the Obama administration's "Regulation Czar." The following is a list of quotes attributed directly to him and comes from the website of Stopsunstein.com.[11] I will cite the sources this particular website used in its own research.

We ought to ban hunting.
    Cass Sunstein, in a 2007 speech at Harvard University

[Humans'] willingness to subject animals to unjustified suffering will be seen...as a form of unconscionable barbarity...morally akin to slavery and the mass extermination of human beings.
    Cass Sunstein, in a 2007 speech at Harvard University

But I think that we should go further. We should focus attention not only on the "enforcement gap," but on the areas where current law offers little or no protection. In short, the law should impose further regulation on hunting, scientific experiments, entertainment, and (above all) farming to ensure against unnecessary animal suffering. It is easy to imagine a set of initiatives that would do a great deal here, and indeed European nations have moved in just this direction. There are many possibilities.

> Cass R. Sunstein, "The Rights of Animals: A Very Short Primer," John M. Olin Law & Economics Working Paper No. 157, The Law School, The University of Chicago.

Do animals have standing? To many people, the very idea seems odd. But several cases suggest that the answer might be yes. In a remarkably large number of cases in the federal courts, animals appear as named plaintiffs....Indeed, I have not been able to find any federal statute that allows animals to sue in their own names. As a rule, the answer is therefore quite clear: Animals lack standing as such, simply because no relevant statute confers a cause of action on animals. It seems possible, however, that before long, Congress will grant standing to animals to protect their own rights and interests. Congress might do this in the belief that in some contexts, it will be hard to find any person with an injury in fact to bring suit in his own name. And even if statutes protecting animal welfare are enforceable by human beings, Congress might grant standing to animals in their own right, particularly to make a public statement about whose interests are most directly at stake, partly to increase the number of private monitors of illegality, and partly to bypass complex inquiries into whether prospective human plaintiffs have injuries in fact. Indeed, I believe that in some circumstances, Congress should do just that, to provide a supplement to limited public enforcement efforts.

> Cass R. Sunstein, Martha C. Nussbaum. Animal Rights: Current Debates and New Directions. (Oxford University Press, USA, 2004). P. 259-260

...Representatives of animals should be able to bring private suits to ensure that anticruelty and related laws are actually enforced. If, for example, a farm is treating horses cruelly and in violation of legal requirements, a suit could be brought, on behalf of those animals, to bring about compliance with the law.

Cass R. Sunstein, "The Rights of Animals: A Very Short Primer," John M. Olin Law & Economics Working Paper No. 157, The Law School, The University of Chicago

The fact that such a left-wing radical Harvard professor of this caliber could remotely be an integral part of the Obama administration is truly scary. On a related note, Cass Sunstein's position on animal rights is not only beyond the pale, as evidenced by his nonsensical comments and views, but his enthusiastic support of other big-government, socialistic entitlement programs is also most alarming. Let us examine this related point in greater detail.

Cass Sunstein has published a book titled *The Second Bill of Rights: Franklin Delano Roosevelt's Unfinished Revolution and Why We Need It More Than Ever* (Basic Books 2004). Yes, you read that correctly! Just like the Animal Liberation Front's absurd "Bill of Rights for Animals," we have yet another farcical example of a former president who advocated another type of Bill of Rights that, according to Franklin D. Roosevelt, was needed beyond what our Constitution provides for the American people. Personally, I didn't even realize that Roosevelt once advocated this sham until I recently came upon it during my research for this book. Here is an excerpt from Roosevelt's January 11th, 1944, message to Congress on the State of the Union. If you have never heard of this message before now, prepare to be just as shocked as I was when I first learned of it. This is part of the "unfinished revolution" Mr. Sunstein of the Obama administration is so fond of promoting:

...This Republic had its beginning, and grew to its present strength, under the protection of inalienable political rights— among them the right of free speech, free press, free worship, trial by jury, freedom from unreasonable searches and seizures.

They were our rights to life and liberty.

As our nation has grown in size and stature, however—as our industrial economy expanded—these political rights proved inadequate to assure us equality in the pursuit of happiness. We have come to a clear realization of the fact that true individual freedom cannot exist without economic security and independence. (emphasis mine) Necessitous men are not free men. People who are hungry and out of a job are the stuff of which dictatorships are made.

In our day these economic truths have become accepted as self-evident. We have accepted, so to speak, a second Bill of Rights under which a new basis of security and prosperity can be established for all—regardless of station, race, or creed.

Among these are:

The right to a useful and remunerative job in the industries or shops or farms or mines of the nation;

The right to earn enough to provide adequate food and clothing and recreation;

The right of every farmer to raise and sell his products at a return which will give him and his family a decent living;

The right of every businessman, large and small, to trade in an atmosphere of freedom from unfair competition and domination by monopolies at home or abroad;

The right to adequate medical care and the opportunity to achieve and enjoy good health;

The right to adequate protection from the economic fears of old age, sickness, accident, and unemployment;

The right to a good education.

All of these rights spell security. And after this war is won we must be prepared to move forward, in the implementation of these rights, to new goals of human happiness and well-being.

America's own rightful place in the world depends in large part upon how fully these and similar rights have been carried into practice for our citizens.[12]

Constitutional conservatives are deeply offended and appalled by the fact that President Franklin D. Roosevelt saw fit to disparage our Constitution's Bill of Rights by stating that it now proves inadequate to assure all of us equality in the pursuit of happiness. Isn't it most telling that this progressive iconoclast didn't seem the least bit concerned with gutting the constitutional civil rights of loyal, patriotic Japanese American citizens during World War II when he had them rounded up and placed against their will in various internment camps in California? Where exactly were Franklin D. Roosevelt's sentiments and convictions when these American citizens had their homes, their land, and their businesses confiscated at the outbreak of our involvement in World War II? So much for FDR's concern with both the political and economic civil rights of all Americans!

So what did Roosevelt—with the enthusiastic support of President Obama's "Regulation Czar," Cass Sunstein—advocate? FDR took it upon himself to arrogantly propose that America needs his socialistic "Economic Bill of Rights" since the original Bill of Rights is supposedly no longer up to snuff with regard to protecting the individual rights of the American people! Roosevelt would have exemplified the perfect Robin Hood of Sherwood Forest had he personally witnessed the fruition of this idealistic utopian crap during his lifetime, and now I am sure he is looking down upon us—tickled pink with delight as Americans are currently witnessing the fruition of his dream in the early stages of the twenty-first century under the leadership of Team Obama! At first glance, his "Economic Bill of Rights" appears to be quite benign and compassionate. After all, who wouldn't desire to obtain or achieve all of the seven components or supposed "rights" mentioned in his vision? Even some American transcendentalists of the nineteenth century attempted to fulfill similar idealistic phantasms of economic security and happiness by establishing various utopian societies such as New Harmony in Indiana and Brook Farm in Massachusetts. Both failed for two very obvious reasons: they succumbed to the stark realities of financial hardship and irreconcilable differences between members of its societies. Such are the best made plans of mice and men.

Our Declaration of Independence guarantees the American people the right to pursue happiness, but nowhere does that document or the Constitution itself guarantee the American people all of the fruits of happiness or to experience perpetual happiness and financial security during their entire lifetime. To my knowledge, no country in the history of the world has ever been able to achieve this, nor will there ever exist any government that can achieve such goals no matter how noble they may be because people are inherently imperfect and come into this world with a sinful nature. The Communists of the twentieth century attempted to establish such utopian societies as well, and look just where it got them. Our country provides its people with the opportunity to seek an excellent education, pursue good employment, obtain outstanding medical care, etc.; however, it would be foolhardy and unrealistic to expect that our own government could miraculously guarantee the American people perpetual immunity to hard times, unemployment, or any other harsh realities of life without facing total bankruptcy in the process.

Simply put, there is one inestimable truth we can all be assured of, and that is: Some people are more industrious than others; therefore, industrious individuals should reap additional benefits and financial rewards over those who are less industrious and less educated. I will use myself as an illustration of this point. When I earned my master's degree in education from the University of

Redlands, I paid for this graduate degree out of my own pocketbook, and nobody assisted me. In addition, I chose to enter a profession that has provided me, in part, with extensive experience and intellectual insight with which to write a book. As a result, I should be rewarded with the choices I have made in life and benefit from those choices and hard work without being required to "spread the wealth." That is part of the American Dream. Why should I, or any other industrious American for that matter, be compelled by both the state and federal governments to share these **extra** rewards with those individuals who have made deliberate choices not to further their education, who have chosen not to work hard and get ahead, who have neglected to take risks, or who have chosen not to get ahead in life through the pursuit of happiness? If the point I am raising makes me out to be some monstrous, insensitive, and selfish ogre, then so be it. However, I believe most Americans would agree with me.

During the presidential election of 2008, when candidate Barack Obama flippantly remarked to "Joe the Plumber" that we all need to "spread the wealth," I immediately thought to myself that I certainly would not be inclined to vote for this Robin Hood, and this is one of the reasons why 48 percent of voting Americans chose not to support Obama for president as well. Many Americans are weary of being lectured to by self-righteous, pompous progressives who somehow believe they have the moral authority to point fingers, assign blame, and portray the rest of us successful Americans as nothing but a bunch of greedy fat cats simply because we believe in pursuing the American Dream. If constitutional conservatives believe in safeguarding one kind of entitlement, it is the one that maintains successful Americans should be "entitled" to retain the vast majority of their acquired wealth so that they may eventually "spread the wealth" to members of their own families and charities and most assuredly not to the likes of many of those lazy freeloaders participating in the Occupy Wall Street Movement throughout

America who advocate socialized "income redistribution." A number of these people would be more than content with pick pocketing that which they do not deserve because they have failed to acquire wealth that requires both hard work and perseverance!

Furthermore, who precisely is to be the arbiter as to what constitutes a decent home, a decent living, enough food, clothing, and recreation for all Americans or useful and adequate remunerative jobs that forever protect us from the economic fears of old age, sickness, accident, and unemployment that are the "rights" advocated by Franklin D. Roosevelt? Why, it is the federal government, of course! Our federal government—under the current socialistic leadership of Team Obama and the Democrats as well as other radicals yielding power and influence over all of us, like Cass Sunstein—are managing to fulfill Roosevelt's vision for America in true tyrannical fashion. Just think about it for a moment. The federal government now controls and regulates many of our banks, much of the car industry, a significant portion of the mortgage industry through Fannie Mae and Freddie Mac, the student loan industry, the education industry, the energy industry, the salaries of CEOs, the retirement industry for most Americans, the Medicare prescription drug industry, and now the health care industry. All told, the federal government is going to run and control roughly 50 percent of the American economy while the Chinese control the rest of it with our massive indebtedness to them. All of these politicians in Washington, DC, are about to saddle our children and grandchildren with huge deficits that they will never be able to repay. As a direct result, our nation is about to go bankrupt while too many unsuspecting Americans give such "Boss Tweeds" their blessing to continue to engage in such unconstitutional shenanigans.

One of my terrific sisters, Carol Thurman, who resides in Texas, sent me the following interesting anecdote on my computer that accurately describes human nature, and it drives home the very point why our nation should avoid European-style socialism as if it were the bubonic plague. Many of the naïve individuals of the Occupy Wall Street Movement, as well as the majority of Democrats and a number of liberal Republicans, would be well advised to pay attention to and learn something from this anecdote:

An economics professor at a local college made a statement that he had never failed a single student before but had once failed an entire class.

That class had insisted that socialism worked and that no one would be poor and no one would be rich, a great equalizer.

The professor then said ok, we will have an experiment in this class on socialism.

All grades would be averaged and everyone would receive the same grade so no one would fail and no one would receive an A.

After the first test, the grades were averaged and everyone got a B. The students who studied hard were upset and the students who studied little were happy.

But, as the second test rolled around, the students who studied little had studied even less and the ones who studied hard decided they wanted a free ride too; so they studied little....The second test average was a D! No one was happy.

When the 3rd test rolled around the average was an F.

The scores never increased as bickering, blame, and name calling all resulted in hard feelings and no one would study for the benefit of anyone else.

All failed, to their great surprise, and the professor told them that socialism would also ultimately fail because when the reward is great, the effort to succeed is great; but when government takes all the reward away, no one will try or want to succeed.

Could not be any simpler than that....

— Author Unknown

America is gradually moving away from the free market system and capitalistic approach to American economics. As stated earlier in a previous chapter, our nation is reaping exactly what we have sowed. Tragically, far too many Americans have forsaken the following wise admonishments expressed by two of our former presidents, John F. Kennedy and Dwight D. Eisenhower:

> Ask not what your country can do for you, ask what you can do for your country.
>
> John F. Kennedy

> A people that values its privileges above its principles soon loses both.
>
> Dwight D. Eisenhower

We all need to take another deep breath as Cass Sunstein, the director of the Office of Information and Regulatory Affairs, reveals his radical views concerning the First Amendment and free speech. He affectionately references FDR's New Deal in one of his quotes.[13]

> A legislative effort to regulate broadcasting in the interest of democratic principles should not be seen as an abridgment of the free speech guarantee.
>
> Cass R. Sunstein, *Democracy and the Problem of Free Speech,* The Free Press, 1995, p. 92

I have argued in favor of a reformation of First Amendment law. The overriding goal of the reformulation is to reinvigorate processes of democratic deliberation, by ensuring greater attention to public issues and greater diversity of views. The First Amendment should not stand as an obstacle to democratic efforts to accomplish these goals. A New Deal for speech would draw on Justice Brandeis' insistence on the role of free speech in promoting political deliberation and citizenship. It would reject Justice Holmes' "marketplace" conception of free speech, a conception that disserves the aspirations of those who wrote America's founding document.

> Cass R. Sunstein, *Democracy and the Problem of Free Speech*, The Free Press, 1995, p. 119

...In light of astonishing economic and technological changes, we must doubt whether, as interpreted, the constitutional guarantee of free speech is adequately serving democratic goals. It is past time for a large-scale reassessment of the appropriate role of the First Amendment in the democratic process.[14]

> Cass R. Sunstein, *Democracy and the Problem of Free Speech*, The Free Press, 1995.

Well there it is! Mr. Sunstein extols the virtue of another socialistic New Deal for free speech while castigating the proper role of free speech in the "marketplace" of ideas, and he wants to reform First Amendment law to reflect his own political agenda. No one can convince me that our current president, Barack Obama, is oblivious of the philosophies of those surrounding him in his administration. Any president, conservative or liberal, is going to appoint individuals to work in his administration who are like-minded, who reflect his own political philosophy, and who are more than willing to carry out his political agenda. President Obama has surrounded himself with individuals who are extremely radical and who want to forever change the political and economic landscape of our country. Before returning to the topic of animal rights, I am going to make some very audacious observations at this particular point in time.

Prior to the elections of 2008 and 2010, I can clearly recall both Democratic and Republican senators and Congressmen warning the American people that Social Security, Medicare, and other big-government entitlement programs are just about insolvent and ready to go belly-up. If that is true, why should the American people naively presume that ObamaCare will somehow be any different? Apparently, liberals would prefer that the American people once again place all of our unquestionable faith, blind trust, and allegiance in the hands of the federal government despite the fact that this behemoth of an entitlement program, the likes of which this country has never seen before, will supposedly be different from other federal programs. So much for transparency and being honest and forthright with the American people! In this country, it is no longer apparent that either the average American or average businessman knows what is best for our country because according to the progressives, we are too naïve and stupid or too full of greed and avarice to handle our own personal and business affairs! Instead, Big-Government Daddy knows best, and we had all better fall perfectly in line to obey this demagoguery daddy lest we all receive a sound spanking. Oh, I forgot; these namby-pambies no longer believe in spanking, but they have, nevertheless, devised a fiendish way to wallop all of us with another type of giant paddle labeled **"Massive Taxation, Regulation, Debt, and Bankruptcy"!** To put it rather delicately folks, be prepared to bear some extremely red and very sore asses for quite some time to come! The way this nation is currently headed, we will not be able to sit down for a hell-of-a-long time as a result of receiving this federal-style blistering!

In Washington, DC, the days of political civility and polite disagreement and discourse are simply a thing of the past. The very survival of our republic is at stake, and the majority of Americans are weary of what the political left and all of its cronies are cramming down the nation's throat! Despite the trouncing the progressives took in 2010, they will continue to go after their opposition with both barrels loaded and guns blazing in the elections of 2012. They will not hesitate for one minute to pull out from their mighty arsenal all of their big guns and other weapons of mass destruction that are at their disposal. So why shouldn't American conservatives, libertarians, independents, and people of devout religious faith be doing the exact same thing? In many ways, this is a type of nonviolent civil war—a war being waged for the very heart and soul of our country between two political and economic philosophies that are diametrically opposed to one another. Only one philosophy is ultimately going to prevail. The question is, which one? Perhaps if John McCain had not turned the other cheek and played the role of the dutiful polite gentleman back in 2008, we would have far better leadership in both the White House and Congress. Conservatives, at the very least, had better wake up to the fact that if we don't continue to fight in the spirit exhibited by the Tea Party movement during the 2010 elections and use it to our complete advantage, we will continue to lose future elections, and we will have no one to blame but ourselves. Many of us are desperately seeking to support devoutly conservative, robust men and women who are running for political office and who are not the least bit hesitant to display some backbone similar to that of the late Republican activist Lee Atwater. Atwater labored tirelessly, and sometimes ruthlessly, against leftist foes of conservative candidates and causes.

This is precisely what the grassroots Tea Party movement is all about as it continues to grow in strength and numbers and fights unapologetically for conservative principles and values. Unfortunately, some conservatives occasionally whine and bemoan the manner in which they are treated by the well-entrenched left-wing establishment, yet we need to aggressively pursue our own conservative equivalents of the liberal George Soros, Move-On.Org, etc. We do have conservative stalwarts such as Sean Hannity, Bill O'Reilly, Rush Limbaugh, Glenn Beck, Tammy Bruce, Laura Ingram, Ann Coulter, Sarah Palin, and Donald Trump—to name just a few—but precisely where are our own conservative equivalents of the leftist lions of the Senate exemplified by the late Ted Kennedy? Just where does a conservative billionaire or two exist who is more than willing to put up some of his own fortune to fund and fight for conservative movements and politicians just as George Soros is so eager to do on behalf of his own beloved left? We need to be willing to fight just as hard and just as formidable, if necessary, for both the preservation and promotion of the values conservative Americans cherish. If we don't, we will eventually lose this political civil war and be compelled to forever forfeit all of that which we hold so dear. At any rate, it is time to return once again to the topic of animal rights.

The animal rights organization PETA is also at the forefront of controversy on a regular basis. This radical organization is a perfect soul mate to the Animal Liberation Front. The following excerpts are just a few general FAQs concerning PETA that appear directly on its own website.[15] As usual, following each ridiculous excerpt, I will offer my own response:

What do you mean by animal rights?

"People who support animal rights believe that animals are not ours to use for food, clothing, entertainment, or any other purpose and that animals deserve consideration of their best interests regardless of whether they are cute, useful to humans, or endangered and regardless of whether any human cares about them at all (just as a mentally challenged human has rights even if he or she is not cute or useful and even if everyone dislikes him or her)."

My response: Oh really? I wonder if PETA would be willing to make a similar statement with regard to protecting the rights of human beings such as children who are diagnosed with Down Syndrome—even if they are not considered cute or useful to those who would prefer to abort them while they are still in their mothers' wombs? I am not holding my breath while waiting for an answer to this question.

It's fine for you to believe in animal rights, but why do you try to tell other people what to do?

"Everybody is entitled to his or her own opinion, but freedom of thought is not the same thing as freedom of action. You are free to believe whatever you want as long as you don't hurt others. You may believe that animals should be killed, that black people should be enslaved, or that women should be beaten, but you don't always have the right to put your beliefs into practice. The very nature of reform movements is to tell others what to do—don't use humans as slaves, don't sexually harass women, etc.—and all movements initially encounter opposition from people who want to continue to take part in the criticized behavior."

My response: I can scarcely tolerate all of this pap and crap! Once again, we see animal rights being elevated to the moral equivalency of slavery, sexual harassment, the beating of women, etc. Why do we even bother to lend any sense of credibility whatsoever to these radical loons by showcasing PETA and its sappy positions on television and other forms of the media? I would prefer that they be relegated to the confines of lunatic asylums where they really belong.

What about all the customs, traditions, and jobs that depend on using animals?

"The invention of the automobile, the abolition of slavery, and the end of World War II also necessitated restructuring and job retraining. Making changes to customs, traditions, and jobs is part of social progress—not a reason to deter it."

My response: Perhaps Team Obama should shy away from this group lest the implementation of PETA's policies add to the already outrageous national unemployment rate. After all, with PETA in their pockets, they could no longer make any claim to "saving" jobs. In the meantime, I will continue to savor the delicious chicken found within Jack in the Box's Chicken Fajita Pita Pockets.

If using animals is unethical, why does the Bible say that we have dominion over animals?

"Dominion is not the same as tyranny. The Queen of England has 'dominion' over her subjects, but that doesn't mean that she can eat them, wear them, or experiment on them. If we have dominion over animals, surely it is to protect them, not to use them for our own ends. There is nothing in the Bible that would justify our modern-day practices, which desecrate the environment, destroy entire species of wildlife, and inflict torment and death on billions of animals every year. The Bible imparts a reverence for life, and a loving God could not help but be appalled by the way that animals are treated today."

My response: Royal subjects of England beware! Queen Elizabeth II—who has "dominion" over you—might just possibly misinterpret this word and pounce upon some British subjects at any moment now in order to have a most sumptuous affair at Buckingham Palace! How about we join together as two great nations to revive the old traditions once practiced in the Tower of London? After all, the Tower once housed a fantastic menagerie, and since the animal rights activists no longer see any distinction between human beings and the rest of the animal kingdom, we may as well imprison them in their own menagerie at the Tower of London. With regard to the Bible, PETA's ignorance of God's divine will and purpose is astounding. Apparently our loving God had no difficulty with establishing animal sacrifice in His Holy Temple—either in the wilderness or in the holy city of Jerusalem. Once a year, the blood of an unblemished sacrificed lamb would be placed by the High Priest on the Judgment Seat of the Holy of

Holies in the Jewish Temple for the remission of sins of the Jewish people. Every year the Jewish people would also purchase doves and lambs with which to participate in ritual animal sacrifice which was required of their religion. When have most of these animal rights nincompoops ever stepped foot inside a traditional conservative Christian church or Orthodox Jewish Synagogue to really learn about God's word? If they were to actually do so, their ranks might shrink considerably. Christian missionaries, you now have a new ripe target for conversion! By all means, evangelize members of PETA not only for their sake, but for ours as well!

Americans in general have no issue with any individual who chooses to be a vegetarian for personal health reasons or for personal moral convictions. Individuals or groups who choose not to buy or wear any products containing fur or leather are behaving totally within the realm of personal freedom and choice. Likewise, if animal rights activists choose not to patronize various entertainment venues that feature the use of animals or they choose not to attend movies where animals are being used for entertainment purposes, again that is strictly their personal choice. No one is twisting their arms to force them to make choices they are uncomfortable with. Where many Americans do draw the line in the sand, however, is when animal rights activists attempt to strong arm or intimidate others into making choices they are uncomfortable with. Many Americans love to eat meat, wear fur and leather, visit zoos and circuses, or hunt and fish. As such, we are most assuredly not going to countenance any behavior on the part of self-righteous animal rights activists that dares to threaten our participating in such legal activities, nor will we tolerate being treated as if we are criminals or second-class citizens should we choose to do so. When these activists and their radical organizations begin to trample upon the constitutional rights of other American citizens who do not agree with their views, or when they attempt to misuse the power of the federal government to achieve their diabolical ends, then they have a real fight on their hands. The majority of the American people are simply not going to tolerate this type of fascism and control over their daily lives, and that is a fact these animal rights activists can take to the bank.

Finally, I would like to conclude this chapter with a tragic factual account as to how far we have come in this nation with regard to the bizarre application of all of this animal rights madness, as well as some sobering facts concerning another unconstitutional power-grab being perpetrated by the federal government.

It is about time the American people and Congress seriously re-examine the Endangered Species Act and the devastating impact it has had on our country during the past several decades. While this act had noble intentions with its inception, it has been maliciously abused and zealously applied by radical environmentalists against Americans of good faith and good will. Let us examine what is currently taking place in the fertile San Joaquin Valley of California or the Central Valley, as it is often referred to.

California is currently experiencing a serious drought because of a lack of sufficient rain and snow. This has had a serious impact on the available water supplies for both farmers and urban areas. The San Joaquin Valley is vital to the food supply of the United States as well as the economic well-being of those who live and work in that valley, not to mention the state of California. Many of the great farms and ranches of that region have been in the same families for generations, yet these very farms are at serious risk of survival not only because of the current drought, but because of what I would boldly claim is the criminal application of the federal Endangered Species Act.

US District Court Judge Oliver Wanger of Fresno ruled that pressure from the massive pumps of two pumping stations being operated by the state and federal governments in the Sacramento-San Joaquin Delta are endangering a tiny minnow called the Delta smelt.[16] Now, this species grows to be no more than three inches and does not live longer than a year under the best of conditions. Other than fish bait, the species does not serve much of any other purpose, yet Judge Wanger has ruled that the pumps have to be shut down. As a result, farm after farm is going bankrupt, people are now unemployed, they rely on government assistance, and some of the food supply for this nation is in serious jeopardy as a result of the enormous loss of some of the best fruits, nuts, and vegetables produced and supplied by the state of California! The Central Valley is becoming a veritable dust bowl reminiscent of the mid-western dust bowl of the 1930s, except that this one is primarily being brought about by the irresponsible actions of mankind. As a direct result of this madness, the cost of fruits and vegetables on grocery store shelves nationwide is going to eventually skyrocket because of the growing shortage of produce being shipped to market from the Central Valley.

When I saw the pathetic plight of these poor farm owners and ranch workers being showcased by Sean Hannity on the Fox News Network during the fall of 2009, my heart just sank because I briefly lived in that beautiful valley for two wonderful years. This tragedy is outrageous, and the federal government should be totally ashamed of itself. To think that farmers, ranchers, and their entire properties—which provide such owners with their very livelihood and function as the progenitors of employment for the people that such properties all serve—are somehow less important in America than some three-inch minnow is just beyond all comprehension and common sense. Well, that is where we currently are with all of this animal rights and environmental business, and what a stinking business it is! This is but another shameful example of just how powerful and tyrannical our federal government and some special-interest groups have become, yet we continue to foolishly elect and reelect progressive patsies of such groups to state and federal office who are directly responsible for imposing all of this havoc upon our great nation! When are we finally going to rise up as a nation and boldly proclaim that enough is enough?

This clear misuse of the Endangered Species Act is illustrative of just how intrusive and all-powerful our federal government has become: meddling in the affairs of states and localities, which according to the Constitution, violates the very premise of limited government. This is quite onerous and does not bode well for the American people with regard to the kind of government envisioned by our Founding Fathers. To further clarify this point, the following excerpt from the *New York Times* News Service is quite revealing:

> The Senate voted Thursday, October 22, 2009 to extend new federal protections to people who are victims of violent crime because of their gender or sexual orientation, bringing the measure close to reality after years of fierce debate....The measure gives victims the same federal safeguards already afforded to people who are victims of violent crimes because of their race, color, religion, or national origin. The measure would also allocate $5 million a year to the Justice Department to assist local communities in investigating hate crimes, and it would allow the agency to assist in investigations and prosecutions if local agencies requested help.[17]

In addition, according to some facts and statistics put out by the Heritage Foundation:

> The Constitution provides for only three federal crimes; piracy, counterfeiting, and treason. Today, there are more than 3,000 federal criminal laws—so many that the Congressional Research Service cannot count them all. More than 40 percent of these were passed since 1970, and there are more than 10,000 separate regulations (estimates run as high as 300,000) that carry criminal penalties.[18]

Thomas Sowell, a favorite conservative African-American news commentator of mine, wrote a very pointed op-ed piece that appeared in one of my local newspapers concerning the colossal monster the federal government has become. Amongst other things, he states:

> Would you have believed that one of the many "czars" appointed by the president, could arbitrarily cut the pay of executives in private businesses by 50 percent or 90 percent?...That there would be plans afloat to subsidize newspapers—that is, to create a situation where some newspapers' survival would depend on the government liking what they publish?...How about a federal agency giving schoolchildren material to enlist them on the side of the president?...President Obama has already floated the idea of a national police force, something we have done without for more than two centuries....Whether enough people will wake up in time to keep America from being dismantled, piece by piece, is another question—and the biggest question for this generation.[19]

Constitutional conservatives couldn't agree more with Mr. Sowell's analysis of the current dilemma facing our troubled nation.

With regard to the agenda of the animal rights activists that is thoroughly exposed for what it truly is in this particular chapter, the American mountain men of the nineteenth century would be appalled with what is currently transpiring in our country. Thank God they are not around any longer to observe all of this lunacy. On second thought, perhaps it would be quite entertaining to actually observe what course of action they might undertake in order to deal with all of this stupidity that has enshrouded our nation. I would speculate that if these brash tough men were still alive in today's "Orwellian" society, they might see fit to corral all of these pompous animal rights and environmentalist activists together in one final grandiose Rendezvous somewhere in the wilderness of Montana. The mountain men heroes of our past might effectively see to it that all of these wimps have an actual rendezvous with destiny by having the entire kit-n-caboodle ghastly stuffed so that their heads may be mounted upon the walls of a number of western establishments. This would leave a lasting impression upon all Americans while effectively serving as a dire warning to the rest of us that we had best behave ourselves! Such a macabre scenario would bring a whole new meaning to the word taxidermy, wouldn't it? It might also inspire the creation of a morbid new episode of the *Twilight Zone* or even serve as a literary topic for a new Stephen King thriller.

Speaking of stuffed mounted heads, here is one magnificent suggestion! Perhaps hunting enthusiasts could offer to make arrangements to book an appropriate site for the next PETA convention. It could possibly take place at the Great Falls International Airport Terminal in Great Falls, Montana, which has very spacious and comfortable conference rooms. Picture the following scenario: As all of the incoming members of PETA disembark from their planes, they might potentially experience a bout of apoplexy as they are welcomed by the impressive array of stuffed animal heads mounted on the walls of the airport terminal lobby. In addition, PETA activists would be aghast with the nightmarish display of a stuffed bear and mountain lion menacingly perched in their natural habitat exhibits throughout the lobby, including the beautiful one that lines the terminal's escalator. As the PETA conventioneers descend the escalator to retrieve their luggage while either fainting or fanning themselves in disbelief and disgust, they would also be treated to the historical display of an auspicious mural painting that depicts the explorers of the Lewis and Clark Corps of Discovery, completely outfitted in their raiment of beaver fur hats and buckskin clothing while attempting to portage the five great falls of the Missouri River, which cascade nearby. All of this hoopla would be way too much for PETA enthusiasts to stomach. Not to worry, ladies and gentlemen, for the city of Great Falls has a very impressive conglomeration of topnotch medical facilities that would sufficiently meet the needs of so many seriously ill PETA enthusiasts! For those conventioneers who may not survive the entire ordeal, Montana hunters would probably see to it that deceased PETA radicals are given a proper funeral at a local cemetery including a fine tribute to them consisting of a gun salute with hunting rifles, which would be a most fitting conclusion. For all we know, such a motley gathering of hunters might even include some actual descendents of the mountain men of the 1800s!

⑥

Cinderella Family

It was and remains an independent place [Great Falls, Montana]. In the center of that place, in the heart of it but not on the sleeve, was God. We didn't always articulate it well, but we knew what was at the heart of times good or bad. That's what the singular vision was all about. There was religious joy at the center.

— Christian D. Stevens

In 2005 a remarkable film, *Cinderella Man,* was released. The film's message is powerful because it exemplifies the spirit of the down-on-his-luck American and how he makes a comeback through pure grit, hard work, and determination. At the very heart of the film is the emphasis on the importance of the family unit, the importance of fatherhood, and the necessity of keeping the family together against all odds and through thick-and-thin. The setting of the true story is in New York and New Jersey during the Great Depression.

A former successful boxer by the name of James J. Braddock, played by Russell Crowe, loses everything with the crash of the stock market. His entire family attempts to survive starvation, cold winters with little heat, illnesses, no money with which to pay bills, and virtually no work. Mr. Braddock refuses to break up his family by sending the children to live with relatives, and he temporarily goes on public relief to help make ends meet. When he eventually returns to the boxing ring and defeats the heavyweight champion of the world, Max Baer, Braddock saves his family, repays the government, and eventually becomes an American hero. It is an inspiring film that has some very important lessons to teach all of us, not the least of which are old-fashioned American self-reliance, the importance of fatherhood, and the importance of the family unit in America. All of these lessons happen to be some of the topics of this particular chapter.

My late uncle, Christian D. Stevens, wrote an article in 1988 titled "There Was No Room for Subtlety in '30s." It was published by the *Great Falls Tribune* to commemorate the 100th anniversary of the incorporation of that city. Chris's article relates much of the struggle my own family faced while trudging through the Great Depression, and it reflects a spirit similar to the one showcased in the true story of *Cinderella Man*. Shortly, readers of this book will have the opportunity to peruse my uncle's heartwarming article. But first, I would like to briefly acquaint readers with this remarkable and distinguished man.

Chris Stevens was and has always remained my favorite uncle, and I loved him dearly. He was a lifelong devout Democrat, and even though Chris and I did not see eye-to-eye on everything politically, he was, nevertheless, one of the kindest and most brilliant men I ever knew. During many summers, Chris would often travel to his beloved hometown of Great Falls—all the way from Dublin, Ireland, where he resided with his lovely family during the latter part of his life. When he would come to visit and board with my father, Chris would often teach summer classes at the University of Great Falls and would also write articles for the local newspaper, the *Great Falls Tribune*. Chris, Dad, and I would have memorable discussions about practically every topic, especially politics. Even though I am a diehard conservative, my uncle and I never raised our voices in anger when we disagreed with each other over matters of politics. I take considerable pride in the fact that I would sometimes get the best of him, which was not an easy task under any circumstance—given the fact that Chris possessed a PhD in English and was a college professor. He was also an accomplished prolific writer and published author of several books.

For example, I recall one particular evening in the 1990s when we were having a casual discussion concerning the proper role the federal government should exert while dabbling in the affairs of the American people. Naturally, my uncle argued on the side of the government having a somewhat larger role in our daily lives, which is a position almost any liberal would advocate. Of course, I argued the opposite point of view, and while Chris and I were at the kitchen sink washing and drying the supper dishes, he continued to press his point with me. I respectfully listened as he reflected upon—rather matter-of-factly—the various "things" Montana's senators did or didn't accomplish for us Montanans over the passage of time while serving in Washington, DC. I then proceeded to reply, "You know what, Uncle Chris? I really wish our senators would do much less for us as I feel we would be stronger as a nation if they would allow us to fend for ourselves." I could tell Chris was somewhat intrigued with my retort because my uncle paused for a few brief moments and reflected upon the point I had just raised. He soon acquired that typical sparkle in his eyes together with the characteristic "Stevens squint," and beamed a wry smile at me as he conceded, "You know what Johnny? You are right!"

I would like to graciously express my thanks and appreciation to the *Great Falls Tribune* for granting me permission to reprint in its entirety my Uncle Chris's quaint and reflective newspaper article, "There Was No Room for Subtlety in '30s." While the specific names and places he cites are for the benefit of the local citizens of Great Falls, the "spirit" of his heartwarming article could have easily transcended Great Falls and soared from coast to coast during the Great Depression. The sentiments and events my uncle recalls could have been reflective of almost any family and any town struggling throughout America during that tempestuous period of time. When I personally reflect upon my uncle's article, I sort of think of it as a companion to Norman Maclean's *A River Runs Through It*, which is a true story of another struggling Montana family, and to the inspiring film *Cinderella Man*. In any event, enjoy reading Chris's article that I have taken the liberty of nicknaming Cinderella Family.[1]

Life in the Thirties in Great Falls, as the late George S. Kaufman might have put it, was full of single-entendres.

There was little time for subtlety in those days. Bankers seldom hid a double meaning in their jokes when they were foreclosing on the mortgage. Come to think of it, they didn't joke at all, and the only thing hidden was the fine print.

Figurative language didn't go down well with the gas company, either. Those people demanded immediate cash in plain diction.

The principal word in a lawyer's vocabulary was "garnishee." If you were looking for a job—and who wasn't?—you had to line up to dig a ditch, and even then you had to call a spade a shovel.

The only credit cards around were wild deuces in a poker game at the Star Cigar Store on Central between Second and Third Streets, and Tuffy Lazanas generally held most of those in his hand close to his chest. He could keep a straighter face at poker than the wooden Indian that stood outside the Star. The only time I ever heard of his losing was when he wandered into the Mint by accident and the proprietor, Charlie Russell's friend and benefactor, Sid Willis, guided him into a pinochle tournament with my dad.

But people who wax nostalgic about the Depression forget that basically it was depressing.

Only kids on the North Side seemed to have chocolate-covered almonds in blue glass bowls in the dining room all day or could wear new gloves in the winter. On the South Side, we had Ex-Lax on the kitchen sink, and that was gone before lunch. As for gloves, I always had to improvise with socks that belonged to my oldest brother, Harvey. It wasn't hard, though. There were always thumbholes where the heels used to be.

For an 8-year-old in the Thirties, cords were out; WPA overalls were in—except mine. They were in at the time, but usually out at the knees.

Still, if you took a clear, singular look at life, survival—in fact, adventure—was likely. It required tunnel vision. The only light at the end of that tunnel for most grownups was Franklin Delano Roosevelt, but he was bright enough for a whole nation, and meanwhile, especially for us kids, there were plenty of sparks along the way.

Sparks were always flying in our family. And family life was intense, close, dramatic, gregarious, united. It was so united, most of our relatives lived with us in the big, rambling house at 1014 2nd Ave. S. I was born there, right on the sofa, on June 30, 1929—the last spark, so to speak, of 10 kids.

That was an ominous date, incidentally. June 30 marked the end of the final fiscal year of what writers later called the Decade of Good Times. A few minutes after I was born, economists were predicting the Crash. My dad called me a fiscal disaster, something he, being a newspaperman, knew a lot about. For years I thought I was personally responsible for the Depression. Mom seemed to get depressed just looking at me.

MY FIRST real memory of the Depression was of rolling down two flights of stairs at 1014 when I was 2. My brother, John, and my nephew, Joe Carroll (who for some reason never fully explained to me, was three years my senior) used to lure me up the stairs with peppermints and then roll me down to watch me bounce. Cynics have often questioned my capacity to recall such an early event. But phrenologists are on my side, as I still have the memory bumps on my skull to prove it.

When I first saw the play, "You Can't Take It With You," I thought it was about our family, and I can remember being surprised to learn that the line, "insanity doesn't run in our family, it gallops," came from "Arsenic and Old Lace." I thought John had invented it.

Mom was usually to be found upstairs in the main bedroom typing away at one of the mystery stories she sold in a series to Daisy Bacon, then editor of Street and Smith's New York fiction magazines, while Dad would be reading galley proofs of his weekly, "The Great Falls News," on the dining room table.

Uncle Rob, who, like "The Man Who Came to Dinner," stopped off from Chicago for a brief visit and stayed through the Depression, usually was rehearsing a piano recital or practicing for a concert at the Grand Opera House on Third Street or a performance on Keep Father Buttrey Busy.

The huge grand piano—a gift from Uncle Rob to Dad and our chief claim to ostentation—was forbidden territory, especially when Uncle Rob was coaching my oldest sister, Alma, through one of our great-uncle Silas's piano pieces like "The Sinking of the Titanic." But I recall how Harvey and John and Joe and I got in trouble one time and hid beneath it. The others escaped, but I fell asleep under there, only to be awakened late in the evening (Uncle Rob liked to rehearse in the gloom) by the crashing left hand of my uncle rolling over the deeper strains of Rachmaninoff.

Harvey was in trouble, I think, for inventing something odious with his chemistry set in the basement—a pastime he abandoned once he had saved up enough to buy a balloon-tired bike for delivering "Leaders." His chief hobby then became one of tantalizing the rest of us by stacking nickels from his route on the kitchen table and meticulously counting them.

I ALWAYS ADMIRED that bike, which Harve raced in a city competition Saturday afternoon in Gibson Park against Norman Nygaard and Hank Elespuru. It made him seem wildly rich. In fact, I always thought the Depression was a time of abundance—in spite of a gut-reaction to mulligan stew—since Harve seemed to be a walking cash register. And he—like all the kids in our neighborhood, like Tiny Frank or Bob Hamer or Richie Hartwig or the Thomas brothers or Carl and Stan Anderson or Bill Gianoulias or Tony Ginalias—was generous.

He would buy a pint of licorice ice cream at the Ice Cream Factory on Ninth and some bananas and a bottle of Lime Rickey at Zipperian's Store on Tenth and throw a party in the attic. We would read his latest issues of "True Detective" to catch up on John Dillinger or Pretty Boy Floyd, and play cards and drink the Lime Rickey, pretending we were getting drunk at the Red Feather Inn.

THE ATTIC, incidentally, was John's main hangout. He had a mania, to put it mildly, for drama, and it was there that I could help be stage manager, dressing up our cat, Tommy Gray, or John's dog, Smokey, in doll clothes commandeered from the old trunk that really belonged to my sister, Faith.This acme of John's attic productions was reached with a performance of "Snow Black," which packed 'em in at the Emerson School-the-Greatest-School-in-the-World.I still wake up screaming over some nightmare about that morbid version of the famous fairy tale in which John played the loathly old hag who has a running feud (and most of the lines) with the Magic Mirror. Carl Anderson starred as the mirror, but later in life he assumed a more electrifying role as a Montana Power executive.While such shenanigans were going on upstairs, I would be practicing my magic tricks (purchased at Prince Wheeler's Novelty Shop on First Avenue South) in the kitchen. Faith would interrupt me

by flitting through the swinging doors of the pantry—her ada-
gio room—on pink satin toe shoes. She was always dressed in
spangled leotards or a Dutch-girl outfit, rehearsing for one of
Miss Wentz's "Follies," annually produced by the Wentz School
of Dance at one of the local theaters.Alma was accompanist for
the Wentz shows and practiced her arpeggios so often that for
the first five years of my life I thought the piano stool was part
of her anatomy and that Faith actually walked on her toes.

THEY WERE marvelous sisters. When they taught the family "The Big Apple," they included me, and I always got a share
of their fudge and divinity and a confection I insisted on calling
Pinocchio. Although we fought like wildcats, I loved my brothers and sisters and still do, because they never left me out.

We closed rank when trouble threatened from outside. I can
remember one time the Molen kids across the street were beating up one of us. I rushed out to witness the action and saw Faith
chasing two of the bigger Molen boys down the street.

Neighborhood scraps were, of course, one of our chief sources of entertainment. When Alma and her friend, Ruth Sims,
dressed me up in Mom's boa and feather-hat and talked me
into imitating Mae West following a squeaky rendition of "It's
an Old Spanish Custom," that was okay for parlor tricks, but
when Bobbie Pierre and Sherman LaRosse peeked through the
windows and gave me the horse laugh, the war was on.

Just for the record, I was the most feisty kid in the first
grade at the Emerson School-the-Greatest-School-in-the-World.
At least, I thought I was until I got tangled up in a free-for-all
with Larry Koleff, Alvie and Ted Hollis, Wally Wadsworth and
the cigar-smoking Cookie Spesock.

When the boys weren't knocking out streetlights from 50
yards with school ground gravel, or sharing their Wings ciga-
rettes (a nickel a pack) behind the school boiler, or pantsing
some unfortunate Northsider on a Friday night, they were

usually helping me graduate from the Kindergarten of Hard Knocks to the real thing.

But the Emerson was a school in the genuine sense of the word. Anyone who went there that I know still thinks of himself as a survivor and is proud of it. I know it's a platitude to eulogize one's grade school teachers, but I doubt if there were any teachers as dedicated—or, for that matter, courageous—as Miss Krause, Miss Stevens, Miss Parker, Mrs. Donegan, Miss Ames, Miss Larson, Miss Kentta and the saintly principal, Miss Martin.

THOSE WOMEN didn't need a liberation movement to establish their superiority. They were superior. They meant business. Anyone who didn't live up to Ralph Waldo Emerson's criterion for American scholarship—experience, books and self-reliance—didn't pass through those hallowed halls, or even from grade to grade.

I don't recall Miss Larson's ever teaching math, but I do remember she always used a ruler; usually on Cookie Spesock. And if you didn't learn how to construct a proper sentence, those teachers seldom overlooked you, no matter what part of the Southside you came from.

Of course, we had our little differences—like the time someone swiped Ted Hollis' horse that he rode to school, or when Oline Kolsrud, Ruth Toy, Donna Mae Ledger and Theresa Mae Carr rushed into the school in a panic to say someone had knocked a sixth grader off the slide and his left eye was lying on the school ground.

It was true.

Then there was the time Dale Forbes and Fenton Burgess and Howie Van Blarcom and Ed Sartain and Bobby Rombough and I went outside to play war with a visiting gang from the Longfellow and found out we had to wage a real one instead.

WE PRODUCED some unusual athletes at the Emerson, but in our grade I think the best all-round athlete was Hal

Webb, although I'd certainly get an argument today from Kenny Campbell or Kenny Power.

Our sports were hardly confined to the school yard. You had to be in good shape just to go trick-or-treating for Halloween which, for us, usually began in late August. Getting to school in winter was a slalom adventure, seeing as how most of us hooked the back bumper of the bus, driven by an amazingly patient Mr. Van Swearingen, and slid all the way from Hess's Grocery down Third Avenue South.

A thrilling night prank was to see if we could get through Mr. Peck's cornfield on Tenth Street, picking up a few ears of corn en route to a neighborhood roast, without being decimated by Mr. Peck's pepper gun. We would roast the corn in a vacant lot where there was a huge cave dug by Marv and Davey Smith or maybe the Richards kids—Gordy, Stan, Roy and Billy.

If Mr. Peck didn't get us, generally Dean Bailey did. He was a sort of unofficial juvenile officer on the police force and took pride in leaping any fence on the Southside without touching it.

I'll lay odds that there are still B-B guns locked away (then the police station was on Fifth Street) that once belonged to the Corontzos brothers or Harold Remus or Delmar Ladd or the Grena boys.

WHEN MOM found out we were up to such pranks, she usually cut them short with her surefire weapon, the hairbrush. If for some reason that punishment didn't last she immediately went to the court of last resort; "Call Guy Palagi!" she would shout to Dad.

Now Dad, being a solid Democrat and staunch supporter of Andy Loberg, Palagi's chief political rival for the county sheriff's office, was not about to contact such a rock-ribbed representative of the opposition on the basis of Mom's imperative mood.

But he didn't have to.

The words, "Guy Palagi!" strike terror in my heart to this day, even though I know that kindly gentleman was on everybody's side. In those days, he was Oz himself. He was sheriff, but he was much worse. He was a Republican.

Neighborhood prejudices were never measured in terms of race or religion or social status or economics or even politics. They were based on territorial rights.

We set our own limits.

OUR SOUTHSIDE, whatever about Paris Gibson's intentions, ran south of the trolley tracks on Central, past the railroad tracks that cut across Fifteenth Street and up to Twenty-fifth. Anyone above that line was a blow-in. Then the limitation ran out to Highway 89 and just beyond. That was Sand Hills country. It contained many more miracles than the Miracle Mile ever produced. Those dunes would inspire a Lawrence of Arabia.

The Ku Klux Klan really did burn crosses out there, although one time a bunch of Irish-descended pranksters fooled the town, including Mayor A. Fousek and old Doc Mayland, into thinking the Klan had spread its aegis by burning crosses all the way to the gravel pit near Dempsey's Inn.

The bigger kids played strip poker out among the sandhills, but mainly it was considered the area ideal as a battleground for neighborhood wars and for weapons-testing. Rabbits and ground-hogs didn't have a chance (Dean Bailey's jurisdiction ended at Tenth), and I remember our excitement over a wooden machine gun invented by Leon Lopach that could fire five inner tube rubber bands in deadly succession—all at Sherman LaRosse, who sufficed as a target when we ran out of groundhogs.

Our naval base of operations was the river, but because of Mom's protestations, we usually settled for Chowen or Giant Springs. Dale Peterson and I designed a submarine out of garbage cans, which we launched early one morning with full baptismal ceremony.

It really sank.

Unfortunately, it never came up, although we did—in a hurry. That was a Chowen Springs caper, but Giant Springs offered greater challenges, seeing as how the authorities kept a close eye on the coins thrown into the pool where specimen trout lolled about like sluggish piranhas.

The South Side ran down Tenth to embrace the Lower South Side that included such marvels as the White Elephant Stables where you could rent a horse all day for two bits.

Then there was Norman Fox's backyard where he showed off his homemade movie machine (years later I recognized more than one of Norman's fiction plots in his novels based on those jejune scenarios).

WE WOULD EYE Mike Mansfield's house, since Mansfield had already become legend as an Emerson School Old Boy. His reputation, however, was not based on any political prowess, but on the fact that he had managed to enlist in the Navy at 14.

Then there was always an excursion through dangerous territory—that ground perilously guarded by the Zadicks and Georges and Teddys—while heading for the Beehive Market on First Avenue where you could find Stan Kimmitt (long before he became secretary of the U.S. Senate) negotiating great blocks of ice from the horse-drawn truck.

Stan was always good for a sliver or two of ice to get the taste of tar out of your mouth in midsummer. The taste of tar came from our epicurean experiments with the freshly paved streets. Street tar always was a useful surrogate for Blackjack gum while you were attending one of the free sandlot games put on by the noisy Furlongs from the Bootlegger Club on Fourth.

But Stan was a good contact later when he advanced to barman at Goodman's Cigar Store on Central and Fourth opposite the Paris-Fligman. We would comb the alleys for steinies (one cent for a small bottle, a nickel for a quart) and cardboard boxes to raise funds for the Saturday matinee at the Alcazar. If we were a bit short of bottles, Stan was always good for the extra pennies for the price of a matinee, and he turned a blind eye if we scooped up a handful of pretzels from the bowl on the bar on the way out.

THE MATINEES were a highlight of the week, of course, ranking with listening to "Hobby Lobby" and "Jack Armstrong" and "Gang Busters" on the radio, or sprawling out on the living room floor after church on Sundays to read how the Katzenjammer Kids fooled the Professor in the comics.

At the Alcazar we would cram into the front row, our dirty tennis shoes propped up on the railing. We would clutch peanut butter sandwiches or sticky root beer barrels or licorice plugs bought at a bargain at Kline's Confectionary, cheering our way through a six-hour orgy of Tim McCoy or Buck Jones or Ken Maynard or Johnny Mack Brown or, if we were lucky, the fingerless Charles Starrett, who always fanned his .44.

The main thing about the matinee was to see someone yet once more gut-shoot dusky Victor Jory as he toppled off the parapet of the Red Dog Saloon.

The mushy stuff would cause an uproar. If Hopalong Cassidy had kissed anything but his horse we would have moaned in our seats. And when Gene Autry made his appearance with his guitar and dancing horse, Champion, we were bored to tears.

The same held true for "The March of Time," which always seemed to feature the jute mills of Bangkok or some equally stimulating subject and which we ranked almost as low as Fitzpatrick's tedious travelogues.

At such barren moments in cinematic production, we spent our time shooting our cap pistols at each other across aisles and seats, or catapulting cottontails at the balding head of the organist who played in the pit—generally Uncle Rob.

I REMEMBER thinking that some sort of an era had passed when we migrated to Bill Steege's Liberty Theater to see our own Gary Cooper in the only western we ever accepted as authentic, even though it was a historic mishmash: "The Plainsman."

Of course, I've only used the microcosm of the South Side to describe a rarefied atmosphere. The above misadventures could be equally represented by Bob Schuman's Westside renegades or the Northside marauders led by the Ryan or the Murphy brothers, or Jim Flaherty's Seventeenth Street streakers, or Rutan's rough-riders from up Boston Heights way. And we all know that Eddie Peressini's Black Eagle machos could offer their own tales of terror.

But ask any kid from the Thirties—ask George Campanella or Marshall Annau or Scotty Warden or Ray Senechal or Chuck Ladd—well, we all have our list, but I think any of them will agree; It was the sense of family, of neighborhood and of school unity that made up what we considered a sure and certain loyalty to the society known as Great Falls.

IT WAS—and remains—a friendly and independent place. In the center of that place, in the heart of it but not on the sleeve, was God. We didn't always articulate it well, but we knew what was at the heart of times good or bad. That's what the singular vision was all about. There was religious joy at the center.

As kids we were proud of the city's arching elms that shaded us in August. We were alert to the slightest civic change and resentful when the statue of Paris Gibson in the center of the oval garden at the beginning of town was shoved over for the Civic Center. We were thrilled to cross the river to the North Montana State Fair to spend our hard-earned quarters and see Happy Sprague dressed up as the Wild Man from Borneo. We marveled atop Gore Hill at the carpet of diamond powder that glittered below us on velvety black nights.

And we lazed our way along our Huckleberry Missouri, which seemed to flow sluggishly past its islands, treacherously over its dams, and mysteriously into our veins.

Mostly, though, we were proud to be part of a society that had been tempered by a depressed economy without losing its warmth or friendship.

At the end of the Thirties I was playing pump-pump-pull away with a bunch of kids from the Lower South Side. It was one of those neighborhood get-togethers that seemed to happen automatically.

We were a ragged crowd. It was a wintry night and mighty frosty. There wasn't a pair of earmuffs among us. We were all warm while we were chasing each other, but after the game, the cold settled into our bones.

I had a long way to walk home.

ONE BOY my age walked along with me and we sang songs all the way up Second Avenue South. I was shivering and so was he. But he had a cap with earflaps that would fit snugly down to his neck. When we were half way to my house, he turned to go back home, but before leaving he insisted that I take his cap. It meant he would have to be cold. But he offered it in a way that was so casual, so natural in its warmth and friendship, that I never forgot his gesture.

I never forgot him, either. He became my best friend. His name was Ronnie Reeves, and I think that he symbolized what I mean about the joy of the Thirties better than any anecdote could do.

Those who knew Ronnie, also know, I think, what made Great Falls great.

Indeed, the children of the Stevens's coterie would often fight like wildcats during the time of the Great Depression, as my Uncle Chris would succinctly put it. My late father, John Temple Stevens, would occasionally recall similar family escapades from that same era. I remember Dad giggling while fondly recounting the following humorous episodes to the family: He related not only the time his older sister, Faith, once struck fear in the hearts of neighborhood boys while chasing them down the neighborhood street in a fit of anger, but also a time when she and my dad actually got into a typical, youthful Irish scrap with each other. During that particular sibling skirmish, Faith was yanking small clumps of hair from my dad's scalp as he was crying in anguish. My grandmother, Temple Stevens, attempted to break up the fight—to no avail—while screaming at the top of her voice to my father with utter exasperation, "Hit her, John! Hit her!" Well, according to my father, he refused to hit his sister, and to everyone's great relief, Faith finally relented. Knowing my father's temperament as well as I do, Dad probably had it coming in the first place as there were a number of times in my own life when I felt like yanking clumps of hair from my father's scalp! In deference to my saintly Aunt Faith, she is beyond question an exceptionally lovely and patient person to this very day. She would unhesitatingly give the shirt off of her back to come to the aid of any relative or friend in need. My Aunt Faith is truly a remarkable woman who I dearly love—so much so that my wife and I named our second-born daughter after her. My own daughter, Faith, is just as feisty as my aunt, and I am very proud of her as I am with my other two daughters, Christa and Bethany. As a matter of fact, nobody messes with my three girls without risking one hell of an Irish fight, be it verbal or physical. At least my three daughters come by it naturally as their wildcat feistiness is most assuredly a part of the Stevens's family DNA.

My father once recalled another endearing episode of the 1930s when his mother handed him a bit of money with precise instructions to mosey on down to the local mom-and-pop store to purchase a few items needed for dinner. After a brief time, my father returned home and gleefully presented his mother with a jigsaw puzzle—together with the remaining change. Missing from his gutsy presentation, however, were the items Dad was instructed to buy and bring home! What with precious money being quite scarce at the time, my grandmother was not the least bit amused. She berated Dad and warned him that she would have to tell my grandfather what had transpired once he returned home from his office, which, of course, she did. Upon receiving the surly news, my grandfather calmly took my father by the hand into the living room, took off his belt, placed my father over his lap, and proceeded to give him a belt whipping he would never forget, and he certainly didn't! After the whipping, my grandfather told my sobbing and contrite dad, "Now son, go and fetch the puzzle you bought, and let's put it together."

My Uncle Chris spoke fondly of the house attic serving as my father's domain and the acme of his various drama productions. My father's mania for drama—as my uncle put it—would come to fruition when he became a graduate of the prestigious Pasadena Playhouse in Pasadena, California. While attending the Pasadena Playhouse as a student, Dad once acted with famous celebrities such as Carolyn Jones of the quirky 1960s television show, *The Addams Family*, when Jones played the kinky role of the matriarch of the family, Morticia Addams.

In the early 1950s, Dad also appeared with Harry Dean Stanton in the Pasadena Playhouse production of *David Garrick*, directed by Vincent Bowditch, as pictured in the following assemblage of family photos. My father is on the far left, while Harry Dean Stanton is second from the right. In another actual performance photograph of *David Garrick*, my father appears in a solo picture.

John Stevens Sr. and Harry Dean Stanton in the Pasadena Playhouse production of "David Garrick"– directed by Vincent Bowditch.

John Stevens Sr. in the solo photo – Pasadena Playhouse production of "David Garrick" – directed by Vincent Bowditch.

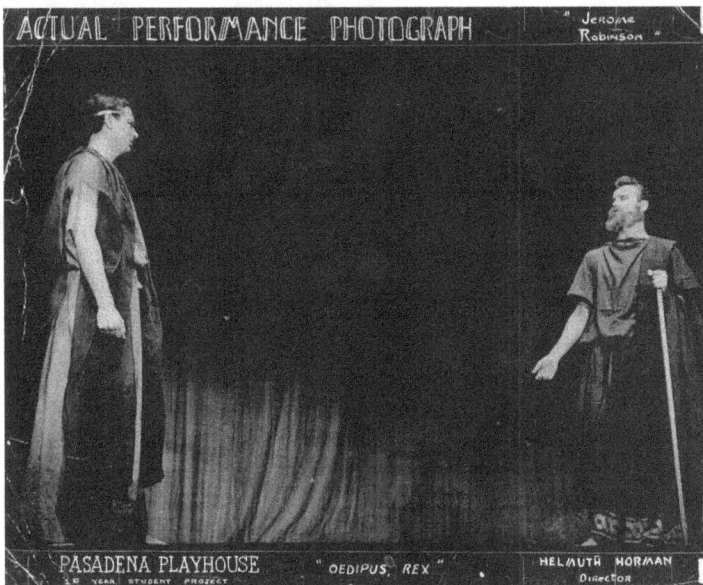

John Stevens Sr. in the Pasadena Playhouse production of "Oedipus Rex" – directed by Helmuth Horman.

John Stevens Sr. in an unidentified Pasadena Playhouse production. John is standing directly to the left of the lamp.

John Stevens Sr. in the Pasadena Town Hall Theater production of "White Sheep of the Family." John is playing the absent minded vicar.

John Stevens Sr. in the Pasadena Town Hall Theater production of "White Sheep of the Family" – cast photo.

Photo of the reunion of Charles Bronson and John Stevens Sr. in Great Falls, Montana during the filming of MGM's "Telefon" in the 1970s.

Faith Stevens Leicht in her twenties.

Christian D. Stevens (1929-2001)

Speaking of Harry Dean Stanton, Dad once related a humorous story to me a few years before he passed away in which the two budding actors supposedly went on a double date in Pasadena while attending the playhouse as students. According to Dad's recollection, he and Stanton seriously considered ditching their dates by escaping through the men's bathroom window because they did not have the money with which to pay for the meals. My father said they both felt guilty and reconsidered taking such ungentlemanly action, and they returned to the table where their two dates were waiting for them. The two young aspiring actors embarrassingly confessed their indiscretion to their lovely dates whereas the ladies offered to pick up the tab for the evening. While I have not been able to verify the accuracy of this tale with Harry Dean Stanton, who is still alive and kicking, my father insisted the incident really did occur some sixty years ago when the two men were in their twenties.

In another actual performance photograph taken at the Pasadena Playhouse, Dad appears on the right in his first-year project of *Oedipus Rex*. Another photo also features Dad in a role the family has not been able to identify. My dapper young father is arrayed in suave clothing, and he is standing directly to the left of the lamp in the middle of the picture (see photos).

In the late 1950s, my father also acted with Ted Knight—famous for his role as the television news anchorman Ted Baxter on the *Mary Tyler Moore Show*. They were both cast in the highly successful Los Angeles Omnibus Center Theatre production of Meyer Levin's crime thriller *Compulsion*. Dad told me that more than 2,000 actors auditioned for the production, and he was one of approximately 21 actors cast. In the production, my father played a hard-hitting news reporter who opened the second act. In 1959, *Compulsion* was made into a riveting feature film that starred Orson Welles, Bradford Dillman, and Dean Stockwell.

My father also played an absent-minded vicar with the English actor Jack Lynne in the Pasadena Town Hall Theater production of *White Sheep of the Family,* as pictured in the assemblage of photos. Dad received several curtain calls from the enraptured audience after one of his performances in that production, as well as rave reviews in a critique from the Alhambra Post-Advocate. The newspaper critique opined in 1958, "The top hit of acting is delivered by John Stevens. He portrays an English vicar and has audiences beside themselves with laughter."

Dad also appeared in several stage productions with Charles Bronson at the Pasadena Playhouse in the early 1950s. A picture that is included in the photo section features a brief reunion of Bronson and my father during the filming of Metro-Goldwyn-Mayer's spy thriller, *Telefon,* which was filmed on location in Great Falls during the 1970s.

George Montgomery was a personal friend of my father as well, and he invited Dad to the old Republic Studio in Hollywood to view the filming of an episode of the NBC television show *Cimmaron City*. Mr. Montgomery arranged to have my dad cast in an episode of that show in 1959, but NBC canceled the series before he had a chance to be viewed on nationwide television.

My lovely late mother, Gwen, who passed away in 1984, was also a native of Montana, and she pleaded with my father to take the family back to Great Falls in the late 1950s because she was not happy living in Pasadena. Mom simply did not like the Hollywood crowd nor did she fit in with the Hollywood culture whatsoever. To illustrate this point, my mother once told me a captivating story where she and my father had attended a posh Hollywood party one evening. My mother was minding her own business while dutifully standing alongside my father at the party when another male actor approached my dad and "hit" on him right in front of my mother! Now, Dad thought the whole episode was quite hilarious, but Mom was not at all amused! Keep in mind, this was during the late 1950s, and this whole affair—no pun intended—was more than my mother could handle. To my father's great credit, he honored Mom's request to haul the family back to Montana, and he did so in an attempt to try and save their marriage. Ironically, their marriage ended in divorce when I was in the first grade, but I eventually gained an additional mother, Anita Padilla, whom I grew to love over a short period of time when my father remarried in the early 1960s. She was always kind to me as a child, and she still is to this very day. I eventually gained a brother, Barney, who is a professional violinist in New York City, as well as two additional lovely sisters, Tianta and Tara. Tianta resides in Great Falls, while Tara resides on the big Island of Hawaii.

Once back in Montana, and prior to the divorce of my parents, Dad started his own production company, which made television commercials for a variety of companies that bought airtime on a local television station in Great Falls. As a young boy, I can remember the joy I experienced playing various roles in the commercials, such as promoting dairy products during my own rambunctious birthday party when I was in kindergarten. This particular commercial also featured my invited neighborhood friends as well as my reliable cousins, dutifully provided by my charming Aunt Katy and Aunt Myrna on my mother's side of the family. My wild cousins, Douglas, Sissy, Nona, and Pete were valuable assets to the commercial as they successfully performed their required duties by merrily stuffing their cheeks with the dairy products we were promoting in the commercial. We thought of ourselves as the "big kids on the block" in Great Falls as we reveled in our celebrity status while viewing ourselves repeatedly on TV. In addition, filming commercials that prompted the boys in town to pressure their parents into purchasing toys from various local stores was an absolute hit with me at the precocious age of five. The compensation I received from Dad was the privilege of being able to keep and play with the toys used in the filming of the commercials which, in my eyes, made Christmas an ongoing celebration throughout the entire year.

In his stirring article, "There Was No Room for Subtlety in '30s," my Uncle Chris would reminisce about how important the sense of family, of neighborhood, and school unity were to the people of Great Falls during the Great Depression. While there is still evidence of the continual existence of these values throughout America, one would have to have his head buried in the sand if he were to attempt to deny the obvious fact that these values are in serious jeopardy as well as precipitous decline throughout our country. In a previous chapter, I alluded to the fact that our nation is now coping with an enormous, morally debased iceberg that conservatives are attempting to circumvent. Our ship of state, which could very well be represented by the *Titanic*, is about to be done in by that iceberg if we don't recapture the essence of what has made our country strong over the passing centuries.

Some may ponder as to how I could possibly be so bleak and austere with my warning. Well, just look at the state of the family unit in America. It is quite depressing and frightening. This chapter will delve into the following related topics: the breakdown of the family unit in America; the absence of fathers in many of our children's lives and the devastating impact such absence is having upon our society; poor parenting skills; the feminization of our nation's culture; the feminization of our schools; and finally, the feminization of both men and boys in America and the tragic consequences these cultural trends are bringing to bear on our nation. First, let us examine the breakdown of the family unit in America and the calamitous impact a "fatherless" culture is having upon our nation as we scrutinize some sobering facts and statistics from a variety of sources and scientific studies.

According to statistics gathered by the National Fatherhood Initiative, we can surmise that the gradual decline of the traditional family unit in America began in the early 1960s.[2] This advocacy group cites statistics that reveal the following: In 1960, the percentage of American households with two parents was at 88 percent. By the year 2004, that percentage had declined to 68 percent.[3] Precisely what is the National Fatherhood Initiative? The following describes its mission and accomplishments that appear directly on its website:

National Fatherhood Initiative's mission is to improve the well being of children by increasing the proportion of children growing up with involved, responsible, and committed fathers. We accomplish our mission through:

- Educating and inspiring all Americans, especially fathers, through public awareness campaigns, research, and other resources.
- Equipping and developing leaders of national, state, and community fatherhood initiatives through curricula, training, and technical assistance.

- Engaging every sector of society through strategic alliances and partnerships.

Or, as we like to say, Educating, Equipping and Engaging. [4]

Here are some additional facts and statistics the National Fatherhood Initiative has provided the public. I will cite the sources it has used in its own research:

"In America, 24.35 million children (33.5 percent) live absent their biological father."
> Source: Krieder, Rose M. and Jason Fields. Living Arrangements of Children: 2001. Current Population Reports, P70-104. Table 1. Washington, D.C.: US Census Bureau, 2005.

Child Abuse

"Using data from 1000 students tracked from seventh or eighth grade in 1988 through high school in 1992, researchers determined that only 3.2 percent of the boys and girls who were raised with both biological parents had a history of maltreatment. However, a full 18.6 percent of those in other family situations had been maltreated."
> Source: Smith, Carolyn and Terence P. Thornberry. "The Relationship Between Childhood Maltreatment and Adolescent Involvement in Delinquency." Criminology, 33 (1995): 451-479.

Poverty

"In 1997, 65 percent of poor children lived in households that did not include their biological fathers, compared to 25 percent of children who were not poor."
> Source: Feeley, Theresa J. "Low Income Noncustodial Fathers: A Child Advocate's Guide to Helping Them Contribute to the Support of Their Children." National Association of Child Advocates Issue

Brief, National Association of Child Advocates, Washington, D.C., February, 2000.

Education

"A study of 1,330 children from the Panel Survey of Income Dynamics showed that fathers who are involved on a personal level with their child's schooling increases the likelihood of their child's achievement. When fathers assume a positive role in their child's education, students feel a positive impact."

Source: McBride, Brent A., Sarah K. Schoppe-Sullivan, and Moon-Ho Ho. "The mediating role of fathers' school involvement on student achievement." Journal of Applied Developmental Psychology 26 (2005): 201-216.

Crime

"Children raised in single-parent families and surrounded by children of single-parent families at school are at the greatest risk of delinquency."

Source: Anerson, Amy L. "Individual and contextual influences on delinquency: the role of the single-parent family." Journal of Criminal Justice, 30 (November 2002): 575-587.

Emotional and Behavioral Problems

"A study using a nationally representative sample of 6,287 children ages 4-11 years old indicated that children in single-parent homes are more likely to experience emotional problems and use mental health services than children who live with both biological parents."

Source: Angel, Ronald J. and Jacqueline L. Angel, "Physical Comorbidity and Medical Care Use in Children with Emotional Problems." Public Health Reports 111 (1996): 140-145.[5]

On May 15, 1997, The Heritage Foundation released a startling report written by Patrick F. Fagan, PhD, titled *The Child Abuse*

Crisis: The Disintegration of Marriage, Family, and the American Community. I have included some excerpts of Dr. Fagan's report that will reveal some disturbing trends:

Introduction

...The underlying dynamic of child abuse—the breakdown of marriage and the commitment to love—is spreading like a cancer from poor communities to working-class communities. As social scientists, community leaders, and legislators consider ways to stop the spread of this cancer, they must focus their attention on the most upsetting byproduct of the disintegration of family and community: the abuse, maiming, and even death of America's infants and young children, about 2,000 of whom—6 per day—die each year.

The Demographics of Child Abuse

- The safest family environment for a child is a home in which the biological parents are married. Contrary to current theory about the effects of marriage on children, recent research demonstrates that marriage provides a safe environment for all family members, one in which child abuse and fatality are lowered dramatically.
- Cohabitation, an increasingly common phenomenon, is a major factor in child abuse...The risk of child abuse is 20 times higher than in traditional married families if parents are cohabiting (as in "common law" marriages) and 33 times higher if the single mother is cohabiting with a boyfriend.
- The incidence of child abuse decreases significantly as family income increases...In 1993, the overall rate of maltreatment (abuse and neglect combined) in the United States was lowest in families with incomes above $30,000 per year; 10 times higher in families with incomes between $15,000

and $30,000 per year; and 22 times higher for families with incomes below $15,000 per year.

- Child abuse frequently is intergenerational. Another generation of child abusers is being weaned by today's abusing parents, and many of these children will never know that children can be treated differently.
- Child abuse is prevalent in "communities of abuse" characterized by family breakdown. These also are communities of crime, characterized by the absence of marriage, the prevalence of drug and alcohol abuse, and a primary dependence on welfare. Children who grow up in the "communities" show signs of permanent damage; moreover, as statistics follow them over time, many prove to have been damaged for life. From these communities of abuse come society's "super predators" (the psychopathic criminals of tomorrow), violent gang members, and other hostile, depressed, and frequently even suicidal young people.
- Child abuse is directly associated with serious violent crime. An increase in the incidence of child abuse precedes an increase in violent crime.

What the Data Means for Americans

The United States will face a continuing rise in the incidence of child abuse because too many Americans continue to tolerate the conditions that debilitate the family and weaken the child... This is particularly true when the compounding effects of two, three, and four generations of broken families have created a subculture of abuse in the local community.

While the United States tries to figure out how to rebuild its broken families and communities, its religious, social, and political leaders must do all they can to keep intact those families that have adhered to a tradition of stable, married life. The family environment provided by married biological parents is the primary resource for tomorrow's well-adjusted children, for the future of the country, and for the protection of both women and children.

Conclusion

...The prognosis is bleak for the United States. The underlying demographic drift in family structure indicates the continuing breakdown of the American family, which can lead only to a continuing rise in child abuse. Until there is a turnaround in the number of out-of-wedlock births and a downturn in divorces, the United States will continue to build a culture of rejection. Nothing other than the fundamental reform of family life and sexual mores can promise a significant change for the better. [6]

In a December 1, 1998, issue of the *Wall Street Journal*, there appeared an article written by Maggie Gallagher titled "Fatherless Boys Grow Up into Dangerous Men" that was based on a study by the University of California and Princeton University. The information reflects further upon the trends previously cited in this chapter with regard to the effects fatherless homes have on crime in America. Here are a few excerpts quoted from Maggie Gallagher's article:

...Boys raised outside of intact marriages are, on average, more than twice as likely as other boys to end up jailed, even after controlling for other demographic factors. Each year spent without a dad in the home increases the odds of future incarceration by about five percent. The study also confirmed the findings of other researchers: Boys living with just their single fathers do not exhibit this increased rate of criminal behavior. [7]

To add fuel to the fire, you will find the following excerpts to be quite illuminating. The first is from a University of California Santa

Barbara study titled *Study Finds Teen Pregnancy and Crime Levels are Higher among Kids from Fatherless Homes,* and it is released by Men's HOTLINE. The other data is from a report put out by fathermag.com titled *Fatherless Homes Statistics.*

Children reared in fatherless homes are more than twice as likely to become male adolescent delinquents or teen mothers, according to a significant new study by two economists at UCSB. Llad Phillips and William S. Comanor based their research on data from random surveys of 15,000 youths conducted annually by the Center for Human Resources at Ohio State University. Their findings suggest that current proposals to provide tax credits and exemptions for single mothers and to collect more child support from absent fathers will have little effect on the problem of delinquency among teenage boys...."A lot of kids get involved in crime long before they are able to make rational choices about crime vs. legitimate work," Phillips says.[8]

Fatherless Homes Statistics RE: Youth Suicide and Divorce/ Single Parent Homes:

"In a study of 146 adolescent friends of 26 adolescent suicide victims, teens living in single-parent families are not only more likely to commit suicide but also more likely to suffer from psychological disorders, when compared to teens living in intact families."
Source: David A. Brent, "Post-traumatic Stress Disorders in Peers of Adolescent Suicide Victims: Predisposing Factors and Phenomenology," Journal of the American Academy of Child and Adolescent Psychiatry 34 (1995): 209-215.

"Fatherless children are at dramatically greater risk of suicide."
Source: U.S. Department of Health and Human Services, National Center for Health Statistics, Survey on Child Health, Washington, D.C., 1993.

"In an earlier study by Kalter and Rembar at [Children's Psychiatric Hospital, University of Michigan], a sample of 144 child and adolescent patients, whose parents had divorced, presented [for evaluation and treatment] with three most commonly occurring problems:

63% Subjective psychological problems (defined as anxiety, sadness, pronounced moodiness, phobias, and depression).

56% Poor grades or grades substantially below ability and/or recent past performance.

43% Aggression toward parents.

Important features of the subgroup of 32 latency aged girls were in the same order:

69% Indicating subjective psychological distress.

47% Academic problems.

41% Aggression toward parents."

Source: *Clinical Observations on Interferences of Early Father Absence in the Achievement of Femininity* by R. Lohr, C. G. A. Mendell and B. Riemer, Clinical Social Work Journal, V. 17, #4, Winter, 1989.

"Among teenage and adult populations of females, parental divorce has been associated with lower self-esteem, precocious sexual activity, greater delinquent-like behavior, and more difficulty establishing gratifying, lasting adult heterosexual relationships...."

Source: *Long-Term Effects of Divorce on Children: A Developmental Vulnerability Model*, Neil Kalter, Ph.D., University of Michigan, American Journal of Orthopsychiatry, 57(4), October, 1987.

"...Criminal behavior experts and social scientists are finding intriguing evidence that the epidemic of youth violence and gangs is related to the breakdown of the two-parent family."

Source: *New Evidence That Quayle Was Right: Young Offenders Tell What Went Wrong at Home*, San Francisco Chronicle (12/9/94).

"Daughters of single parents are 53% more likely to marry as teenagers, 164% more likely to have a premarital birth, and 92% more likely to dissolve their own marriages. All these intergenerational consequences of single motherhood increase the likelihood of chronic welfare dependency."
Source: Barbara Dafoe Whitehead, Atlantic Monthly (April 1993).

"The National Fatherhood Institute reports that 18 million children live in single-parent homes. Nearly 75% of American children living in single-parent families will experience poverty before they turn 11. Only 20% in two-parent families will experience poverty."
Source: *Fatherhood in the 90's: Kids of Absent Fathers More "at risk,"* Melinda Sacks, San Jose Mercury News (10/29/95).

"The feminization of poverty is linked to the feminization of custody, as well as linked to lower earnings for women. Greater opportunity for education and jobs through shared parenting can help break the cycle."
Source: David Levy, Ed., *The Best Parent is Both Parents* (1993). [9]

All of this startling data is certainly not shrugged off by actor and comedian Bill Cosby. In recent years, he has taken the inner-city, African- American community to task over these disturbing trends, and not without considerable criticism and condemnation being lobbed at him by various members of African-American associations or groups for being so outspoken and honest with regard to his own assessment of the current situation affecting children of his own race. Bill Cosby is anything but a sissy! I really admire him for his tenacity and straight-talk as well as his willingness to stand up and be counted. On May 17, 2004, Mr. Cosby delivered an address at the NAACP's Gala to Commemorate the 50th Anniversary of Brown v. Board of Education. Here are some hard-hitting, blunt excerpts from his impassioned speech:

...Ladies and gentlemen, these people set—they opened the doors, they gave us the right, and today, ladies and gentlemen, in our cities and public schools we have 50 percent drop out. In our own neighborhood, we have men in prison. No longer is a person embarrassed because they're pregnant without a husband. No longer is a boy considered an embarrassment if he tries to run away from being the father of the unmarried child....

In the neighborhood that most of us grew up in, parenting is not going on....I'm talking about these people who cry when their son is standing there in an orange suit. Where were you when he was two? Where were you when he was twelve? Where were you when he was eighteen, and how come you don't know he had a pistol? And where is his father, and why don't you know where he is? And why doesn't the father show up to talk to this boy?...

...50 percent drop out rate, I'm telling you, and people in jail, and women having children by five, six different men....All this child knows is "gimme, gimme, gimme." These people want to buy the friendship of a child, and the child couldn't care less. Those of us sitting out here who have gone on to some college or whatever we've done, we still fear our parents. And these people are not parenting. They're buying things for the kid—$500 sneakers—for what? They won't buy or spend $250 on Hooked on Phonics....

...Brown versus the Board of Education is no longer the white person's problem. We've got to take the neighborhood back.... It's standing on the corner. It can't speak English. It doesn't want to speak English. I can't even talk the way these people talk. "Why you ain't where you is go, ra." I don't know who these people are. And I blamed the kid until I heard the mother talk. Then, I heard the father talk. This is all in the house. You used to talk a certain way on the corner and you got into the house and switched to English. Everybody knows it's important to speak English except these knuckle heads. You can't land a plane with, "Why you ain't..." You can't be a doctor with that kind of crap coming out of your mouth. There is no Bible that has that kind of language...."

I'm telling you Christians, what's wrong with you? Why can't you hit the streets? Why can't you clean it out yourselves? It's our time now, ladies and gentlemen. It is our time. And I've got good news for you. It's not about money. It's about you doing something ordinarily that we do—get in somebody else's business. It's time for you to not accept the language that these people are speaking, which will take them nowhere. What the hell good is Brown V. Board of Education if nobody wants it?.... [10]

Can we take a giant leap of faith and presume Mr. Cosby will probably not be invited to speak at the Rev. Jeremiah Wright's church anytime soon? Neither, I presume, would Mr. Juan Williams of Fox News. Mr. Williams is another standup guy who is African-American and the author of a recent book, *Enough*. In his book, the liberal political commentator assails what he refers to as "phony" black leaders. Here are some of his hard-hitting comments given in an interview with Ronald Kessler of NewsMax concerning his book:

Victimhood Not a Black Tradition

"That says to an individual, 'You can't help yourself, you can't help your family, and therefore all you can do is wait for the government to do something for you....I think it is a message of weakness and ineffectual thinking that is absolutely crippling the poor and especially minorities in the United States....Cosby comes across as a real hero....

Culture of Failure

"That culture says that you are acting white if you're a good student, that says that going to jail is just a rite of passage, or that crime is acceptable in the black community. You know, you celebrate drug dealers and gangs, and you say, 'That's authentically black' when you see criminal behavior. How self-defeating! What a negative image to take on to yourself, but even worse, to put on your children."

Just Say No

"Bill Cosby said he's never seen the NAACP lead a march against drug dealers. You change the culture by getting groups like the NAACP to start admitting that what's really undermining the success of black families and black children is when a crack house opens in the neighborhood and people tolerate and allow that to happen....If you finish high school or go to college, if you make sure that your kids have wonderful experiences instead of sitting in front of the TV, if you teach them to work hard, this is a country that will reward you....These are basic steps that almost guarantee that you will not live in poverty in this country. You never hear that message." [11]

At this particular moment in time, I would like to make a personal observation concerning single parents in our country. There are many single moms and dads amongst us who are doing an outstanding job with raising their children and under the most daunting circumstances at that. Those single parents who take their parental responsibilities seriously and discharge their duties responsibly are the unsung heroes amongst us because they often do so with little support or encouragement. Having said that, however, sound facts, statistics, and scientific reports do not lie. The reports cited in this chapter paint a very ugly and horrifying picture about the dire consequences communities throughout America are being compelled to deal with, such as alarming adolescent suicide rates, poverty, crime, sexual abuse, physical abuse, poor academic performance of adolescents in schools, teen pregnancy, adolescent rebellion against authority, as well as disrespectful in-your-face behavior being shamefully exhibited toward elders as a direct result of the breakdown of the traditional family unit and the absence of fathers in homes. If that weren't bad enough, there is a great spiritual void in the souls of too many of our nation's children. I see it every day as a public school teacher. Conservatives are appalled with the manner in which various progressive special-interest groups fight tooth-and-nail to promote and defend the supposed "separation between church and state" as well as progressive laws, regulations, federal and state programs, and unconventional lifestyles that inherently ignore or sidestep the very root of the problems confronting society today.

So what precisely are the proactive solutions being advocated by our federal government with regard to all of this? We now find ourselves in a vicarious predicament whereby additional financial burdens are being levied on already financially stressed taxpayers and families by a government that thinks the solution to all of these problems is to fund various social child welfare programs. But these programs are merely attempting to fill the void being left by an ever-increasing cabal of irresponsible and selfish parents who should never have had children in the first place! Their irresponsibility now becomes a cumbersome burden upon the rest of us who are doing our jobs as parents!

How often do we hear altruistic progressives crying about the "children—it's all about the children?" If they were truly concerned about the welfare of our nation's children, they would fight fervently for both state and federal policies that would seriously advocate on behalf of the traditional two-parent family unit economically, socially, educationally, and religiously. And it is not entirely about money and the plethora of child welfare programs. None of these societal programs will ever serve as adequate substitutes for what intact, happy, two-parent households can better provide, including (but certainly not limited to) both loving parents sharing the responsibilities of providing a strong, supportive environment for their children; both parents firmly disciplining their children when necessary instead of making unending lame excuses for their children's poor behavior and bad choices; parents holding their children accountable for maintaining respectable grades throughout school; parents assisting their children with their homework while supporting their teachers at school by attending various school functions; parents attending church or synagogue together as a family in order to provide children with essential spiritual nourishment for their eternal souls; parents attending their children's music performances such as choral and band concerts, attending their children's dance performances, or taking their children to parks, museums, and other educational venues; both parents supporting their children at the baseball and football games and other sport competitions; parents enrolling their children in Girl or Boy Scouts, sending their children to church camps or sending them to summer Vacation Bible School; and most importantly, both parents providing children with comforting and nurturing shoulders to cry upon when they are suffering and going through the trials and tribulations associated with growing-up—especially during adolescence.

All households, regardless of whether they are ones consisting of a single parent or two parents, bear the full responsibility of providing a variety of many of the above elements for their children, and being poor in this nation is certainly no excuse for neglecting children because it does not take money to discipline, love, nurture, and encourage their children. Neither does it require very much money on the part of the poor to assist their children with completing their homework or seeing to it that their children attend public school on a regular basis so that they do not fall behind academically. Parents who fail to engage in these parental responsibilities are, in this author's opinion, guilty of true child abuse!

Furthermore, when parents fail to do their jobs, the best thing government can endeavor to accomplish is to try and fill a pathetic void in children's lives by functioning as the proverbial evil "stepmother" exemplified in Walt Disney's story of *Cinderella,* which is in stark contrast to the examples of *Cinderella Man* and Cinderella Family discussed at the beginning of this chapter! What innocent child in his or her right mind would ever aspire to be reared by the evil stepmother in Disney's *Cinderella*? On the contrary, a huge segment of today's neglected and abused children would rather advocate for a return to the old-fashioned family values exemplified by *Cinderella Man* and Cinderella Family if they were to have any say about the matter. There wasn't a great deal of money flowing about the nation during the Great Depression, yet during that era, millions of parents somehow managed to get by with very little while carrying out their proper duties of being good and responsible parents. Oh, by the way, bringing children to church and synagogue is still free, last I checked.

The kind of change President Obama so proudly professes is not change for the better, unless such change is actually a return to the nonpartisan values we once cherished as a nation prior to the turbulent 1960s. America, like any other nation in history, is going to ultimately be judged by the manner in which we raise and treat our children, and as of right now, I would opine that we have purchased a one-way ticket to Hell. How could anyone seriously believe otherwise given the depressing data that has been put forth in this chapter, which is empirical evidence of the collective maltreatment of our nation's children during the past fifty years? In addition to the breakdown of the traditional family unit, the neighborhood, and school unity, poor parenting itself is rearing its ugly head and is, in large part, responsible for much of the current tangled web America finds itself trapped in.

In March of 2009, there appeared an excellent op-ed piece in a local newspaper where I currently reside that was written by a liberal political commentator, Ruben Navarrette, for the Washington Post Writer Group. He correctly assesses the current state of many of our children being raised by indulgent parents. It is titled "Spoiled Kids Will Doom This Country." Here are some excerpts of Mr. Navarrette's article:

One of the great long-term threats to the security and prosperity of the U.S. is a growing sense of entitlement....

...I'm talking about the sense of entitlement that many of us have unknowingly instilled in our children, the consequences of that kind of thinking, and the threat it poses to the ability of our population to be productive and globally competitive in the years to come...

...Researchers at UC Irvine have produced a study called "Self-Entitled College Students: Contributions of Personality, Parenting, and Motivational Factors."

It found that a third of students surveyed said they expect a B just for attending lectures, and 40 percent said they deserved a B for completing the required reading....

...The lead author of the study speculates that this sense of entitlement comes from parental pressure, peer competition or increased anxiety about achieving good grades.

I think most of it comes from how these young people were raised. A lot of parents spoil and coddle their kids, constantly telling them they're special and the center of the universe.

They instinctively use praise to inject them with high self-esteem but often fail to teach them that the best way to feel good about yourself is by working hard and accomplishing something in life....

...Former Labor Secretary Elaine Chao was right in 2007 when she noted that young workers "have to be able to accept direction...(since) too many young people bristle when a supervisor asks them to do something."

One would hope that the current recession would change some of that thinking and teach young people to bring their attitudes down a notch. That would lead to a stronger work ethic and less sense of entitlement.... [12]

As a public school educator, I certainly concur with the statements expressed by Mr. Navarrette. While I will reserve the majority of my comments and observations concerning educational issues as they pertain to today's youth and parents for the next chapter, it is imperative that I address a number of these thorny issues in this chapter because they go directly to the heart of the topic of poor parenting skills. My wife and I, as public school educators, are confronted on a regular basis with a prevailing attitude amongst today's generation of parents that implies their cherubs are "entitled" to practically everything under the sun. This is due, in great part, to society's "entitlement" mentality that has been imbued in the psyche of our nation throughout the course of the past fifty years, especially with the emphasis being placed on the intrusive role big-government and the "nanny state" plays in our daily lives. This thinking contrasts with the conventional wisdom of earlier generations of Americans that promulgated attributes of personal responsibility, individual achievement, the American work ethic, competition, personal accountability, and good moral character. To illustrate this point, the following anecdote is currently circulating about the Internet, especially between teachers within the public school community. While meant to be a humorous account of the current state of affairs in our public schools, there is, nevertheless, a great deal of truth embedded within it with regard to what public schools are compelled to put up with on a regular basis from the "entitlement" throng currently haunting us. Every middle school and high school in the nation should adopt this fictional message even though it is politically incorrect. Enjoy this anecdote as it is most humorous yet, ironically, rings quite true:

Hello! You have reached the automated answering service of your school. In order to assist you in connecting to the right staff member, please listen to all of your options before making a selection:

To lie about why your child is absent - Press 1

To make excuses for why your child did not do his work - Press 2

To complain about what we do - Press 3

To swear at staff members - Press 4

To ask why you didn't get information that was already enclosed in your newsletter and several flyers mailed to you - Press 5

If you want us to raise your child - Press 6

If you want to reach out and touch, slap or hit someone - Press 7

To request another teacher, for the third time this year - Press 8

To complain about bus transportation - Press 9

To complain about school lunches - Press 0

If you realize this is the real world and your child must be accountable and responsible for his/her own behavior, class work, homework and that it's not the teachers' fault for your child's lack of effort: Hang up and have a nice day! [13]

— Author Unknown

My wife is the choral director at a local high school in the community where we reside in California. She directs many different choral ensembles—some of which are audition only and quite competitive to get into. Her select chamber choir has performed in choral festivals and competitions throughout the country, including Carnegie Hall in New York City, as well as throughout Europe, and her chamber choir has garnered numerous awards and top honors. She has been amazed at the number of parents who have called her over the years to whine and complain when their children did not make it into the chamber ensemble after the first try. She has to educate the parents that this particular choir consists mostly of juniors and seniors who have excellent voices and singing abilities which are necessary requirements in order to be selected as members to not only sing in this select choral ensemble, but to also fulfill the very demanding duties and responsibilities required of them throughout the school year. She has also had to explain that it is necessary for students to pay their "dues," so to speak, by singing in other choirs under her direction in order that they may acquire the necessary skills and experience to warrant singing in her top choral ensemble.

Now, one would think all parents would possess the common sense to realize this, but most of the time my wife's explanations fall on deaf ears. A number of parents feel their children are "entitled" to be in the most advanced choral ensemble—even as entering freshmen—regardless of whether or not they have the necessary talent and skills required to be a member of this elite choir, or whether or not their children have worked long and hard enough to carry out the responsibilities inherent with serving in the chamber choir. It is no different than the varsity football team. In order to make the varsity team, boys need to gain experience by playing on both the freshman football team and junior varsity team—then perhaps they **might** make the varsity team if they are good enough as players. Even then, not all players are "entitled" to make first string. Not all players can be the star quarterback either. The same is true for advanced choir, band, drama, mock trial, speech and debate, or any other competitive endeavor in high school. That is the way life is and should continue to be in America!

Apparently, poor parenting skills that are prevalent throughout our nation today are not confined only to the poor or middle-class families. The crisis has hit the affluent as well. The following information comes from a 2007 edition of Campus Report, published by Accuracy in Academia. Deborah Lambert, writing for Campus Report states:

Out Sourcing Parental Irritants

"There's good news for parents who wish they didn't have to put up with mundane family tasks like potty training a toddler or convincing a teenager to choose a more demure prom dress.

Now, they turn those chores over to a consultant. That's right.

According to the Council on Contemporary Families, there is an increasing call for outside services aimed at quieting screaming babies, teaching kids to ride a bike, and potty training...

...Recently, the Soho Parenting Center in lower Manhattan reported that there had been a 50% increase in parent 'consultations' on all aspects of parenting, from getting kids to sleep better, to eating his/her veggies.

Another company, Nannies and More, reports that they have experienced 'a tripling in placements of baby nurses' to help with newborns. After that, parents turn to another kind of consultant, namely 'parent coaches,' who 'for about $75 an hour, will do such things as help you say 'no.'...."[14]

Unbelievable, isn't it? I suppose the next evolution in our parenting skills will be the invention of androids perfectly capable of cleaning our homes and raising our children so we can further indulge ourselves with selfish whims and other priorities while we neglect our children, however misguided they may be! Perhaps these future nanny androids will do us all a huge favor by not turning out to be the mollycoddled examples many parents currently are. In fact, we can name all of these clever androids, Rosie, which is right out of the futuristic cartoon family, *The Jetsons*! God help us!

Another disturbing trend that is having a devastating impact on the culture of America is the feminization of our nation's schools, our nation's boys, and our nation's men. Let me be more specific. Christina Hoff Sommers is the W.H. Brady Fellow at the American Enterprise Institute who wrote an excellent article for the *Atlantic*

Monthly in May of 2000 called "The War Against Boys." Here are some intriguing excerpts from her article that will help support the premise that we are feminizing our nation's boys and schools:

> ...For many years women's groups have complained that boys benefit from a school system that favors them and is biased against girls. "Schools shortchange girls," declares the American Association of University Women...
>
> ...Data from the U.S. Department of Education and from several recent university studies show that far from being shy and demoralized, today's girls outshine boys. They get better grades, they have higher educational aspirations. They follow more rigorous academic programs and participate in advanced placement classes at higher rates. According to the National Center for Education Statistics, slightly more girls than boys enroll in high level math and science courses. Girls, allegedly timorous and lacking in confidence, now outnumber boys in student government, in honor societies, on school newspapers, and in debating clubs. Only in sports are boys ahead, and women's groups are targeting the sports gap with a vengeance. Girls read more books. They outperform boys on tests for artistic and musical ability. More girls than boys study abroad. More join the Peace Corps. At the same time, more boys than girls are suspended from school. More are held back and more drop out. Boys are three times as likely to receive a diagnosis of attention-deficit hyperactivity disorder. More boys than girls are involved in crime, alcohol, and drugs....
>
> ...The performance gap between boys and girls in high school leads directly to the growing gap between male and female admissions to college. The Department of Education reports that in 1996 there were 8.4 million women but only 6.7 million men enrolled in college. It predicts that women will hold on to and increase their lead well into the next decade, and that by 2007 the numbers will be 9.2 million women and 6.9 million men. [15]

The Department of Education's predictions have become reality. Jonathan Rauch is a senior writer and columnist for *National Journal* and a frequent contributor to *Reason*. I read with considerable interest his op-ed piece which appeared in a local newspaper on January 27, 2008. Here are some excerpts that reaffirm the observations revealed by Christina Hoff Sommers in her 2000 article. The title of Jonathan Rauch's article is, "Face New Gender Gap-Men, Watch Out: More Women With College Degrees Are Passing You By":

...By about 1980, the gender gap in college enrollment had vanished. Young women had reached educational parity, with the promise of social parity not far behind...

...Projections by the National Center for Education Statistics show a 22 percent increase in female college enrollment between 2005 and 2016, compared with only a 10 percent increase for men. In 2006, according to the Census Bureau, about 27 million American men held a college degree; so did about 27 million American women.

Women's superior education will increase their earning power relative to men's, and on average they will be marrying down, educationally speaking...But women will not stop wanting to be hands-on moms.

No, men are not about to disappear into underclass status. They will not become mothers anytime soon, and they will not stop secreting testosterone. Men's ambition will ensure ample male representation at the top of the social order, where CEOs, senators, Nobelists and software geniuses dwell.

Women will not rule men. But they will lead. Think about this: Not only do girls study harder and get better grades than boys, high school girls now take more math and science than do high school boys. If there is a 'weaker sex,' it isn't female." [16]

As a public school teacher, I can absolutely vouch for these observations. For seven years, I taught English and US history honors classes at the middle school level, and I can attest to the fact that there were consistently more girls than boys enrolled in those classes on a year-to-year basis. The principal of the middle school where I taught at the time was a member of the American Association of University Women herself, and she once confided to me that she was very concerned with the declining trend of male enrollment in honors classes. In fact, every year in February, the American Association of University Women holds a symposium at our local university for eighth grade middle school girls for the purpose of encouraging them to enroll in more math and science courses in high school and college. I must admit, I personally saw to it that my own three daughters participated in this annual event while they were attending middle school because as a parent, I saw value in the subject matter being presented and discussed at the symposium. However, here are some pointed questions I would like to pose not only with the AAUW, but my own school district as well. Why are they still continuing to hold this annual symposium? According to all of the data and research I have gathered, girls are not suffering at all with regard to access to math and science classes or careers associated with these core academic areas. And why are they excluding eighth grade middle school boys from attending? This smacks of outright sexism and discrimination to me, especially given the fact that our boys are the ones who are now at serious risk academically in middle school, high school, and college. It kind of makes one wonder, doesn't it? Something is definitely amiss with this current scenario. The following account sheds additional light on the subject of the feminization of our nation's boys:

Over the past twenty years, I offered an incredible adventure for both my male and female students to participate in while attending either elementary or middle school. A personal friend of mine, Captain Greg Clinton, owns a traditionally rigged tall ship called the *American Pride* of the Children's Maritime Institute, which is moored at Long Beach Harbor in California. For years, I took hundreds of my students on exciting overnight trips on the tall ship, during which we participated in a living-history program called Manifest Destiny, or we participated in a Civil War reenactment on the Island of Catalina in Southern California. The purpose of such adventures was to not only bring history alive for my students by having them actively participate in hands-on activities that were very engaging and quite challenging, but to also put my students in touch with their maritime past that would leave an indelible impression with them.

Captain Greg and his excellent sailing staff would put on quite the maritime show while compelling my students to live and work precisely as professional tall ship sailors were commanded to do throughout the 1800s. The students quickly learned to labor diligently under the strict orders and loud commands of a tyrannical captain who did not spare punishing the young lads and lassies if they failed to fulfill their duties to his demanding satisfaction. They strived to earn the status of becoming real "Salts" as they learned to reeve a block-and-tackle so that they could be hoisted up the mainmast in a swinging Bosun's chair. In addition, they also weighed anchor, hoisted sails, navigated the ship's helm on the open seas, stood their night watches, and cleaned the ship from bow to stern. Robert Clinton, the ship's cook—or "Cooky" as he prefers to be called, prepared hearty fare for the young sailors to consume as they accumulated quite the appetite while engaging in the arduous physical labor required aboard a tall ship. Obviously, the duties required of the students while sailing the *American Pride* were quite complex and demanding, especially given the fact that the students were partially responsible for the safety of the ship and all hands on board! The students had a marvelous time, and they accumulated memories they would treasure for the rest of their lives.

Prior to the sailing trips, I would do my part as a teacher by thoroughly preparing my students to accomplish the following feats at school: having them memorize sailor's vernacular; requiring them to memorize all of the essential parts of a merchant tall ship; teaching the students the significance of US maritime history; requiring my students to read Richard Henry Dana's classic novel, *Two Years Before the Mast*; compelling them to write maritime journal entries using creative writing; instructing the students in the art of ringing ship's bell time accurately; demonstrating for the students how to tie important sailing knots quickly and accurately while giving them time to master the skill themselves; instructing them to sing sea shanties with vim and vigor; and assisting the budding sailors with acquiring the other necessary skills with which to function and survive on such a physically, mentally, and emotionally draining program. In order to accomplish all of these tasks, I utilized a highly effective and motivating classroom simulation called *Clippers* from the Interact Company that the children absolutely treasured year after year! As soon as my students were thoroughly prepared for the adventure of a lifetime, I would take sadistic delight in warning all of my young "Greenhands", that once the actual sailing adventure was about to commence aboard ship while they were being mustered by the tough and demanding First Mate, **"That's when school really begins!"** I would always chuckle as my students would stare at me from their desks while displaying that frightened "deer in the headlight look!" The sailing adventures never disappointed us!

What deeply concerns me as a teacher, however, is the current trend I see whereby a declining number of my male students show interest in participating in the tall ship adventure. I have no difficulty with recruiting female students for the trip, yet I have seen a gradual decline over the past ten years in enthusiasm with the boys. When I was their age, I would have practically sacrificed my left arm to be given the opportunity to participate in such an amazing hands-on, living-history program—especially if it meant participating in an overnight adventure far away from the confines of a traditional classroom environment! So what gives here? Well, I maintain that it is a direct result of too many of our young boys not growing up under the vital influence of their fathers, hence they are often being denied rich experiences such as scouting as well as other male-bonding activities that build character and self-esteem in boys. In other words, this disturbing trend is a direct result of the feminization of our families, our schools, our culture, and our boys!

Over the passage of time, I have been dismayed as many over-protective single moms have repeatedly shared with me their concerns and trepidation with sending their boys out to sea on a tall ship—worrying that some tragedy might befall their sons and therefore effectively contributing to the feminization of their own boys. Most assuredly I would do my level best to reassure many of these single mothers that we were not sailing around treacherous Cape Horn. On the contrary, we were only going to sail about Long Beach Harbor or the short distance to Catalina Island—within shouting distance of the Coast Guard! I would tell the single moms that it is important for their boys to participate in an activity that would help build character, give them a sense of purpose, build self-esteem, and put them in touch with their past, yet my pleas would often fall upon deaf ears.

I even went so far as to query some of my female students as to what they believe may be the reasons as to why a number of boys these days are not as interested in sailing a tall ship as girls are, and their honest responses have been most revealing. They perceive many of the boys to primarily be interested in playing video games, sitting at the computer while logged on to Facebook or You Tube, or watching hour-after-hour of mindless programs on the boobtube—which was my grandmother's preferred word of choice for the television set. That is precisely what many girls have related to me over the years! With the exception of participating in athletics, far too many of our boys no longer want to be boys and engage in the type of activities that have traditionally been a natural draw for them.

As discussed earlier, many schools throughout the nation are willing participants in this plot to feminize our boys. Deborah Lambert, writing for *Campus Report*, reveals the following ridiculous yet factual account that lends additional credence to this fact:

Shadow Tag

Schools across the country are falling all over each other to ban childhood games that might cause bumps and bruises to the current generation of kids, according to the Arizona Republic.

The latest target of education administrators is tag, "which joins the list of childhood games such as dodge ball and tackle football no longer allowed...because of too many injuries and squabbles."...

...To eliminate that possibility, schools around the country have substituted another form of tag for the traditional game. "Children can play tag, but they can't touch each other. They stomp on each other's shadow instead. The bans are for safety and civility, though some worry that kids may not get enough exercise or enjoy a childhood rite of passage."

Acacia School Principal Christine Hollingsworth says her school started a "no-touch" policy several years ago, which drastically reduced the number of injuries on the playground. Hollingsworth said that she is "no longer called upon to settle fights that had escalated from an unintentional too-hard game of tag."[17]

Come to think of it, when is the last time anyone has seen an old-fashioned merry-go-round in a city park or elementary school playground where kids would hang on to the metal bars and run as fast as they could to give it the necessary momentum with which to jump on at just the right moment? As young children, didn't we have an instinctive realization that if we let go of the bar, we might fall off of the equipment and be injured? During the hundreds of times I had joyfully played on these now banned jewels of fun, I cannot recall any child or friend of mine ever being injured, and even if someone were to potentially be hurt, we simply would have chalked it up as a rite of passage into adulthood. In my old neighborhood, you wouldn't have dared whine or cry about any such injury less you be taunted and branded a momma's boy or sissy!

To be fair to schools and cities throughout America, they now have to contend with the intimidating threats of frivolous and costly lawsuits being filed in the court system by overprotective "helicopter" parents in the event that their children get hurt or injured for any innocent reason. That is precisely why our schools and communities have found it necessary to ban such equipment and games. The bloodsucking lawyers who are ambulance chasers are more than likely waiting outside the school gates hoping to make a fast buck off of the backs of the local school districts with the full support and cooperation of spineless progressive judges who have lost all sense of proportion and common sense. Nevertheless, we are now setting the stage for transforming our children into future sissies in their own right because as a society, we are now too timid to engage in any type of risk-taking endeavors with our children on school playgrounds or city parks.

Because of this feeble trend toward the feminization of our culture, I predict it is just a matter of time before all contact sports such as football, wrestling, hockey, baseball, soccer, and basketball, are banned in our local high schools, colleges, and professional sports teams and leagues because of potential injuries and costly lawsuits! So we had all better be prepared to sit in our various sports stadiums only to watch and cheer our favorite football players as they engage in "Shadow Football" where they stomp on each other's shadows rather than engage in the traditional, tougher, riskier acts of physically tackling their opponents who possess the football. That is, until we progress to the point in America where we are afraid of our own shadows! But have no fear, my fellow citizens, because until that particular point of time is upon us, we will probably rename the National Football League the National Shadow Football League. Once we are afraid of our own shadows and can no longer engage in "Shadow Tag" or "Shadow Football," we will have an athletic alternative whereby all contact sports will be confined to various **video** sports games. We can all invite our friends and relatives over to play such video games in our garages and other "man caves" on Saturdays and Sundays while drinking beer, eating pretzels, and fondly reminiscing about the good old days—assuming, of course, that the nation's progressive "food fascists" and politically correct "thought police" have not banned supposedly unhealthy beer and pretzels as well as improper thinking!

To use a science fiction analogy, Americans will then be held captive in our own cages or menageries that are similar to the one that confined Captain Christopher Pike in *Star Trek,* when all of his thoughts and actions were controlled and manipulated by the powerful Talosians of Talos IV. When Captain Pike resisted the demands of his captors, they temporarily placed him in a horrifying and painful illusion where he was being burned in Hell. The Talosian leader told Pike, "From a fable you once heard in childhood." "If you continue to disobey, from deeper in your mind, there are things even more unpleasant." "Wrong thinking is punishable; right thinking will be as quickly rewarded." This science fiction scenario is currently coming to pass in our own country, as many of America's own Democratic Talosians, who currently comprise progressive activists, lawyers, judges, and politicians, are attempting to control, manipulate, punish, and reward the rest of us who are under their direct control. Such American-style Talosians will more than likely be content with converting all of the nation's sports stadiums into safe, benign, environmentally friendly, vegetarian, vegan, family picnic peace menageries!

Next, it will be the military's turn. We all had a good laugh in 2004 when the now retired conservative US Democratic Senator Zell Miller of Georgia questioned the conventioneers attending the Republican Convention in New York City as to whether or not Democrats within his own party would want our armed forces to fight future wars with spit balls. At the time, the line was quite humorous as Miller mocked members of his own political party, especially presidential candidate John Kerry of Massachusetts. But you know what? With the way events are currently unraveling in America, I am no longer laughing!

Don Closson received his BS in education from Southern Illinois University, his MS in educational administration from Illinois State University, and his MA in Biblical Studies from Dallas Theological Seminary. He served as a public school teacher and administrator before joining Probe Ministries as a research associate in the field of education. He is the general editor of *Kids, Classrooms, and Contemporary Education*. The following are highlights of his article, "The Feminization of American Schools," distributed by Probe Ministries:

There is growing recognition that American school-age boys are not doing well. In fact, many of our sons are experiencing significant problems both inside and outside of the classroom...

...The majority of those receiving master's degrees are now women and the percentage of males seeking professional degrees is declining every year....Boys are three times more likely to be a victim of a violent crime and between four to six times more likely to commit suicide....

...The 1990's brought to bear a number of powerful ideas on the way schools look at and treat boys....Successful lobbying of Congress resulted in passage of the Gender Equity Act in

1994 that categorized girls as an under-served population, placing them on par with other oppressed minorities. Since then teachers and administrators have been deluged with gender equity materials and conferences sponsored by the Department of Education....

...Feminist philosopher Sandra Lee Bartky writes that human beings are born bisexual and through conditioning are "transformed into male and female gender personalities." William Pollack, a Harvard psychologist, argues that by doing away with traditional male stereotypes the next generation of boys "will be able to safely stay in the doll corner as long as they wish, without being taunted.".....

...A teacher in San Francisco is going one step further. She has transformed her classroom into a woman-centered community of learners. All the images in the classroom are of women, and as one feminist noted "perhaps for the first time, boys are the ones looking through the window."...Schools are denying the very behavior that makes little boys boys. In Southern California, a mother was stunned to find out that her son was disciplined for running and jumping over a bench at recess....Sixty percent of American high schools no longer use class rankings or announce valedictorians. Referring to the hostility towards honor rolls, one principal has stated, "It flies in the face of the philosophy of not making it so competitive for those little kids.... We even frown on spelling bees." [18]

Is it any wonder that we are currently witnessing the demonization of business as well as the outright hostility being exhibited toward the economic forces of free-market competition by the Obama Administration and the progressives in Congress when a significant percentage of our nation's schoolchildren is being brainwashed into thinking that competition is inappropriate? This anti-competition culture being promulgated in many of our public schools manifests itself throughout high school and college, and its lingering philosophy then permeates our political culture as well. Now, certainly this is not occurring in the majority of our schools, but it is prevalent enough that our own federal government is partially responsible for the feminization of our schools by virtue of the very policies it supports or does not support—as the case may be.

Prior to the fall elections of 2010, one could hardly watch an evening cable news program without observing the callous manner in which the current administration and the 111th Congress would criticize the salaries of CEOs as well as the profits of various companies as if they were all obscene and evil. You would have thought the Greek goddess of divine retribution, *Nemesis,* whom I prefer to call the former Speaker of the House, Nancy Pelosi, was lurking about the country while poised to pounce upon any business for daring to turn a handsome profit. This was being branded as "corporate greed." What kind of message did this outrageous behavior send to our high school and college students, the future leaders of America? We are currently witnessing such a message being echoed loud and clear right before our very eyes with the Occupy Wall Street crowd with the complete blessing of Team Obama, the Democratic Party, the labor unions, and the cheerleading section of the mainstream media! Is it any wonder Nancy Pelosi publicly praised such a conglomeration of deadbeats?

In addition, these same progressive government officials who see fit to rant and rave publicly about the evils of "corporate greed and avarice" are the same hypocrites who would more than likely whine and bellyache the loudest if their own bloated salaries, lavish perks, Cadillac health care benefits, and obscene pensions—courtesy of hard-working taxpayers—were to be put on a restrictive diet by the American people! What is so appalling is the fact that such limousine liberals have the audacity to portray themselves as the supposed "champions of the common man," yet they too are members of the 1 percent of Americans the Occupy Wall Street protestors love to vilify. Indeed, such pontificating liberals are multimillionaires in their own right, and they most certainly live opulent lifestyles that are unlike the lifestyles of any of the common men and women I hobnob with! At least Republican multimillionaires, such as Donald Trump, do not pretend to be anything other than what they truly are, and their transparency is front and center for all to see. One would certainly not observe Donald Trump or other conservative multimillionaires denigrating the instruction of free-market principles in our public schools and universities either.

If that were not bad enough, observe just how "green" all of these supposed enlightened progressives are as they promote curricula in our public schools that extol the virtues of environmentalism while such "green" politicians fly about the United States and the world in their private jets in order to attend various "global warming" conferences. They are also perfectly content with being chauffeured about in gas guzzling SUVs or limousines, and they reside in lavish mansions while consuming more energy and leaving a much larger carbon footprint than all of the rest of us combined! Yet, how they do love to point fingers and have the mitigating gall to lecture the rest of the American people about the necessity of going "green" while demanding that we support legislation—such as cap-and-trade—that would effectively kill vital jobs, strangle the nation's economy like an Anaconda snake, astronomically drive up the costs of fuel and electricity on homes and businesses alike, and place regulatory burdens not only on the unsuspecting poor and lower-class citizens of America, but middle and upper-middle classes of Americans and businessmen as well. And all of this hogwash is for our own good and the general welfare of the nation?

If all of these progressive, elitist, and crafty Artful Dodgers were to have it their own way and be permitted to pick our wallets clean with unfettered hands, they would effectively see to it that all of the rest of us hapless saps would be compelled to live in tenements under the willy-nilly supervision and financial benevolence of none other than the sneaky villain Fagin of Charles Dickens's *Oliver Twist.* Can't you just picture this lovely scenario? All of these wily, smug, know-it-all liberal Artful Dodgers would be delighted with banning together while joyfully singing a lovely little ditty from the musical, *Oliver,* that goes something like this: "Consider yourself, at home. Consider yourself, one of the family!" You bet, such big-government liberal thieves and pickpockets are indeed the "champions of the common man" all right—so much so that they would drive the entire nation into the "poor house" while at the same time seeing perfectly fit to protect their own interests and lavish lifestyles in order to guarantee that all of them would continue to live high on the hog in progressive posh communities such as Beacon Hill of Boston and Beverly Hills, California. In the meantime, the rest of us naïve and destitute Olivers would be confined to living in abject poverty and squalor under the continual tutelage of Fagin as he merrily enjoins: "You've got to pick a pocket or two-oooooh; you've got to pick a pocket or two." The American people are simply fed up with the progressives' hypocrisy and double standard in this regard.

Isn't it noteworthy that it was during the Clinton Administration that the Gender Act of 1994 was handed down by the federal government, which contributed to the feminization of our boys and schools? Where is our current administration's concern for the welfare of America's boys who are at serious risk? I have seen President Obama admirably proclaiming the importance of fatherhood on a public service announcement on television, and for that he deserves both credit and respect. I also admire the manner in which Barack Obama and his wife, Michelle, have served as positive role models for the nation with regard to parenthood and positive family values. But I have yet to see our current administration address the stark reality that our nation's boys are at serious risk socially and academically.

Precisely how are our young boys going to grow up to be responsible fathers and providers for their own families when they do not have many role models themselves anymore? For a large segment of our nation's boys, the only role models they see in many communities scattered about are the various gangs roaming the streets at all hours of the night! After all, if their needs are not being met at home, boys will eventually turn to some other kind of family, even if that family consists of a violent gang and all of the criminal activities that come with it. As a direct result, our nation will certainly have no difficulty with providing its own cast of pathetic characters to play the appropriate gang of violent pickpockets in our own upcoming production of *Oliver Twist*—American-style, that is. Has anyone in government seriously pondered this fact? I never hear Congressmen or senators jumping into the fray with regard to the feminization of our boys and schools. To be fair, I cannot recall any similar concern being expressed by the Republicans when they were in control of Congress under the administration of George W. Bush. They were preoccupied with writing and passing the unconstitutional *No Child Left Behind Act* with the gleeful assistance of the late Senator, Ted Kennedy, and his fellow Democrats.

Bill Barnwell is a pastor in Swartz Creek, Michigan, and has a master of ministry degree from Bethel College. On September 1, 2003, he penned an excellent article titled "The Feminization of Men." Mr. Barnwell hits us right between the eyes with his provocative article. His sagacious thoughts are most blunt and revealing. Here are some excerpts of his excellent article:

> Whatever happened to the virtue of masculinity? It is long gone if today's popular culture is any indicator. There was once an era where a man was supposed to be a man. He looked like a man, he talked like a man and acted like it. Not so anymore. Today, if you want to be an appealing, attractive male, then you had better feminize yourself, and feminize yourself quick....
>
> ...Each sex puts on his or her best face and package themselves to attract the opposite sex. What do women find attrac-

tive today? Sissies. Women are CONSTANTLY trying to get men to look more like women. Dye or highlight your hair, be real slim and wear form-fitting clothing, get an earring, get rid of excess body hair, etc., etc., etc...

...If I'm wrong then what exactly was that whole boy band craze about? A bunch of singing and dancing pretty boys who when they weren't whining in their songs about the girl they loved or missed tried to occasionally act like bad boys...? But guys will continue to open up their wallets, because it allows them to look like wimps and that's what girls want. Then you can add the cute little white hats (with the college initials on them) that a lot of guys wear, add some blonde streaks to your hair, throw on an earring, and bam, you can be completely sissified and attract women to you.

Now just because women want guys to look like wimps doesn't mean they want them to totally act like wimps....No, a girl likes a guy who is sensitive but strong. Humble but cocky. Nice but arrogant....

...So in conclusion, young women want a man who has feminine physical traits, but a combination of feminine and masculine character traits. It is in many ways a contradiction, and the seeking male has to walk a fine line between looking like a sissy and actually being a sissy. The proper balance between being a wuss and being a loudmouth tough guy must be maintained...

...Those of us single men who do not like the way this trend is going are forced to do one of three things: (1) Sell out and pretty ourselves up, (2) Bite the bullet and refuse to feminize ourselves and attract a fewer number of women to ourselves than we could if we sold out, and (3) Find some sort of middle ground....Hopefully one day we can go back to acting like true men. [19]

Mr. Barnwell has hit the nail right on the head with regard to this whole issue of the feminization of men. It certainly is not in the best interest of our nation's boys when the culture of America promotes and perpetuates an image of wimpy, brainless men. How often do we see males of all ages maligned and poked fun of by Hollywood and the media? For example, I personally find some of the shows my youngest daughter likes to view on television to be quite offensive because they often portray teenage boys as nothing but a bunch of blockheads, acting subservient to their superior female counterparts who are portrayed as bright and witty sages who have all of the solutions to life's problems. We are constantly subjected to commercials on television where male studs are pictured carrying females in elevated royal litters as if they were slaves catering to the demands of their queens. How about the cutesy and feminine image of a man flying about the house dressed up as a ballerina-type fairy—complete with delicate wings and leotards—advertising various cleaning products with the wave of his precious magic wand? What about the degrading image of a shirtless African-American man scrubbing the bedroom floor with a mop while he obediently caters to the whims and commands of either his spouse or girlfriend lounging in bed while eating her fruit? Let us not fail to mention how our boys are being exposed to other supposed male role models such as the prissy looking Adam Lambert, simulating sexual acts with another man during some concert on television! The old saying "a picture is worth a thousand words" really rings true, now doesn't it? When our sons are constantly being bombarded by such garbage in our culture, how can it not have a debilitating impact on them? Gone are the images of the masculine Marlboro Man or the sailor advertising the men's cologne Old Spice.

My daughter, Faith, was recently married to an apple farmer, Tim Riley, who owns an apple ranch up in the mountains of Oak Glen, California. He certainly doesn't concern himself with being prissy for anyone. In fact, he actually does resemble the sailor who once advertised the product Old Spice. After all, he was cast as one of the British sailors in the hit film, *Master and Commander.*

Faith is perfectly content, as are her mother and father, with Tim epitomizing the rugged Renaissance man that he is: farmer, construction worker, professional actor, bagpiper, music instructor, entrepreneur, Christian, and conservative intellectual. My wife and I sincerely pray our other daughters, Christa and Bethany, will also be fortunate enough to hook up with men very similar to Tim. If this blessed nation of ours is ultimately going to survive, we had better recapture the essence of what made America great—namely the strength of the intact, traditional American family. As a nation, we need to hearken back to the "spirit" of the era that gave us *Cinderella Man* and Cinderella Family.

> *It was the sense of family, of neighborhood and of school unity that made up what we considered a sure and certain loyalty to the society known as Great Falls.*
> — Christian D. Stevens

7

Every Child Left Behind

Learning is not attained by chance; it must be sought for with ardor and attended to with diligence.

— Abigail Adams

LET ME SEE IF I'VE GOT THIS RIGHT...

You want me to go into that room with all those kids and fill their every waking moment with a love for learning. Not only that, I'm to instill a sense of pride in their ethnicity, behaviorally modify disruptive behavior, and observe them for signs of abuse, drugs, and T-shirt messages.

I am to fight the war on drugs and sexually transmitted diseases, check their backpacks for guns, and raise their self-esteem.

I am to teach them patriotism, good citizenship, sportsmanship and fair play, how and where to register to vote, how to balance a checkbook, and how to apply for a job, but I am never to ask if they are in this country illegally.

I am to check their heads occasionally for lice, maintain a safe environment, recognize signs of potential antisocial behavior, offer advice, write letters of recommendation for student employment and scholarships, encourage respect for the cultural diversity of others, and, oh yeah, teach, always making sure that I give the girls in my class fifty percent of my attention.

I am required by my contract to be working, on my own time, summer and evenings and at my own expense, towards additional certification and employment status.

I am to collect data and maintain all records to support and document our building's progress in the selected state mandated program to "assess and upgrade educational excellence in the public schools."

I am to be a paragon of virtue larger than life, such that my very presence will awe my students into being obedient and respectful of authority.

I am to pledge allegiance to supporting family values, a return to the basics, and my current administration.

I am to incorporate technology into the learning, but monitor all websites for appropriateness while providing a personal one-on-one relationship with each student.

I am to decide who might be potentially dangerous and/or liable to commit crimes in school or who is possibly being abused; and I can be sent to jail for not mentioning these suspicions to those in authority.

I am to make sure ALL students pass the state and federally mandated testing and all classes, whether or not they attend school on a regular basis or complete any of the work assigned.

I am to communicate frequently with each student's parent by letter, phone, newsletter, e-mail, and grade card.

I am to do all of this with just a piece of chalk, a computer, a few books, a bulletin board, a 45 minute or less plan time, and a big smile on a starting salary that qualifies my family for food stamps in many states.

Is that all?

And you want me to do all of this and expect me to do it:
WITHOUT PRAYING?

— Author Unknown

This absorbing anecdote partially describes the dilemma American public school educators face on a daily basis in today's classrooms, and it is certainly not a cakewalk! In other words, today's society expects its public school teachers to function as none other than demigods! No teacher, regardless of whether he or she is a conservative or a liberal, pursues this noble profession for the purpose of becoming independently wealthy. The simple truth of the matter is this: Educators choose to enter this profession because the vast majority of us are devoted to children, and we have a passion and gift for teaching. Furthermore, we choose to forgo becoming successful American entrepreneurs so that we may be of public service to the nation because teachers help prepare and inspire our children to become successful and productive individuals in their own right.

This final chapter will delve into the controversial issues surrounding the current state of public education in America, and as a direct result, perhaps the readers of this book will gain a deeper appreciation as to what teachers are truly up against in today's dysfunctional society. Hopefully the majority of the American people will find my frank and honest assessment of such issues to be refreshing for a change because I will be challenging both progressive and conservative assumptions with regard to the current quagmire engulfing America's public school teachers. I am certainly not beholden to liberal teachers' unions nor am I an apologist for liberal dogma and its accompanying eduspeak in the field of education any more than I am beholden to all conservative viewpoints with regard to this particular profession. There are a few positions that are advocated by the teachers' unions that I agree with just as much as there are many aspects of the teachers' unions that I find absolutely abhorrent. Likewise, I wholeheartedly agree with the majority of the objections and concerns conservatives have with public education just as much as I disagree with a few of their erroneous assumptions. This is an extremely complex topic, and there are no easy answers when it comes to "fixing" what ails public education. Many of our schools and school districts are in decline simply because America itself is in serious decline, and the two are not mutually exclusive.

I will begin my analysis by emphatically stating the following: I have been most proud to serve in the trenches of America's public school classrooms for over twenty-five years, while doing so with distinction. Accordingly, I possess the expertise, leadership, and experience with which to intelligently comment upon the myriad of controversies surrounding public education in America. I will do so with forthright honesty—supported by sound research and facts—and as a result, the general public, the nation's politicians, and many of my colleagues will either concur with a number of my observations and suggestions as to how we might improve our public schools, or they will be shocked and taken aback as to the chutzpah that is inherent with my proposals for solving some of the toughest issues plaguing many of our nation's schools.

My views will most certainly reflect those coming from a conservative teacher's perspective, yet liberals and conservatives alike will find something to appreciate as well as criticize within the pages of this chapter. Indeed, both sides will most assuredly grapple with my intemperate viewpoints. Nevertheless, I promise the American people to not only be an "equal opportunity offender" as I prepare to fire warning shots across the bows of both left-leaning and right-leaning ships moored alongside the banks of the educational isle, but I also promise all readers of this book that they are about to be taken on a wild roller coaster ride—Harry Potter style. In addition, while perusing this chapter, the readers will continue to be presented with a number of delightful educational anecdotes that have crisscrossed my desk over the course of many years. Some anecdotes are humorous and sardonic while others are serious and profound, yet all of them, in their own unique way, shed some light on the current state of American public education from a **teacher's point of view,** which will be refreshing for a change.

The American people are continually bombarded with a barrage of platitudes coming from a variety of sources concerning the so-called "deplorable state" of America's public schools. Some criticisms are justified while others are not. However, there certainly is no shortage of supposed "experts" in the complicated field of education as these know-it-alls include the following: highfalutin politicians, psychologists, judges, parents, university professors, journalists, preachers, op-ed commentators, radio talk-show hosts, civil libertarians, and cable television news commentators. They all claim to be oracles of divine wisdom when it comes to this particular arena, yet rarely does one ever hear an actual teacher's perspective on any of the educational issues confronting us today.

Teachers across our fruited plain just love it when politicians of all political stripes chime in during every single state and national election as to what needs to be done to "fix" our schools, as if the nation's teachers and schools were nothing better than pitiful pawns to be moved and manipulated about on the latest political chessboard! Now bear in mind, these political paragons of educational expertise are the same incompetent ninnies who are bankrupting their own state economies as well as our national economy, and they are the same cast of characters who are woefully mismanaging the people's business while displaying incompetence and malfeasance of duty on a grand scale. Yet they have the unmitigated effrontery to point and wag their fingers at the nation's public school teachers and lecture us as to how we are collectively failing the nation's schoolchildren! It very much reminds me of a couple of old sayings of the Lord Jesus Christ (and I am paraphrasing here): "Before you point to the splinter in your brother's eye, behold the plank in your own," or "He who is without sin, let him cast the first stone."

As practicing educators, why should any of us seriously listen to or pay heed to such political yokels who are incapable of properly discharging their own duties as governors, legislators, judges, or even presidents—both past and present—of the United States! Perhaps if they were to keep their own castles of political wizardry in respectable functioning order, teachers might be inclined to listen to some of their suggestions, but such pompous politicians have very little credibility with me and many of my colleagues on both sides of the political aisle. Besides, precisely how many of these loquacious political windbags are experienced educators themselves? Do they hold advanced degrees in education? Do they have so much as a smidgen of experience teaching in any of our nation's public elementary, middle, or high school classrooms? I would be willing to bet the family farm (if I had one) that the vast majority of them do not. No, what we have instead are a bunch of overweening know-it-all politicians who are peering through rose-colored glasses as to how their own classrooms of yesteryear may have possibly looked when compared to the classrooms of today. Our society has changed enormously and quite radically over the past fifty years as this book has effectively illustrated throughout its chapters, yet according to these political sages, America's current classrooms should magically reflect the culture, curriculum, and values of, say, *Leave It To Beaver, Father Knows Best*, or *Ozzie and Harriet* of the 1950s and 1960s. Amazing, isn't it? We are certainly no longer living in the land of *Father Knows Best,* as was clarified in chapter six of this book. On the contrary, we are occupying the land of *Father Knows Nothing*! The following anecdote, while both humorous and somewhat exaggerated, effectively drives home this very point:

SCHOOL DAYS 1970 VS. 2007

Scenario: Jack goes quail hunting before school, and he pulls into the school parking lot with his shotgun in the gun rack.

1970 – The vice-principal comes over, looks at Jack's shotgun, goes to his car and gets his shotgun to show Jack.

2007 – The school goes into lock down, the FBI is called, Jack is hauled off to jail and never sees his truck or gun again. Counselors are called in for traumatized students and teachers.

Scenario: Johnny and Mark get into a fist fight after school.

1970 – A crowd gathers. Mark wins. Johnny and Mark shake hands and end up best friends. Nobody goes to jail, nobody is arrested, nobody is expelled.

2007 – The police are called, the SWAT team arrives, they arrest Johnny and Mark and charge them with felony assault. Both are expelled even though Johnny started it.

Scenario: Jeffrey won't be still in class and disrupts other students.

1970 – Jeffrey is sent to the office and is given a good paddling by the principal. Jeffrey returns to class, sits still and does not disrupt the class again.

2007 – Jeffrey is given huge doses of Ritalin; He becomes a zombie; He is tested for ADD; The school gets extra money from the state because Jeffrey has a disability.

Scenario: Billy breaks a window in his neighbor's car and his dad gives him a whipping with his belt.

1970 – Billy is more careful next time, grows up normal, goes to college, and becomes a successful businessman.

2007 – Billy's dad is arrested for child abuse. Billy is removed to a foster care home and joins a gang. The state psychologist tells Billy's sister that she remembers being abused herself and their dad goes to prison. Billy's mom has an affair with the psychologist.

Scenario: Mark gets a headache and takes some aspirin to school.

1970 – Mark shares some aspirin with the principal out on the smoking dock.

2007 – The police are called, and Mark is expelled from school for drug violations. His car is searched for drugs and weapons.

Scenario: Johnny takes apart some leftover firecrackers from the 4th of July and puts them in a model airplane bottle. He blows up a red ant bed.

1970 – Ants die.

2007 – BATF, Homeland Security, the FBI, and PETA are called. Johnny is charged with domestic terrorism, PETA has Johnny charged with felony animal cruelty, the FBI investigates his parents, siblings are removed from the home, computers are confiscated, Johnny's dad goes on a terror watch list, and Johnny is not allowed to fly again.

Scenario: Johnny falls while running during recess and scrapes his knee. He is found crying by his teacher, Mary. Mary hugs him to comfort him.

1970 – In a short time, Johnny feels better and goes on playing.

2007 – Mary is accused of being a sexual predator and loses her teaching job and credential. She faces 3 years in state prison. The school eliminates recess to avoid potential lawsuits from angry and overprotective parents. Johnny undergoes 5 years of psychotherapy.

— Author Unknown

America's public school teachers also bemoan the manner in which many of our nation's ills are placed right at the gates of our schools. Indeed, our state and national politicians love to scapegoat the nation's teachers for practically everything gone awry with today's society. Didn't you realize this is entirely our fault? I must confess: I am certainly participating in some level of whining and bellyaching here, but as a result of serving as an educational foot soldier in the trenches of American public education for almost three decades, perhaps I can be granted some degree of latitude and succor to continue to do so. As teachers, we would have greater respect for politicians running for office or for the ones currently serving in government of both political parties if they were to actually have the gumption to conduct a very frank conversation with the American people, look them squarely in the eyes, and at least put **some** measure of blame for the lack of a significant number of our current students' progress or their academic failure on those who primarily bear the responsibility for it—namely, parents and their own children! But no, we certainly wouldn't want to offend any of the voters or actually hold any of them and their children accountable in any manner now would we? To berate or chastise the very source of many of these problems might deny our disingenuous and lily-livered politicians the desperate votes they need every two to four years in order to get elected or reelected to public office. They would prefer to scapegoat the nation's teachers and schools because it is politically expedient and popular for them to do so. Consequently, we are continuing to countenance the decline of the virtues of self-reliance and personal accountability with parents and their children in America. With regard to this specific educational issue, both progressives and conservatives need to plead, "guilty as charged."

My dear people, having taught school for more than twenty-five years myself, I have discovered one truth to be of paramount certainty: Show me concerned and proactive parents who take an actual interest and role in their children's education, and I will show you successful, industrious, and well-adjusted children in school. These same children will not grow up to be lazy deadbeats nor will they become economic dregs on society because of any entitlement mentality. Instead, they will be industrious, entrepreneurial businessmen and businesswomen who will be the movers and shakers of America's future, unlike many of the children discussed in the previous chapter who fall into the various categories of neglected, abused, and fatherless homes, who through no fault of their own, happen to carry all of their usual negative baggage with them that ends up being deposited at the doorstep of American society.

Every semester during the school year, I frustratingly observe that as much as 25–30 percent of the students in my history classes receive "D" or "F" grades in middle school. What is more disappointing is the fact that with rare exceptions, their parents neglect to take the time to contact me to express any concern for their children's lack of success! It is as if these parents have forsaken their children. The majority of these same indifferent parents of failing or underperforming students neglect to attend our school's annual Parent Open House at the beginning of the new school year to meet with their children's teachers in order to obtain vital information as to what parental strategies are easily available to them at home to help their own children become successful students or, at the very least, achieve average grades in their core academic classes. This is truly irresponsible on the part of such offending parents because what they are effectively communicating to their children, either directly or indirectly, is that education is not of primary interest to them. Naturally, how can education be a priority of the children of such parents when this underlying message is being conveyed to them? I suppose that is the fault of teachers as well.

Since a huge number of our effete politicians, as well as a generation consisting of many very pampered and bleeding-heart parents who support them, are not willing to be transparent here, permit me to be completely frank and brutally honest with the American people—somebody ultimately needs to take the bull by the horns in order to do so. Many politicians, parents, and even a majority of progressive educators will not be willing to either acknowledge or admit to the simple truth of what I am about to reveal because sometimes the truth can be quite troubling and really sting, especially when such truth delivers a rather harsh slap across the face. So be prepared to offer the other cheek as well.

The real problem with the **majority** of failing and underperforming students attending our nation's public schools is not always predicated upon reasons of failure due to poverty; or because such students are perpetual victims of social injustice; or because they are incapable of being successful in school because they lack qualified instructors, the best facilities, or the best materials with which to succeed. On the contrary, most failing students across our great nation actually fail because of the following reasons: they do not read and study sufficiently at home; they are not intrinsically motivated; they do not receive enough support, guidance, and supervision—much less discipline—from their parents; they do not take school seriously enough to try and be successful because too many of them perpetuate a destructive youth culture that says it is "hip" to fail, and many of these students would rather squander away their time and God-given abilities and talent in the classroom while making the deliberate choice to fail; they do not complete their homework on time—if at all—and many do not devote the necessary time to study for their quizzes and tests because they are outright lazy and simply do not care.

Now, there are certainly exceptions to what I have just stated, such as students who occasionally fail certain core classes because they are truly struggling academically with certain subjects. There are also students who fall into the debilitating categories detailed in the previous chapter that can impede their academic progress, yet many of them still manage to overcome obstacles despite such feeble conditions. Nor am I referring to students who are diagnosed with specific learning disabilities or students who are not yet proficient with the English language. Nevertheless, the majority of the students who fail their core academic classes on a consistent basis are unconcerned about their poor grades. To make matters worse, many of these students often walk about the campus as they freely display big-time attitudes with chips on their shoulders while bragging and extending high-fives to their like-minded friends when they receive poor grades, as if such lackluster achievements are some type of unwonted cultural badge of honor! I should know because, as a teacher, I observe this happening on a regular basis when a number of these individuals proudly react with a haughty giggle or sneer as they are handed their failing test papers and report cards prominently displaying one-legged "A" **(F)** grades. And I teach in one of the best school districts in the state of California with some of the highest and most respectable standardized test scores as compared to those of other school districts in the state!

To be sure, there are progressive individuals and advocacy groups throughout America, both inside and outside the educational community, that will vehemently deny the fundamental truth I have just shared with everybody, and such liberal ostriches will continue to keep their naïve and idealistic heads buried in the sand. They will collectively persist in making every kind of politically correct, lame, pathetic excuse under the sun for these lazy, failing miscreants and their inept parents—claiming that they are all victims of a variety of circumstances and social injustice. As these enablers continue to proceed down this fickle path, they will most assuredly contribute ad infinitum to the crippling of such students for life as they exacerbate the problem by justifying failing students' behavior, excusing their sense of victimization, and promoting their entitlement mentality. Nevertheless, what I have just illustrated is the absolute truth whether progressives or conservatives choose to admit it or not. Sometimes teachers wish they could put the following brazen report card comments on a third of our students' report cards each semester. Enjoy this next humorous—albeit harsh educational anecdote:

TEACHERS' REPORT CARD COMMENTS:

01. Since my last report, your child has reached rock bottom and has started to dig.
02. I would not allow this student to breed.
03. Your child has delusions of adequacy.
04. Your son is depriving a village somewhere of an idiot.
05. Your daughter sets low personal standards and then consistently fails to achieve them.
06. Your child has a "full six-pack" but lacks the plastic thing to hold it all together.
07. This child has been working with glue too much.
08. When your daughter's IQ reaches 50, she should sell.
09. The gates are down, the lights are flashing, but the train isn't coming.
10. If this student were any more stupid, he'd have to be watered twice a week.

11. It's impossible to believe the sperm that created your child beat out 1,000,000 others.
12. The wheel is turning but the hamster is dead.

— Author Unknown

The following excerpts are from an op-ed piece that appeared in one of my local newspapers in August of 2009. The title of it is "Government Programs Can't Fix Irresponsible Behavior," and it is written by Thomas Sowell, a conservative intellectual who has already been quoted in chapter five of my book. To his prodigious credit, he is one of the few conservative intellectuals who has come down on the side of public school teachers—at least in this particular article—rather than throwing all of us under the bus. Mr. Sowell validates everything I have addressed thus far.

Many of the issues of our times are hard to understand without understanding the vision of the world that they are part of...
...Education is usually discussed in terms of the money spent on it, the teaching methods used, class sizes or the way the whole system is organized. Students are discussed largely as passive recipients of good or bad education.

But education is not something that can be given to anybody. It is something that students either acquire or fail to acquire. Personal responsibility may be downplayed in the "nonjudgmental" age, but it remains a major factor nevertheless.

After many students go through a dozen years in the public schools, at a total cost of $100,000 or more per student—and emerge semiliterate and with little understanding of the society in which they live, much less the larger world and its history—most discussions of what is wrong leave out the fact that many such students may have chosen to use school as a place to fool around, act up, organize gangs or even peddle drugs.

The great escape of our times is escape from personal responsibility for the consequences of one's own behavior....

...It is not just the "nonjudgmental" ideology of the intel-
ligentsia but also the self-interest of politicians that leads to
so much downplaying of personal responsibility in favor of
external programs to "solve" the "problem"... [1]

Mr. Sowell certainly does not mince words with regard to the stark
reality Americans need to face and own up to. A particular point
Mr. Sowell raises in his brilliant article needs further examination,
and that is the brusque fact that many students and their parents
are squandering the taxpayers' money. As of the year 2007, it costs
California's taxpayers $9,760 per student to educate him or her
every school year! Let us assume a student attends school in California all thirteen years (K-12) and the dollar figure remains fixed.
That would mean the taxpayers have effectively awarded every
student's parents a scholarship worth **$126, 880.00** to pay for
their child's K-12 public schooling. Now that is a significant sum
of money! In addition, depending on the number of dependents
a family has, multiply that figure by two, three, four, etc., and
you might see where I am about to go with this salient observation. Over the course of thirteen years, a family with four children
would have been awarded more than a half of a million dollars of
taxpayers' hard-earned money to educate their children! It is worth
noting that no average couple in California pays anywhere near
that amount of tax money to the state over the course of thirteen
years in order to cover the cost of educating four of their children
in California's public schools.

It is high time we raise some very serious and pertinent questions
with regard to all of this. Given what it currently costs taxpayers to
educate our children, does any child and his or her parents have a
moral right to squander that kind of money away by apathetically
taking advantage of the situation or by abusing the system? Most

Americans, if they were to give this question serious consideration, would probably chime in with a resounding "no!" Similarly, is it fair or even tenable for the taxpayers of this nation to continue to pony up that tidy sum of money year after year, only to have it wasted by at least a third of our lazy failing students and their indifferent parents, many of whom do not give any consideration whatsoever as to whether or not the rest of us are compelled to share our hard-earned tax dollars on their behalf, and watching such children and their irresponsible parents basically "partying" on our dime for thirteen years? Again, most of the public would probably say "no!" But remember, according to President Obama, we all need to "spread the wealth," and we most certainly are!

This is what shamefully occurs when, as a nation, we promote and tolerate an entitlement mentality that has been permitted to run amok in America during the course of the past fifty years and counting! Here is another prime example that illustrates this very point: Parents are obligated to provide meals for their own children, yet in all of our public schools, we are simply letting too many of them off the hook by providing their children with free breakfasts and lunches every school day, and I have even read recent articles in the newspapers whereby politicians are advocating that schools should expand this program to include dinners for "poor" schoolchildren every evening! My sweet Lord! The federal and state gravy trains are operating quite abundantly now aren't they? Many of us in the teaching profession, both conservative and liberal, are absolutely appalled by the fact that a number of these supposed "poor" children who are waiting in line for such handouts are also listening to music on their expensive I Pods and talking to or texting their friends on their fancy cell phones and smart phones while conveniently wearing designer clothing as they walk about the school campuses. Nevertheless, according to the advocates of the progressive social justice doctrine, the rest of us taxpayers have absolutely no right to be "judgmental" or call into question the manner in which such individuals of less financial means choose to spend their money. We should all unquestionably march to the progressive ideological drumbeat of the Democrats and gleefully follow Drum-Major-In-Chief, President Obama, while bombastically blaring the tune of "Spreading the Wealth." Well pardon me, but if such "poor" people feel they are "entitled" to various societal freebies, then the rest of us taxpayers should have a right to voice our opinions and help determine precisely how our tax dollars are to be spent on such supposed poverty-stricken individuals, even if it does appear to be "judgmental."

My wife complains to me every year that she finds it most disingenuous on the part of a number of the parents of supposed "poor" children when they bellyache that they allegedly do not have the money with which to pay the modest $40 rental fee for their children's choral uniforms for the school year—uniforms that continually need to be cleaned, repaired and replaced every year—yet such "poor" families conveniently manage to conjure up $500 or more for the extravagant cost of sending their children to the annual junior-senior prom. What precisely does the $500 or more buy them? Well it pays for their dance tickets, the rental of tuxedos or the purchase of formal dresses, flowers, sumptuous dinners in the most expensive fine dining establishments, and the rental of lavish limousines with which to cart their "poor" teenagers off to the dance in true royal splendor! Doesn't your heart just cry out to these supposed "poor" families who then claim they simply do not have the means with which to pay a modest $40 rental fee for the maintenance and use of a choir uniform each year, while at the same time, arrogantly demanding that the school's choral department scholarship their children the uniform rental fee as if this were some kind of "entitlement." It is only a matter of time before such freeloaders demand that the school districts also fund their children's costs for attending extra-curricular school functions such as the junior-senior prom—claiming that such activities should be a part of a "free" public education!

Yee gods, when I was a teenager in the 1970s, I had to throw newspapers before school and cook at McDonald's after school and on the weekends as well as during the holidays, flipping burgers day in and day out in order to pay for such opulent school functions. As a result, I really learned the value of a buck and came to respect and appreciate the long hours that would be required of me to labor in the workplace so that I could pay for and participate in these various high school functions as well. My mother and my sister and I did not expect any school handouts, nor did we ask for or depend on any government assistance program whatsoever. In addition, I paid for my own lunch every day by working as a cashier in the cafeteria at Villa Park High School in Orange County. My family took personal pride in our strong work ethic, and all three of us carried our own weight—earning meager livings while residing in a very modest apartment in Orange, California. My tight-knit family managed to get by with much less or we simply went without as compared to what others of greater financial means were able to enjoy in life, and we did so without complaining or despising the more affluent families who were living in Orange County in Southern California! Class warfare was simply not a part of our vocabulary! By the way, as a young teenager, the wages I earned while working at McDonald's also paid for my weekly piano lessons, since my mother could not afford such a luxury on her very limited income working as a legal secretary!

Be that as it may, is it any wonder our country has drifted down the scurrilous path whereby a significant percentage of our citizens feel that they are "entitled" to continually feed off of the state and federal gravy trains? Conservatives really resent this outlandish abuse of our generosity, and it must come to a screeching halt once and for all because our children in public schools are being brainwashed from an early age into thinking that they are some-how "entitled" to free handouts by the general public for practically everything under the sun, especially if their parents whine loud and long enough, and such specious thinking follows them into adulthood. Most of our states as well as the federal government are teetering on the brink of bankruptcy as a direct result of America gradually transforming into a "sissified" nation of deadbeats and freeloaders rather than a nation that is dominated by enterprising entrepreneurs and hardworking individuals! In all aspects, the traditional American work ethic is gradually becoming a thing of the past! Of course, those Americans who do manage to work very hard, who take patriotic pride in their efforts, and who handsomely succeed financially are lectured to by self-righteous Democrats about not paying their "fair share" of taxes! Americans need to reject such folly!

In this author's opinion and the opinion of many other Americans, the decadent "entitlement" philosophy that is being extolled by our current president and his socialistic political party is outright deleterious, and it is most assuredly contributing to the decline of our great country! Republicans are not entirely blameless for some of this fatuous tomfoolery either because they too have been guilty over the past several decades of perpetuating this "gimmee-gimmee-gimmee" philosophy by promoting various Congressional earmarks and entitlement programs that are "Democrat-light," rather than behaving as responsible politicians who are more than willing to show some backbone by simply saying "no" to their own pampered constituents.

Most people would not take issue with the supposition that every child in America has a right to a "free" public education, and the vast majority of conservatives would generally agree with this premise so long as it isn't abused in the manner just described. However, the fallacy that public education is supposedly "free" is certainly a misnomer as it is one of the most costly items in any state budget. I would also add the following caveat to the above proposition: Society should provide any student a supposed "free" public education so long as he carries his own weight in school. If that condition is not consistently met by the student and enforced by his parents, then society ought to provide an alternative "free" educational experience for any habitually failing and disruptive misfit. Well, this public school teacher certainly has some suggestions as to how we can possibly remedy this problem, and such suggestions will be shared with the readers toward the end of this chapter. What is more, these solutions will absolutely drive the progressives and other bleeding-heart sissies of this nation insane, so stay tuned, folks!

As a direct result of my blunt and honest assessment of the current situation facing all of us in America, my detractors will no doubt attempt to portray me as a caricature of some pathetic burned out or disgruntled educator, but nothing could be further from the truth. I really do love my job, and I command the respect of the vast majority of my colleagues, my parents, and their students, and I have the empirical evidence with which to prove this declaration. Furthermore, as a dedicated educational professional, I am happy to acknowledge the fact that the vast majority of my students— even those with substandard or failing grades—not only like me personally, but they are also engaged with the various educational activities occurring within my classroom. If I didn't have a positive and lasting impact on their lives, they would never take the time to repeatedly drop by my classroom and graciously extend to me their warmest regards while thanking me for being their favorite teacher in school. This is the primary reason that I have chosen to remain in this profession. It is certainly not because of the abundance of adulation and gratitude being expressed to me over the years by politicians as well as those who scorn public school education, nor is it because of the bountiful financial rewards my wife and I have received as a result of our dedication and devotion to our students in elementary school, middle school, and high school! My wife and I are certainly not holding our breath waiting for that kind of grati- tude, and it will probably be a cold day in Hell before public school teachers in general will ever be afforded that kind of courtesy, appreciation, and respect in this country. Am I in any way defending or making excuses for poorly performing or "bad" teachers out and about who should never have become teachers in the first place and need to be discharged? Certainly not! This is one of a number of sins I hold against the various teachers' unions. A teacher would have to practically be fornicating in public before the unions would finally come to the conclusion that such an educator ought to be terminated. Due process rights of all teachers need to be protected and enforced, but sometimes, it seems, such protection goes far beyond all reason and common sense, which leads me to the next point.

Teacher preparation and credential programs at various universities have to bear some of the responsibility for the placement of less-than-stellar teachers in various school districts. My wife and I have served as mentor teachers over the years in our own school district, and even when we have supervised the training of a number of student teachers, our recommendations to schools of education have, at times, been ignored. For example, there have been a couple of instances when we have not made entirely positive comments on student teacher evaluations to their university supervisors, thereby recommending that such individuals either repeat student teaching or, in some cases, be denied the awarding of preliminary teaching credentials because they do not show evidence of becoming potentially effective educators. This student teaching process is most critical because it is an important moment when both teachers and schools of education can truly police our own ranks by weeding out those who have no business entering the teaching profession. This doesn't imply that certain individuals are bad or even lazy people. To the contrary, some teaching candidates simply need to be counseled into pursuing another line of work or an alternative field of study. Schools of education and teacher preparation programs need to be reevaluated, and their education classes also need to transcend beyond the realm of liberal orthodoxy and social justice educational dogma. For example, my oldest daughter, Christa, has a master's degree in music as well as a bachelor of arts degree in English. In 2010, she was awarded her preliminary teaching credential in English by successfully completing her student teaching requirements at a local university. However, while she was attending education classes necessary to fulfill the requirements of earning her teaching credential, she often complained to me about the number of liberal "social-justice" and "touchy-feely" classes she was forced to endure, and she could not recall so much as one conservative-leaning professor instructing the students in any of her education classes at the university level. So much for diversity!

The following scenario is another disturbing trend occurring in our schools that many teachers are very concerned with—that is, the emerging addiction being exhibited by our children to modern technology, such as computers, the Internet, video games, and especially smart phones. Obviously, these high-tech devices are quite marvelous, and they are absolutely necessary for all of us in order that we may compete and function in today's global economy. When used in moderation, all of this technology is beneficial to everyone, but in my opinion and the opinion of many of my colleagues, certain aspects of modern technology are actually working to the detriment of our children. We are currently rearing a generation of children who are literally **addicted** to technology—so much so that they can hardly survive a moment throughout the day without having continual access to such technological devices. For example, my wife and I have had some difficulty experiencing an entirely relaxing choral retreat with our high school choir students in the pristine forests of our local mountains every August without the kids being joined at the hips with their smart phones, constantly texting and accessing the Internet 24-7. When we attempt to encourage our students to take a walk through the forest and experience what nature has to offer them without their smart phones, they look at us, smile, and roll their eyes as if we were old fuddy duddies asking them to engage in an activity that goes entirely against the grain of their own nature—namely, to enjoy another type of adventure without text messaging. My wife and I have simply given up trying to influence today's students in this regard, including our youngest daughter, as we have begrudgingly come to the realization that we have lost this battle. Perhaps my wife and I really are old fuddy duddies because there are fleeting moments in time when we wish the things had never been invented!

As teachers, we see another negative and alarming aspect to this dilemma. Recreational reading, much less required reading in the core academic subjects, is currently becoming a real challenge for too many of our students. The majority of our students are no longer interested in reading a good classic novel anymore, and they detest reading from the school textbooks even when today's textbooks contain interesting stories and excellent graphics as well as colorful pictures to accompany those narratives, which, by the by, are a significant improvement over the textbooks my generation was forced to endure when we were students. As a consequence of this dire trend, students' reading comprehension levels are declining dramatically, and their acquisition of a sophisticated and extensive vocabulary is in serious jeopardy. For example, when I first began instructing American history fifteen years ago at the eighth grade level in middle school, my students were reading and studying from a textbook adoption I now see being utilized on college campuses with college-level history courses! Every seven years, when our school district adopts a new textbook series, I observe that the reading level is significantly easier for the kids, and the text is in much larger print, accompanied with pictures and graphics that utilize almost 50 percent of the textbook pages rather than the smaller print and text that once utilized at least 80 percent of the textbook pages of previous adoptions. I predict that before my wife and I retire from teaching, our students will be learning the core academic subjects from comic-style books or magazines wherein the text will be encircled with balloons suspended above colorfully illustrated characters and utilizing simplistic English or contemporary slang. Do you think I am kidding? I have already been shown examples of such material, and it is very disconcerting! When we eventually progress to that point in public school education, I will most definitely be hanging up my hat while bidding "adios" to the teaching profession, and I will then offer the following proposition to my own grown children: I will be more than happy to homeschool my future grandchildren from my yet-to-be-purchased motorhome as my wife and I travel about America during our retirement!

Our federal government has now established the utopian goal through the president's *Race to the Top* initiative of having 100 percent of our students attend college in order that they may excel in both math and science. Now this may be a laudable goal, but how is this going to possibly occur when a significant percentage of our youth is too lazy to read, much less tackle the level of reading proficiency, comprehension, and analysis required of such lofty pursuits? Too many of our children today would rather while away their spare time playing video games, spend countless hours on the smart phone or sit at the computer for hours on end communicating on Facebook, Twitter, and YouTube! Certainly not all of our children are obsessed or preoccupied with spending an inordinate amount of time engaging in such activities, but to deny such realities would be foolish and naive. Our children currently have way too much extra time on their hands if they are engaging in all of this social networking, and the negative impact all of this is having upon our nation's children is certainly cause for concern. For example, we continually read articles in various newspapers reporting on the alarming increase of cyber-bullying that happens to be contributing to teenage suicide! What about the deleterious influence sexting is having upon the declining morality of our children? We have already witnessed how this new phenomena has been expanded all the way to the halls of Congress with the shocking example of former Democratic Congressman Anthony Wiener of New York!

There certainly is a downside to all of this modern technology, and the nation is just beginning to grapple with these new problems. These are explicit examples of how the decline of public education and the decline of the federal government in America are not mutually exclusive: children are sexting in school while Congressmen are sexting in Congress!

The goals of President Obama's utopian *Race to the Top* remind me of the same foolish and unrealistic goals that were established with President George W. Bush's *No Child Left Behind Act* whereby **100 percent** of our children are supposed to be proficient in language arts and math by the year 2014! I see! Well, the Pope in Rome has about as much chance of converting to Protestantism by the year 2014 as are the odds of all of America's students achieving the goals of *No Child Left Behind* by the same year! Some may opine that I am being mean-spirited and unfair with regard to such criticism of both presidents. On the contrary, I am not being unfair or mean-spirited, nor am I being a pessimist. Having served the nation in the capacity as a teacher for over twenty-five years, I am simply being a realist and maintain we should set rational goals for our children that can be realistically attained within a reasonable amount of time. I am now prepared to confront the controversial *No Child Left Behind Act,* which happens to be the bane of both liberal and conservative educators alike—and for good reason!

State governors have the potential of becoming excellent and productive presidents because the duties and responsibilities of both offices are quite similar, yet there are striking differences as well. When George W. Bush became President of the United States in 2000, he forgot one basic fundamental truth. The US Constitution provides for one rather annoying, nagging, and bothersome principle our Founding Fathers insisted upon including in that remarkable contract. That principle is called Federalism. What exactly is Federalism and why is it so important? It is one of the seven principles of our Constitution that clearly dictates how power is to be shared between the federal government and the respective states. Some powers are reserved exclusively for the states, some powers are delegated exclusively to the federal government, and some powers are shared between the states and the federal government.

The following fact may actually come as something of a surprise, not only to former President Bush, but to President Obama as well: The education of America's children is a responsibility reserved exclusively for the states or the people (parents). If you were to carefully examine Articles I, II, and III of the Constitution, you would find that such articles specifically describe the responsibilities and functions of the Legislative, Executive, and Judicial Branches of the federal government. Absolutely nowhere will we find any reference to Congress, the president, or the Supreme Court being charged with the responsibility of educating our nation's children or even establishing educational goals or policies, much less establishing a federal Department of Education. However, the following is exactly what the Tenth Amendment to the Constitution clearly states:

> The powers not delegated to the United States by the Constitution, nor prohibited by it to the States, are reserved to the States respectively, or to the People.

Since Articles I, II, and III clearly do not delegate any educational tasks to the federal government whatsoever, the Tenth Amendment comes into play, which authorizes only the states or parents themselves to handle the task of educating the nation's schoolchildren. Why then, are the states permitting the federal government to intrude upon their sovereignty? Education policy has been under the purview of the states for the past couple of centuries. So precisely when did the federal government begin to stick its nose where it doesn't belong with regard to education policy?

The first unconstitutional intrusion of the federal government into states' rights or states' sovereignty as far as education policy is concerned occurred during the Lyndon B. Johnson Administration of the 1960s. During Johnson's Administration, Congress passed *The Elementary and Secondary Education Act* on April 11, 1965.[2] This act was the first federal government aid to education law and was designed to address the needs of poor and underperforming children throughout the United States. The second major unconstitutional intrusion of the federal government in education policy occurred during the Jimmy Carter Administration of the 1970s when President Carter and Congress elevated the Department of Education to full cabinet status, complete with its first Secretary of Education.[3] Of course, the states were perfectly content at the time with tolerating all of this heavy-handed nonsense and power-grab by the federal government because the Legislative and Executive Branches began to sing a delightful tune made famous by Abba called "Money, Money, Money." Such parlor tricks being performed by the federal government had the intended effect of luring the states into becoming dependent on a more than fifty-year-old federal-style money addiction. Rest assured, when money is involved, there are always many strings attached to it. Furthermore, isn't it ironic how the educational progress or lack thereof, of America's schoolchildren began to decline significantly once the federal government got entangled with education policy? Prior to 1965, our nation's public schools were considered to be exemplary. For the most part, the nation's fifty states seemed to be operating independently and quite respectably. Were our public schools perfect? Not by any means, yet we will never be able to achieve perfection with public education, just as private schools are not perfect with their operational results. Indeed, we still had to face issues of poverty, etc., but overall, our public schools were the envy of the world prior to 1965.

To be fair, federal intrusion upon public school education is not entirely responsible for the decline of America's schools. The decline of our nation's core values and Judeo-Christian influence during the course of the past fifty years have also played a significant role in the ebb of our schools, as this book has thoroughly documented throughout its chapters. Our nation's schools are an accurate reflection of our society in general. How can we seriously expect this to be otherwise? As people of a great nation, if we truly desire to restore our public schools to the place of greatness that they once occupied in society, then we had better get serious, cease behaving like muddled blockheads, apply some very tough love with our students and their parents, and restore **all** of America's virtues of exceptionalism to their proper place in American society. Only then will we ultimately be successful in rekindling "A City upon a Hill." This must be accomplished through shared sacrifice by electing representatives of both political parties to public office who will not only adhere to these virtues while they govern, but who will see fit to restore fidelity to our Constitution as well. In addition, the American people must insist that judges at all levels respect and adhere to these American virtues themselves by enforcing the principles of the Constitution as originally written by our Founding Fathers.

Not to be outdone by the Johnson and Carter Administrations, the Bush administration and the Republican-controlled Congress passed the *No Child Left Behind Act* in 2002. This federal law went one step further and established federal guidelines as to what criteria would be required of all of the nation's public school teachers in order for them to be considered "highly qualified," as if the various states' own credential programs and state teacher exams, such as California's CBEST, were somehow inadequate. Of course, the federal government compelled the states to implement this poorly funded and unconstitutional mandate under the guidance and supervision of the National School Board (the Department of Education), and all of the states have been struggling to meet the unrealistic goals of *NCLB* for ten long years.

For those of you who may not be completely up to speed with the mandates of this intrusive act, let me illustrate the absurdity of some of the harebrained goals of *NCLB*. The states are required to administer standardized testing to their students every spring in order to measure whether or not the public schools are doing their jobs in educating and assessing the progress of the nation's schoolchildren. Fair enough. Standardized testing, in one form or another, has been required and implemented in our schools for decades, and most teachers really do not object to the administering of these tests per se. But here is the problem with *NCLB*: The federal government has established five levels of criteria with which to measure students' progress on these exams. They are:

Advanced – The equivalent of an "A" grade – mastery of content.
Proficient – The equivalent of a "B" grade – mastery of content.
Basic – The equivalent of a "C" grade – average grasp of content.
Below Basic – The equivalent of a "D" grade – below-average grasp of content.
Far Below Basic – The equivalent of an "F" grade – failing.

If one were to examine the following two charts which were provided to all of the teachers in my own school district in 2006, one will notice that the federal government is demanding that 100 percent of the children attending our nation's public schools achieve minimally at the proficient level in English Language Arts and mathematics (which is mastery level) on state and federal standardized tests by the year 2014.[4]

Annual Measurable Objectives - Percent Proficient
English Language Arts Grades 2-8

100.0%

89.2%

78.4%

67.6%

56.8%

46.0%

35.2%

24.4%

13.6%

2001-2002 | 2002-2003 | 2003-2004 | 2004-2005 | 2005-2006 | 2006-2007 | 2007-2008 | 2008-2009 | 2009-2010 | 2010-2011 | 2011-2012 | 2012-2013 | 2013-2014

Annual Measurable Objectives - Percent Proficient
Mathematics Grades 2-8

100.0%

89.5%

79.0%

68.5%

58.0%

47.5%

37.0%

26.5%

16.0%

2001-2002 | 2002-2003 | 2003-2004 | 2004-2005 | 2005-2006 | 2006-2007 | 2007-2008 | 2008-2009 | 2009-2010 | 2010-2011 | 2011-2012 | 2012-2013 | 2013-2014

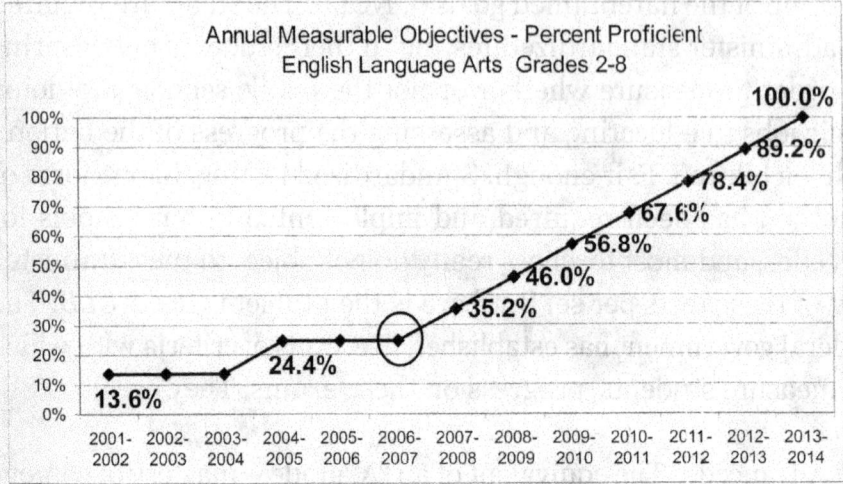

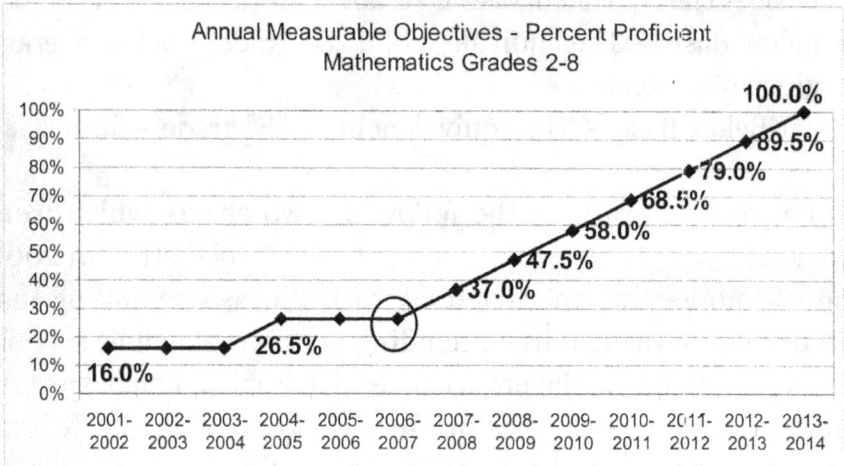

What an asinine pipe dream! The goal may be laudable, but no public school in America that is legally compelled to educate every kind of child imaginable could ever attain such unrealistic outcomes without sacrificing standards of educational excellence! As a direct result, *NCLB* is setting up the nation's public schools for failure!

As both a professional teacher and a parent, I would like to approach this dilemma from another angle. How many of you, while attending school as children, sat in any classroom in which 100 percent of the students earned all "A" and "B" grades in math, English, science, and history on their report cards? Did any of you have friends in school that received "C" grades or below? Why, of course you did! According to the utopian delusion of *NCLB,* the law is effectively dictating that as of the year 2014, it is no longer acceptable for any child in America to score basic or below on standardized tests in these core academic subjects, which, according to the federal government, serve as its equivalent of "report cards" for the nation's teachers and schools. Oh, by the way, isn't it quite convenient that private schools and academies as well as homeschooled children, are not required by the federal government to participate in all of this claptrap and play by the same rules of engagement that are required of the rest of us in public education? Now, if public schools do not achieve these unattainable goals by the year 2014, we will all be judged to be abject failures and should therefore be replaced immediately by those who can supposedly achieve this perfection! To the federal government, public school teachers all across the fruited plain will be more than content to respond in kind: **Good luck and God speed! Since you know everything, let's just see how you can make this miracle come to pass, and should you fail to measure up to your own unrealistic expectations and criteria, do not come back to the rest of us supposed "failures" cap-in-hand, begging for our forgiveness while pleading with us to return to the nation's classrooms in order to clean up the mess you have managed to leave behind!**

There are some additional facts that need to be disclosed with regard to *NCLB.* Incredibly, children in special education subgroups with diagnosed learning disabilities in language arts or math are also required to take the same tests that are administered to regular education students—at least in history, and they must achieve similar results by the year 2014 as well! If that weren't bad enough, what about the millions of students sitting in our nation's classrooms who are not yet proficient with the English language? After just a few short years from initially being enrolled in school, English Language Learner (ELL) students are administered the same standardized tests, whether or not they can functionally read the questions and answers at all, much less comprehend them! It would be the exact same situation as plopping all of us Americans on our butts in schools throughout France for a couple of years and requiring all of us to read and comprehend sophisticated French exam questions and answers and pass such exams with the same level of proficiency as native French speakers! How many Americans would appreciate being placed in such an insufferable position?

In addition, public schools have to continually contend with what I like to refer to as "the revolving door syndrome" whereby we are legally compelled to enroll numerous transient students in our respective schools throughout the school year regardless of their educational background or disciplinary history. In other words, the teachers in my own school district are constantly striving to educate failing transfer students who arrive at our doorsteps from other school districts, from God knows where, and we are being judged and evaluated by the federal government with their lousy test scores even though these students have scarcely been present within our schools or our school district the majority of the school year. Consequently, why should our teachers, schools, and school district be judged by the substandard test scores these transferring transient students produce when we have had very little to do with their education in the first place? Lovely, isn't it? Now, some politicians would argue that all school districts must contend with such nonsense, and that would be factually correct. However, it still does not make it reasonable or tenable to subject any teacher, school, or school district to such outrageous drivel.

Educators are also legitimately concerned about the fact that we are being held accountable by *NCLB* for the test results of students under our tutelage who are chronically absent from the classrooms and who are conveniently being excused and kept home by their parents for a variety of reasons such as the following: family outings, extended family vacations taken during the school year, the baby-sitting of younger siblings at home, or students conveniently attending highly educational activities such as amusement theme park excursions with their friends and family members during the school week. This is what teachers and administrators commonly refer to as outright ditching and truancy! We are not moaning and groaning about student absenteeism due to legitimate illnesses or family emergencies that may arise from time to time. We are talking about the lame excuses many parents repeatedly make to school officials when they deliberately choose to abuse the system in order to keep their children out of school so that they may "play" at a plethora of activities during the school week when their children's energy would be better spent attending school at the properly appointed time. These abundant and enjoyable activities should be reserved for weekends, holidays, and the traditional Christmas, Spring, and Summer Breaks. After all, rest and relaxation from school is part of the purpose of such breaks. But abusing the system in such a callous and habitual manner as we are currently witnessing does not help promote the traditional American work ethic with our children, now does it?

Of course, these are some of the same "helicopter" parents who will whine and complain the loudest to local school officials when their children do not receive grades on their report cards that are as good as other children's, and they will most assuredly blame the teachers for their children's lackluster performance on standardized tests while claiming their children are the victims of substandard education and discrimination! Such parents will arrogantly demand that alleged insensitive, unreasonable, and mean-spirited teachers do everything under their power to make all kinds of exceptions for their children so that their important schoolwork may be made up and completed at some later date for full credit rather than supporting teachers by having their children complete assignments and other school obligations during the properly appointed time.

As can be expected, some of these "helicopter" parents—in conjunction with their full complement of sympathetic political representatives, as well as their reliable "cheerleading team" of the judicial system and the ACLU—will collectively come flying to the rescue when they seek to emulate a children's cartoon hero of the 1960s as they thump their chests and boldly proclaim: **"Have no fear, *Underdog* is here!"** Furthermore, just how fair is this to the rest of the students who are present in school on a regular basis, diligently laboring on their schoolwork and learning to the best of their abilities while completing their assignments and projects on time? Precisely where is their Underdog waiting in the wings to come flying to their protection? All of this ballyhoo is trying the patience of the nation's public school teachers, especially given the fact that **we alone** are the ones who are being compelled to answer for the outcomes of such students' grades and standardized test scores while parents and their children are being exonerated of all personal accountability in this particular arena!

How can academic excellence be consistently achieved in our country when some children and their parents repeatedly exhibit such cavalier attitudes toward school attendance and are permitted to get away with it? Why are parents and students themselves not being held responsible or accountable for such behavior by *NCLB*? America's teachers would greatly appreciate it if our state and national politicians were to seriously address some of these germane questions and concerns. Then again, these career politicians wouldn't want to offend the sensibilities of their voting constituents, now would they? The trite and predictable reactions of politicians is to order all teachers and schools to cease their whining, suck it up, and devise their own proper courses of action to follow in order to solve such problems. When we do attempt to apply some level of accountability to the equation, we are continually thwarted by state and federal legislation that defends the indefensible or by the court system—under the usual and predictable prodding of the ACLU—which orders schools not to discriminate against children or violate their civil rights or the rights of their parents as a result of frivolous lawsuits being brought to bear against the supposedly oppressive and unfair school districts. Going up against the authority and power of **"Underdog"** is most daunting to say the least! Sweet Jesus, there are those precious moments in time when teachers and school administrators simply want to toss their collective arms and hands up into the air in order to surrender to the powers that be, or at the very least stand upon some precipice and scream at the top of their voices in utter exasperation and anger the following quote from the movie, *Network*: "We're as mad as Hell, and we're not going to take it anymore!" I personally contend that God has a very special place reserved for all of us educators in Heaven because of all of the stupidity we are being compelled to put up with! Be that as it may, there are no easy solutions for how best to solve many of these problems! Because progressive governors, legislators, and judges continue to perpetuate the status quo while pretending these problems will somehow eventually go away or get better in due time, many conservative parents feel they have no other alternative but to beat the drums of "vouchers" and "school choice," and conservative public school teachers like me really cannot blame them!

In the meantime, here are a few other myths associated with the *No Child Left Behind Act,* courtesy of the California Teachers Association:[5]

MYTH – Schools and educators are spending more time helping students learn and less time filling out forms.

REALITY – Educators and school personnel are spending millions of additional hours and dollars doing paperwork as a result of NCLB. This means less time preparing students and drawing up lesson plans. It means more time drafting compliance plans to submit to Washington bureaucrats. FACT: According to the U.S. Department of Education, states and schools are expected to spend 6,457,586 burden hours and $135.9 million to comply with the paperwork requirements of NCLB.[6]

MYTH – NCLB is on track to eliminate the achievement gap by 2014.

REALITY – According to UCLA's National Center for Research on Evaluation, Standards, and Student Testing (CRESST), the "most serious problem is that the NCLB expectations for student achievement have been set unrealistically high, requiring that by the year 2014, 100% of students must reach the proficient level or above in math and reading. Based on current improvement levels and without major changes in the definition of adequate yearly progress (AYP), almost all schools will fail to meet NCLB requirements within the next few years."[7]

MYTH – NCLB is improving teaching and learning in America's classrooms.

REALITY – Teaching to the test and narrowing the curriculum are only two of the unintended consequences of the fundamentally flawed law. School districts are spending more time on reading and math—the two subjects on which tests are based under NCLB—sometimes at the expense of other subjects not tested.

According to the Center on Education Policy, 71 percent of districts are reducing time spent on other subjects in elementary schools, and 60 percent of districts require a specific amount of time for reading in an elementary school.[8]

The Partnership for 21st Century Skills said: "The No Child Left Behind Act risks losing relevance if an innovative approach to reauthorization is not pursued...." One of its recommendations is that NCLB's assessment and accountability system should be based on multiple measures of students' abilities that include 21st century skills.

According to the Thomas B. Fordham Institute, "...is anybody prepared to tackle one of that law's most damaging unintended consequences? We refer, of course, to 'the big squeeze,' the compression of the curriculum to little but reading, math, and sometimes science."9

Here are a few quotes concerning the *No Child Left Behind Act* retrieved from a few conservative sources. Neal McCluskey is an education analyst at the Cato Institute and author of the recently published *Feds in the Classroom: How Big Government Corrupts, Cripples, and Compromises American Education.*

In early 2002, Republicans passed the No Child Left Behind Act, the most intrusive federal education law in American history....

In the end, neither Republicans nor Democrats should fight for NCLB. It hasn't helped either party, and it has hurt children all over the country. Indeed, if NCLB has taught one thing, it is this: When Washington gets involved in education, no one wins.10

Robert B. Bluey is director of the Center for Media and Public Policy at The Heritage Foundation. Mr. Bluey's article, *Another Revolt on the Right*, first appeared in Townhall.com on July 2, 2007. Here are a couple of excerpts retrieved from his article:

...It's a markedly different political climate from when the bill (NCLB) was first debated. Then, few conservatives put up a fight. NCLB won approval in the House, 381-41, and passed the Senate on an 87-10 vote....

In a paper released last week, Hickok and Ladner of the Goldwater Institute analyzed what has gone wrong with the law and how it could be fixed. They recommend that Congress shift greater policy making authority to states. Not only would it give parents and citizens more meaningful information about how well local schools were performing, it would also "begin to restore citizen ownership of American education"—something Hickok and Ladner say was lost with NCLB.[11]

The criticisms of *NCLB* just cited from both liberal and conservative sources are absolutely correct. The following humorous anecdote also illustrates the absurdity of *NCLB*:

NO CHILD LEFT BEHIND – THE FOOTBALL VERSION

1) All teams must make the state playoffs and all MUST win the championship. Any team that does not win the championship will be held on probation until they are the champions, and the coaches will be held accountable. If, after two years, they still have not won the championship, their footballs and equipment will be taken away UNTIL they do win the championship. The head coach of any team that doesn't win the championship after several years on probation will be sent to coach another team, as will the assistant coaches.

2) All kids will be expected to have mastered the same football skills at the same time, even if they do not have the same conditions or opportunities to practice on their own or with their coaches. NO exceptions will be made for kids who are good at soccer but not at American football, or good at swimming, gymnastics, baseball, basketball, or dodge ball. NO exceptions will be made for lack of interest in football or in performing athletically. NO exceptions will be made for kids with disabilities, or whose parents have disabilities. Coaches will be expected to resolve all these issues for the players.

3) ALL KIDS WILL PLAY FOOTBALL AT A PROFICIENT LEVEL!

4) Talented players will be asked to work out on their own, without coaching. This is because the coaches will be using all their instructional time with the athletes who aren't interested in football, have limited athletic ability, or whose parents don't like football.

5) Games will be played year-round, but statistics will only be kept in the 4th, 8th, and 11th games. Teams that do not play out the games that do not have statistics kept will be subjected to the standards in #1, above.

Remember, if no player gets ahead, then no player will be left behind. Parents who dislike this system will be encouraged to vote for voucher schools, and to support private schools that will screen out the non-athletes and prevent their children from having to go to school with bad football players.

— Author Unknown

The education of our schoolchildren nationwide has become quite truncated and all for the sake of the pursuit of the "almighty standardized test score." Even in my own school district, the scope and sequences of our core academic subjects are tighter than a fat lady's girdle, as they dictate to teachers precisely what curriculum is to be taught, the manner in which it is to be taught, exactly when it is to be taught on a week-by-week basis, and precisely how it is to be tested and evaluated with district common assessments, etc. While this highly structured and regimented policy of curriculum delivery and student assessment may propagate uniform compliance to state standards throughout the district's schools, it also de-emphasizes the thorough incorporation of time-honored and highly successful pedagogical components of creativity and higher-level thinking skills in the lesson plans of teachers that would otherwise include—but not be limited to—the following: problem-solving, complexity, depth, novelty, acceleration, evaluation, analysis, synthesis, point-of-view, and synectics (the joining together of different, unrelated elements); and the icons of depth and complexity that embrace scholarly pursuits in children, such as language of the discipline, topics across disciplines, topics as they relate over time, multiple perspectives, big ideas, ethics, unanswered questions, trends, rules, patterns and details. *NCLB* also fails to take into consideration the important fact that children acquire and display their mastery of knowledge and standards through the use of multiple intelligences that cannot possibly be measured on standardized tests; these intelligences include the following: linguistic, logical mathematical, spatial, musical, bodily-kinesthetic, interpersonal, and intrapersonal intelligences. Any excellently trained and experienced veteran teacher worthy of respect will incorporate the aforementioned pedagogical elements into his or her lesson plans despite the constrictions of *NCLB*, yet many **new** teachers to the profession are not being adequately trained in these vital teaching techniques due to the lack of state funding as well as the truncated and myopic approach *NCLB* places on the education and testing of our children. This is ultimately what transpires when the federal government unconstitutionally intrudes upon the education of the nation's schoolchildren!

Many of us veteran teachers truly bemoan the fact that as a nation, we are turning our kids into nothing but factoid automatons who may potentially qualify as future contestants on the television prime-time game show Jeopardy. But regurgitating facts impressively and in a timely manner on some high-tech trivia game board does not necessarily make for a well-rounded, highly educated individual. One may be able to win some fast bucks on such a game show, but in today's complex society, our children certainly need to effectively demonstrate mastery of most of the other essential skills mentioned in the previous paragraph in order to compete and survive in today's dog-eat-dog world. The ability to regurgitate a bunch of relevant facts and knowledge before one's boss is one thing, but it will be problematic if a person lacks the necessary skills to demonstrate creativity, to analyze and apply relevant facts to one's task, to engage in effective problem-solving, or to cooperatively work with one's peers or one's team in order to accomplish difficult tasks on a strict corporate time schedule. Simply put, recalling facts, figures, and other data isn't everything! America's corporations are already expressing deep concern with this dilemma as well as frustration with the fact that a number of our students who are graduating from both high school and college are ill-prepared for such demanding tasks that are required of them in today's workforce. The veteran teachers of this nation could just as easily have warned our federal politicians that such would be the case because of *NCLB*, but then what do we know? We should just continue to shut up and obediently goosestep to the marching orders of the know-it-alls in Washington, DC, correct?

I would like to take the time to address a few other controversial issues concerning public education because the following issues have been given considerable attention in the news, and they have also been topics of heated discussion and debate for quite some time now.

Controversy #1: Should we adopt merit pay for teachers?

The controversy surrounding merit pay being used as an evaluation tool and method for compensating public school teachers is quite fascinating. The vast majority of conservative politicians that I have seen interviewed on the subject definitely come down on the side of a resounding "yes" with regard to this question. Even President Obama and other liberal politicians have recently expressed their own desire to implement some form of merit pay in our nation's schools. Therefore, this particular issue currently transcends partisan politics. Here is where I stand on this issue.

I am personally not in favor of merit pay for teachers because it does not take into consideration certain germane factors. For example, when I instructed honors English and honors American history classes for seven years at a middle school in my school district, I instructed seventy highly motivated youngsters on the eighth-grade honors team every year who had very high academic expectations for themselves—as did their parents. Of those seventy students, on a year-to-year basis, 95 percent of them consistently earned A's and B's in English and history, and the majority of them scored at the advanced level on standardized tests. Rarely would there exist a case wherein homework was submitted late or not submitted at all because such negative attributes were simply not part of the proclivity of these students. Certainly, this was to be expected, since the students were enrolled in honors classes.

On a merit pay system, I would have been paid a higher salary or bonus over that of regular education teachers because, naturally, the standardized test scores of my accelerated students would rank significantly higher when compared to the scores of students in regular education classrooms. Does that mean that I worked any harder than my colleagues, or that I necessarily put in longer hours at both school and at home grading papers and preparing lesson plans, or that I was necessarily a better, more competent teacher? My own answer to these questions would be "no."

In addition, regular education teachers' classrooms are filled to capacity with the following categories of students: those students who are still in the process of learning to read, write, and speak English (ELL); students who are diagnosed with learning disabilities in either language arts or math that require teachers to modify such students' lessons and assessments due to their IEPs (individualized educational programs—Special Education); students who must have their lessons and assessments modified to meet the legal requirements of their 504 plans (as per the two federal laws, The Rehabilitation Act of 1973 and Americans With Disabilities Act of 1990); students who are high achieving; GATE (Gifted and Talented Education) and underachieving GATE students; average and below-average students; an alarming and explosive growth of students who are diagnosed with various degrees of autism, including those high-functioning autistic students who often experience emotional "meltdowns" in the classroom; students with Asperger's Syndrome; students with ADD (attention deficit disorder) or ADHD (attention deficit hyperactive disorder); students who have other physical disabilities whose medical needs must now be serviced by regular education teachers rather than medically trained professionals; and last, but certainly not least, students who are dysfunctional and display disruptive behavioral problems within all of the above categories. If politicians and the general public were to step foot in today's classrooms for a few consecutive days and not just fleeting staged moments, they might actually come away with a greater appreciation and understanding as to what public school teachers are up against in today's educational environment! The above working environment is by no means an exaggeration. My colleagues and I face this reality on a daily basis, and despite all of this, we still remain faithful and dedicated public servants who continue to teach all of these students with a passion, despite the fact that we are recipients of unrelenting criticism and diatribes spewed forth by politicians and other critics of public education!

Now, bear in mind, all of the above categories of children are to be found sitting together in the same classrooms like one big happy family, while teachers are doing their level best to meet the educational needs, emotional needs, physical and medical needs, and the legal requirements of all of these children combined because our politicians, judges, parents, civil rights activists, and school administrators—in their infinite wisdom—contend it is in everyone's best interest to group all of these students together in a one-size-fits-all educational environment! And teachers' compensation should supposedly be directly linked to the test results of all of these various categories of students as if their achievements should miraculously produce **equal outcomes** on all of their standardized test scores? Perhaps the general public and politicians might finally "get it" and come to an understanding, or at least some degree of appreciation, as to why the vast majority of teachers—be they conservative or liberal—are opposed to merit pay.

There is another way to look at this merit pay approach to compensating teachers. Since the current compensation and benefit packages of public school teachers are incessantly compared to that of the private sector, let us make a comparison between public education and business as we journey down that path for a short while! Suppose a small business entrepreneur is entirely dependent upon the productivity of all of his employees as a necessary requisite for him to remain competitive and generate the greatest profits possible. What would happen to an employee if he were to habitually arrive to work tardy, if he were to chronically miss work for a variety of reasons, if he were to perform his assigned duties with a bad attitude and huge chip on his shoulder, or if he were complicit in failing to perform his duties to the owner's expectations because of sheer laziness? Such an individual would deservedly be terminated because if he weren't, the business owner would lose customers, which would decrease his profit margins. Nobody would blame any businessman for terminating such a substandard employee, nor would anyone force him to retain such an ineffective and nonproductive individual in the hope that said employee might get his proverbial act together. Naturally, any employer who desires to make a serious go of his business could not possibly countenance a myriad of excuses as to why such an ineffective employee should remain in his hire because if he were to foolishly do so, such a business owner would not be operating in the black for any significant length of time, and his business would eventually come to a screeching halt.

Likewise, it would be logical to assume that if public school teachers were to have their compensation packages strictly linked to the standardized test results of students who are exhibiting the exact same characteristics described above with the business owner's problem employee, such scores would negatively impact the profitability of teachers' income. However, here is the prime difference when comparing the two. Public school teachers currently do not have the legal means or the luxury of "terminating" or removing failing and underperforming students within their classrooms if such students do not attend school regularly, or if they are habitually tardy throughout the year, or if they fail to do their homework or don't bother to study for their tests. If teachers could remove such students from their classrooms and place them in alternative educational facilities, their test scores would skyrocket. These are but a few of the "external factors" Thomas Sowell alluded to in his article when he illustrated that students need to take responsibility for their own efforts in school and shoulder the negative consequences should they fail to carry their own weight over the course of thirteen years. Politicians of both political parties love to bark at the American people just like a bunch of annoying, snipping Chihuahuas that teachers' compensation and benefit packages need to reflect that of the private sector and, therefore, all teachers should be placed on some type of merit pay scheme as if we were running our own businesses. Yet isn't it quite convenient that we are not legally permitted to operate by the same rules of engagement that are afforded the private sector? All of this may sound good and make for good politics while providing talking points for a bunch of dunderheads who are truly ignorant of today's realities in the nation's classrooms, but the truth is, comparing public education to the private sector in this regard is the equivalent of trying to compare apples to oranges.

As I stated earlier in this chapter, teachers do not pursue a career in the field of public education with the hope that we will one day become the most affluent amongst us as a result of our commitment to educating America's children. We wish we were paid the same bloated salaries together with the Cadillac health benefits for life, the lavish pensions, and the perks all of our state and national politicians receive for their public service, but that is never going to occur—nor should it—because the American public simply cannot afford to pay for this through taxation. However, teachers deserve to be adequately and fairly compensated for putting in their time earning and paying for their expensive professional college degrees, for their hard work in juggling the numerous and daunting obstacles they are compelled to confront on a daily basis in today's classrooms, and for their years of valuable accumulated teaching experience while serving in the nation's public schools. Indeed, adequate and fair compensation is open to interpretation and is also in the eye of the beholder. Yet providing decent and competitive compensation packages for public school teachers is not too much to ask of the public—provided we are doing our jobs to the best of our ability in the classrooms. The solution to dealing with poorly performing or incompetent teachers is to see to it that they are ultimately terminated and replaced, but we should not punish the entire profession by reducing educators' compensation packages in general or by implementing merit pay schemes as a panacea for dealing with all of the ills within the profession.

The American people repeatedly hear politicians of both the federal and state governments pounding the drumbeat, proclaiming that if our young students desire to pursue careers that provide excellent and competitive salary packages, then they had best seek a college education with advanced degrees. Fair enough. However, why should the teaching profession be exempt from this? It requires a minimum of five to six years for an individual to attend college full time—including a semester of unpaid student teaching—in order to earn a preliminary teaching credential. This is both very expensive and time consuming, and there are many other hoops teachers must jump through at their own time and expense in order to obtain a clear teaching credential, not to mention a master's degree in education in order to advance on the pay scale. Given the current climate of discontent being exhibited towards teachers in general, the politicians and public would probably prefer that teachers work for minimum wage as if we were employees of some fast food restaurant, but that is never going to occur, ladies and gentlemen! Teachers are professionals who possess college degrees and professional credentials just like medical doctors, attorneys, dentists, accountants, etc., and we should be compensated with competitive wages and benefit packages as are other highly educated professionals. In addition, the vast majority of teachers carry their own weight in their respective communities—volunteering their spare time to work for a variety of local organizations as well as supporting the local, state, and national economies through our taxes and consumer spending. Furthermore, we occupy a very important niche in American society, especially given the fact that there are some choice moments when teachers feel we are actually teaching in classrooms occupied by a number of children of the likes of Morticia and Gomez Addams or Lily and Herman Munster. Thank the good Lord that we also have classrooms occupied by very sweet, well-behaved, and conscientious students who are supported by very caring and loving parents, or there simply would not be so much as a single soul who would be willing to enter the teaching profession and put up with all of the hogwash that is currently demanded of us, and that is the God-honest truth!

Indeed, for the most part, teachers in my own school district do earn adequate compensation as well as decent health and retirement benefits, but such benefits are really not so lavish or as posh as pundits try to make them out to be. The annual reports my wife and I receive from the privately run State Teachers Retirement Service (STRS) reveal that we will, on average, receive approximately 60 percent of our current salaries upon retirement, certainly not

100 percent as some pundits and cynics like to fabricate. Maybe I'm unreasonable, but I don't believe that 60 percent is either lavish or unfair for our decades of devotion and public service to the nation! When I recently looked at our pay warrants, I verified that we contribute 8 percent of our gross income into private retirement accounts (STRS) while my school district contributes an additional 8.2 percent. This is very similar to what was required of us when we worked in the private sector for a number of years. During the 1960s, 1970s, and most of the 1980s, we contributed a percentage of our monthly income that was required by the federal government into our personal Social Security accounts, while our private-sector employers contributed matching percentages into the same accounts. This is money we will most likely never see during our retirement because over the decades, the federal government has misappropriated and misused the Social Security trust fund, driving it into insolvency! Personally, I interpret this looming scenario to be not only a serious breach of trust between the American people and the federal government, but outright theft, fraud, and malfeasance of duty on the part of politicians who are responsible for this imminent fiscal disaster. In this author's humble opinion, such politicians are deserving of some serious jail time in a federal penitentiary.

Teachers in my school district are also required to render a portion of their monthly salaries unto Caesar in the form of payments toward the premiums of our health care provider as well as for Medicare. Once my wife and I reach the age of sixty-five, we will no longer be covered by our school district health benefit plan. We will be dependent on Medicare at that point just like everyone else, and we will also need to supplement Medicare with an additional medical plan of our choice and pay for it out of our own retirement income once we retire. That should dispel once and for all the wild rumors flying about implying that teachers will retire with pension plans that pay 100 percent of their salaries while they were teaching, or that we will retire with Cadillac health benefits until the macabre Grim Reaper pays us a mercurial visit.

In addition, we have taken our own hits financially during these hard economic times like everyone else. We have seen our incomes reduced significantly by having to take furlough days as a result of shortened school years because of the financial crisis in California, so we are certainly doing our part in making the necessary sacrifices just like everyone else is in the private sector, including the paying of higher state and federal income taxes as well as having to cope with the effects of inflation. Our homes have lost significant value, our privately run retirement accounts that are independently managed by the STRS have taken tremendous hits financially due to the wild speculation and peaks and valleys of the Stock Market, and we have seen our personal estates wither at the vine through no fault of our own just like other Americans. In addition, many teachers are losing their jobs, at least in California, and they are feeling the pinch just like our fellow citizens in the private sector. We are certainly not immune to the fiscal realities that are staring all of us in the face.

It must also be clarified that the vast majority of teachers do not receive any compensation for working beyond our contract day. Most professionals who work overtime on evenings and weekends, such as firemen and police officers (to cite just a couple of examples), are handsomely compensated for their overtime work, but such is certainly not the case with the majority of teachers. For example, I personally log in a minimum of 500 to 700 extra hours per school year as the assistant choral director at the high school where my wife teaches, and I receive absolutely no compensation whatsoever from my school district for these extra hours, even though I am school board approved as the assistant choral director! Now, I am not whining, as no school administrator is holding a gun to my head forcing me to do so. I am simply stating the facts as they truly are. And such is the case with most teachers who devote uncompensated time on evenings and weekends grading papers and projects as well as working to assist and supervise students in a variety of extracurricular endeavors.

Because of the specific time demands required of her job, my wife does receive a paltry stipend from our school district in her capacity as a high school choral director for the 700 extra hours per year she works beyond her contract day during evenings, the weekends, and even holiday breaks. My wife and I have sat down together and actually done the math in order to calculate the precise amount of money she earns for her overtime work, and the results are most pathetic. If she were to be paid by the hour with her overtime stipend, she would be earning only $7.42 per hour for her extra time and effort! So much for the accusations of greed and avarice that have been leveled against public school teachers most recently by a number of critics! Try to convince other professionals such as firemen and policemen to work for that pitiful wage for the overtime hours they put on the time clock. Even nonunion workers would balk at that rate of compensation, unless the nation was engulfed in a full-scale economic depression! The general public as well as our state and national politicians also tend to look the other way or choose to ignore the fact that teachers continually pony up various amounts of out-of-pocket funds over the course of their careers to purchase materials with which to supplement the curriculum as well as the various items needed to attractively decorate their classrooms. For example, my own classroom is adorned with approximately $3,000 worth of extra books, furniture, and decorations that I have provided at my own expense over the years in order to provide my history students with a very attractive and professional environment in which to work.

I am also opposed to merit pay for public school teachers for the following important reasons: The previous chapter went into considerable detail concerning the devastating impact fatherless homes and the breakdown of the traditional family unit are having upon children and American society as a whole. Children who are the victims of divorced parents and fatherless homes struggle a great deal more in school when compared to children being raised by both biological parents. The statistics and studies bear this out. Far too many of these children being raised by single parents suffer with a significantly higher degree of severe depression, higher suicide rates, higher pregnancy rates, greater antisocial behavior, lackluster academic progress in school, lower self-esteem, involvement in gang activities, etc. Add to that factual scenario a certain element of youth culture that exhibits alarming traits of laziness, chronic absenteeism, a sense of entitlement, apathy, and other external circumstances that teachers have absolutely no control over, and one might better appreciate why most teachers would resent having their compensation packages tethered to the test scores of students coming from many of these dysfunctional circumstances and who bring such negative external factors with them into the classrooms.

For some very peculiar reason, America has forgotten the fact that the primary function of teachers in school is to **"instruct"** curriculum and **"evaluate"** student progress. Indeed, teachers should also strive to the best of their ability to encourage and motivate their students to excel academically to the greatest extent possible, and some teachers do a better job at this than others. We are not, however, miracle workers or demigods, and last I heard, we have not collectively been bestowed with the title of "Sainthood" by the Pope in Rome or with the ceremonial title of "Knighthood" by Queen Elizabeth II in London, England. I will remind every American of the old adage that states, "You can lead a horse to water, but you can't make him drink from it." Thus, I am going to beat this dead horse one more time in the hope that it will finally sink in with those who choose to continually scapegoat this nation's public school teachers for most of the nation's woes, especially with regard to education.

Once again, teachers cannot control all of the various negative external factors children bring into our classrooms, as was pointed out by the conservative commentator, Thomas Sowell, nor should we unrealistically be held accountable for the absence of intrinsic motivation with at least a third of today's student population. As teachers, we cannot force the students to complete their homework, we cannot force them to attend school regularly, and we cannot force them to study at home for their quizzes and tests because we are not their parents. We are their teachers, no more, no less! Simply put, at some point, and the teachers of this nation certainly hope it is in the very near future, poorly behaved miscreants as well as lazy students must ultimately be held responsible for their own actions and academic failure, and many of their irresponsible parents must also be held accountable for their own poor judgment and atrocious child rearing tactics. In the overall scheme of things, ladies and gentlemen, very little will change for the better in America unless we all take responsibility for this as concerned and informed citizens—regardless of political persuasion. We must seize the auspicious moment and act decisively upon it. Our nation could have classrooms scattered about coast to coast, staffed with the most brilliant and highly educated teachers with multiple graduate degrees, and they could also be the world's best instructors, communicators, and entertainers. Yet it will not make a lick of difference if, as a society, we refuse to own up to this fact and ultimately affix blame where it primarily needs to be placed—namely, upon the backs and shoulders of students themselves as well as their parents. What has just been authoritatively stated by this author and experienced public school teacher will probably draw the ire of both liberals and conservatives alike because it is going to rock their boats, challenge their conventional way of thinking, and rattle many of their special-interest cages. Nevertheless, to metaphorically use the game of baseball as a comparison, it is about time the American people step up to the plate so we may collectively hit a home run of truth, proceed to run from base to base with boldness, and collectively sing an educational rendition of "Take Me Out to The Ball Game" before it is too late. The ninth inning is almost over!

Finally, it is definitely worth noting that we have some empirical evidence that indicates merit pay schemes have already failed in the state of Texas, which, by the way, is a conservative-leaning state. The *Dallas Morning News* reported, that "for the $300 million spent on merit pay for teachers over the last three years, Texas was hoping for a big boost in student achievement. But it didn't happen with the now defunct Texas Educator Excellence Grant (TEEG), according to experts hired by the state."[12] Researchers from Texas A&M University, Vanderbilt University, and the University of Missouri studied "flaws in the way the program was designed and did not conclude whether merit pay for teachers in general is a good idea." However, they did say, "There is no systematic evidence that TEEG had an impact on student achievement gains in Texas." The *Dallas Morning News* notes that TEEG, "which provided incentive pay for teachers at about 1,000 campuses a year in lower-income neighborhoods, was discontinued by the legislature after the 2008-09 school year because of design problems."[13]

The following profound anecdote pretty much summarizes everything I have had to say with regard to merit pay:

I MAKE A DIFFERENCE

The dinner guests were sitting around the table discussing life.

One man, a CEO, decided to explain the problem with education. He argued, "What's a kid going to learn from someone who decided his best option in life was to become a teacher?"

He reminded the other dinner guests what they say about teachers: "Those who can, do. Those who can't, teach."

To stress his point he said to another guest, "You're a teacher, Bonnie. Be honest. What do you make?"

Bonnie, who had a reputation for honesty and frankness replied, "You want to know what I make?" (She paused for a second, then began...)

"Well, I make kids work harder than they ever thought they could."

"I make a C+ feel like the Congressional Medal of Honor winner."

"I make kids sit through 50 minutes of class time when their parents can't make them sit for 5 without an I Pod, Game Cube or movie rental."

"You want to know what I make?" (She paused again and looked at each and every person at the table.)

"I make kids wonder."

"I make them question."

"I make them apologize and mean it."

"I make them have respect and take responsibility for their actions."

"I teach them to write and then I make them write. Keyboarding isn't everything."

"I make them read, read, read."

"I make them show all their work in math. They use their God given brain, not the man-made calculator."

"I make my students from other countries learn everything they need to know about English while preserving their unique identity."

"I make my classroom a place where all my students feel safe."

"I make my students stand, placing their hands over their hearts to say the Pledge of Allegiance to the Flag, One Nation Under God, because we live in the United States of America."

"Finally, I make them understand that if they use the gifts they were given, work hard, and follow their hearts, they can succeed in life."

(Bonnie paused one last time and then continued.)

"Then, when people try to judge me by what I make, with me knowing money isn't everything, I can hold my head up high and pay no attention because they are ignorant....You want to know what I make?"

"I MAKE A DIFFERENCE. What do you make Mr. CEO?"
His jaw dropped, he went silent.

— Author Unknown

Controversy #2: Should we eliminate seniority and tenure with public school teachers?

My reply to this question is this: Not entirely. Teacher seniority and tenure should be conditionally protected. Certain protections of seniority should apply to veteran teachers while other factors should be given consideration when granting a certain degree of latitude to school districts to terminate some senior teachers more easily when necessary, provided certain reasonable conditions are met. Again, there are germane factors that need to be taken into consideration with regard to this issue.

According to the Center for the Future of Teaching and Learning, 20 percent of all new teachers leave the classroom in California within three years because of stress, and in urban districts, 50 percent of new teachers flee during the first five years of teaching.[14] In addition, one third of the teacher force in California is approaching retirement age, and the state will need an additional 100,000 teachers over the next decade to replace those who are retiring.[15] As we reflect upon such sobering statistics, we must ask: how are we going to be successful with recruiting new college graduates into the teaching profession when teacher compensation is a significant deterrent to recruitment compared to other professions that require comparable education, training, and skills, yet pay significantly higher? Again, earning a college degree as well as the necessary teaching credential required for the teaching profession is both expensive and time consuming; therefore, what college graduate would seriously risk entering the profession if he knows he could be subject to the ax at any given moment—if he is not assured of some degree of job security on the part of his employer, especially as he ages and fulfills his required duties admirably and successfully? Now, certainly any commitment to job security is not a constitutional right by any means, whether it be applied to either the public or private sectors, but it is a factor potential recruits consider when making career decisions in the marketplace of competition. In addition, why would our youth be inspired to pursue such a thankless career, a career that is replete with unending criticism, disrespect, and controversy due to the dour disposition currently being displayed by our politicians and the general public towards the nation's public school teachers?

Veteran teachers in my own school district are very concerned with the following scenario: Over the past four years, our school district has been forced to eliminate approximately 30 million dollars from its operating budget due to the financial crisis California has been struggling through. School boards across the state are being compelled to deal with their bottom line, and that is: what precisely do they cut from their budgets? Naturally, the majority of any school district's budget is linked directly to its personnel. Veteran teachers, such as myself, are quite concerned that if school boards are given a free hand by our governors and state legislators to either ignore or eliminate altogether their seniority and tenure agreements with their teachers, they would effectively dismiss their most experienced teachers, not because of any supposed lackluster job performance in the classrooms, but because experienced veteran teachers are the most expensive to keep on the payroll when compared to new teachers hired directly out of college. Some might argue that school district administrators would not possibly be so callous as to recommend such drastic action be taken by their respective school boards. Oh, really? My own school district has already, on two occasions, offered our most experienced and senior teachers early retirement incentives and "golden handshakes" in order to save the district some very serious money so that it may retain less costly teachers who have only been working a few years in the school district. If anybody were to naïvely believe some district administrators and school boards throughout California, confronted with the difficult choices of making serious budget cuts, wouldn't dismiss or "sacrifice at the altar" veteran teachers when push came to shove in order to keep younger, inexperienced, and much cheaper teachers on the payroll, then I have a Brooklyn Bridge in New York City I would like to sell to such doubting Thomases for several million dollars!

On the other hand, school districts should be given some degree of latitude to remove a percentage of teachers with tenure and seniority who have become "dinosaurs" and are intransigent or remain closed-minded with regard to implementing new ideas and effective pedagogical strategies that are designed to help motivate today's students to excel in their academic studies. I have personally witnessed a small number of senior teachers at various school sites who have definitely overstayed their welcome and need to move on to greener pastures. They sometimes make no effort to remain team players on a school's staff and are resistant to new ideas as well as new technology, and the teachers' unions need to quit coddling and protecting such ineffective teachers. Teachers who have overstayed their welcome, however, should be examined and dealt with on a case-by-case basis. If negative empirical documentation of teacher malfeasance of duty exists within the personnel files of such offending teachers, then they should be escorted to the school gates in order to be given a proper and permanent bon voyage. This is not only fair, but it is absolutely necessary to preserve the integrity of the teaching profession. However, excellent veteran teachers who have been loyal employees of their respective school districts and have provided such districts many decades of faithful and effective service ought not be terminated and replaced by less expensive teachers simply because school boards need to make financial cuts to their budgets or prefer to keep a greater percentage of younger and less expensive teachers on their payrolls.

Controversy #3: Should we provide government funded

"vouchers" to parents who desire to send their children to private schools?

As a proud veteran public school teacher approaching almost three decades of dedicated public service, I must confess to the American people that I have been grappling with this particular issue during the course of the past several years while writing this book because I genuinely appreciate the arguments of both sides with regard to this highly controversial topic. Nevertheless, as far as this conservative educator is concerned, I must declare that I have crossed over to the **dark side and am now a willing advocate of the pro-voucher and school choice crowd.** No doubt, many of my progressive colleagues will probably think I am a traitor to public school education, and I can appreciate their position in this regard. However, the fact of the matter is this: I am not the public school educator who is a traitor to public education as I have served this profession faithfully and enthusiastically for several decades—and with great success, I might add! On the contrary, it is the secular liberals who are guilty of betraying public education for the following reasons:

First, it was the progressives who initially ignored the Constitution when they threw their enthusiastic support behind the federalization of public education during the Johnson Administration of the 1960s. This set in motion a series of events that contributed to the gradual decline of public education in this country as this author has discussed within the various chapters of this book. Second, the liberals are the ones who have used public school classrooms at all levels with which to promote their own political and social agendas for fifty years. The purpose of the school system is to instruct the core academic curriculum to our children, evaluate student progress, and prepare our children for college and the American workplace in order that they may function as productive and patriotic citizens within our society. It is not the purpose of public schools to be a functioning subsidiary of the Democratic Party that is actively infusing controversial topics within the curriculum, such as the promotion of gay marriage, global warming, and global citizenship, as well as advocating for the election of liberal politicians running for political office. In addition, public education should not be complicit in the instruction of an altered American history curriculum that downplays the importance of the Constitution as well as this nation's historical virtues of American exceptionalism. Third, the secular progressives have done everything in their power to diminish—if not outright abolish—the Judeo-Christian heritage that is embedded within the American culture and its sacred national holidays. Finally, liberals have ignored the fact that they are not just educating children of progressive parents, but conservative and independent parents as well. The curriculum should be free of political bias, yet liberals have turned a blind eye and a deaf ear to the legitimate needs and concerns of parents of various political persuasions while running roughshod over the concerns of such parents and their children who do not necessarily ascribe to liberal political and social issues. The sneaky agenda of the liberals is to use the public school system to convert all of America's children into thinking and behaving like little devout Democrats who will then proceed to grow up to be big devout Democrats, and the pathetic truth is this: Their agenda is working. Secular progressives have had a monopoly on education in this nation at all levels—from kindergarten all the way through college—for way too many decades, and we have finally progressed to a point where this must come to a grinding halt. Progressives are not only contributing to the serious decline of our public schools, but they are contributing significantly to the decline of the rest of the country as well. The tragedy of all of this is the fact that conservative, independent, and moderate Americans are simply permitting radical liberal judges, liberal special-interest groups, liberal politicians, liberal teachers and their unions, and liberal parents to get away with all of this chicanery!

If all of the nation's public schools were reflective of the district I am currently employed with, we would certainly have no need for vouchers as the vast majority of parents in my school district are pleased with our schools—even conservative parents. Our school district is certainly not perfect, but many people deliberately choose to make the city where I reside their home because of the excellent quality and reputation of our schools. The same is true for the majority of public schools throughout Orange County in Southern California—a very conservative county within our state. As such, all I can really accomplish for the reader at this particular point is to reflect upon the conflicting, yet legitimate viewpoints of both sides of the voucher debate, as well as continue to explain to the American public why it is I am for vouchers and school choice. In addition, I will propose a number of plausible solutions for the American people to take under serious consideration with regard to improving public education throughout our country.

Private schools operate independently of most state regulations, education codes, and most federal mandates. They establish their own criteria for the admission of potential students to their schools, and they determine the content of their own curriculum free from the interference of the government. Parents who enroll their children in private schools are usually required to sign contracts stating that they will support such schools and their teachers by seeing to it that their children behave during the school day. Parents of students in a number of private schools also need to agree that they will permit corporal punishment to be administered to their children by the principals when necessary, and such contracts make it abundantly clear that parents are to support and assist their children with their homework as well as foster good study habits with their children at home. Many private schools require their students to wear uniforms, and most private schools require parents to work a minimum number of predetermined volunteer hours every year on their campuses in order to assist the schools with whatever chores administrators deem to be necessary and in the best interest of all of their stakeholders. If parents do not agree to submit to such demanding terms, the schools have the freedom to deny their children admission to such educational facilities. Also, if the children and their parents do not consistently abide by the terms of the signed contracts, students can be removed from these private schools at the discretion of the administrators—at any time during the school year. When such a situation occurs, it then becomes incumbent on the part of parents to seek an alternative educational environment for their misbehaving and failing children to actively haunt, which is usually the nearest dumping ground—namely the neighborhood public school.

I have frequently observed former private schoolchildren sitting in my own classrooms over the years who, for a variety of reasons, have struggled academically with me as well. However, here is the telling difference. I do not have the luxury of going to my principal and unequivocally demand that poorly behaved or failing students be removed from my classroom should such students fail to measure up to my stringent academic standards and my high expectations of behavioral excellence. Public school teachers must pick up their crosses every school year and cope with all categories of students whether they like it or not! Would that teachers had the wonderful option at our disposal of having misfits removed from our classrooms, for our lives would be much easier to manage, our stress levels would diminish significantly, and we would be in much better physical and mental health!

Legislation has recently been passed by the California State Legislature that permits the following claptrap: Parents are now being given some element of authority to determine whether or not teachers and administrators can be terminated in their local public schools if they feel such educators are not doing a satisfactory job educating their children. On the face of it, this idea sounds good and quite reasonable. However, my reaction to such piffle is this: Fine, what is good for the goose is good for the gander! Are teachers and administrators going to be given reciprocal authority to initiate legally binding contracts between schools, their parents and their children, and in turn be permitted to kick students out of public schools should some parents fail to see to it that their children study at home, complete their homework on time, attend school regularly, achieve respectable grades, score minimally at the proficient level on standardized tests as required by the federal government, and behave properly at school? After all, this is totally expected of students and their parents in private schools with the exception of the requirements demanded by the federal government with regard to *No Child Left Behind*. Furthermore, are public school officials going to be permitted to make these decisions free from the threat and interference of bleeding-heart political sissies, of all frivolous lawsuits being brought to bear by the insidious ACLU, and of the incessant interference of know-it-all magistrates when parents whine, bellyache and cry "foul" or "discrimination?" Call me cynical if need be, but somehow I seriously doubt it!

Public school teachers and administrators in California **should** be permitted to make such decisions, but we will not be holding our breath, nor will we be chomping at the bit waiting for such reciprocal legislation to be handed down from the progressive or conservative cast of characters in Sacramento granting us such legal authority. If parents are going to be permitted to make decisions and take action of the aforementioned nature with regard to our schools, educators deserve to make similar decisions as well. Otherwise, I can safely predict that California will be facing a much greater teacher shortage in the very near future than already exists. No reasonable teacher in his or her right mind will tolerate this unfair, lopsided drivel for very long.

I have personally maintained for the majority of my teaching career that if parents choose to send their children to private schools, especially religious ones such as Christian, Catholic, or

Jewish academies, they should pay for the tuition of such schools out of their own pockets because private schools are not required to play by the same rules of engagement that are required of public schools, nor are private schools tethered to most of the same stringent federal regulations that legally hamstring our public schools. Having said that, however, I have complete empathy for conservative parents who are quite alarmed with the frightening direction many of our nation's progressive public schools are continually embarking upon, as evidenced by a number of contemptible examples that have been cited throughout this book.

For a brief period of just four years, my wife and I had enrolled our oldest daughter in our own church's private elementary academy during the late 1980s because it was our sincere desire for her to be instructed by teachers upholding Christian values, and we thought that the incorporation of Bible lessons within the core curriculum would be of tremendous value to her. After several years, however, we pulled Christa out of Christian school and reenrolled her in public school within our own school district because we were not at all content with the quality of education she was receiving with inexperienced and non-credentialed teachers in private school. By the time our daughter had reached the end of her fifth-grade year in Christian school, she was sorely deficient in the application of proper writing skills as well as higher-level thinking skills inherent with gifted and talented accelerated students. Fortunately, her sixth-grade public school teacher, a colleague of mine who was a real battle-ax if ever there was one, was able to quickly whip Christa back into shape academically—figuratively speaking that is. My daughter's formidable sixth-grade teacher didn't cut her any slack whatsoever! Christa's sixth-grade school year was most arduous to say the least, yet it was worth all of the trials and tribulations both she and her parents were required to endure during that particular stressful year.

My wife and I, through personal experience, ultimately came to the conclusion that the quality of education in private schools is not necessarily better than public schools, and neither is the behavior of all students attending Christian school. For example, when my wife and I cautioned Christa that the school environment of the public elementary school she would be attending in sixth grade would likely exhibit somewhat coarser attributes by its student population in comparison to Christian school—what with public schoolchildren frequently engaging in cussing on the playground as well as occasionally participating in fighting and bullying, etc.—she immediately and nonchalantly replied, "Dad, I heard cussing going on all of the time on the playground at private school, and you and Mom would be surprised to find out what occasionally occurred with the kids at Christian school!" At any rate, being a proud product of public education myself in both Montana and California, I subscribe to the belief that our society is better served when we learn to associate with and work with people of diverse cultural and religious backgrounds, and I fundamentally believe that to this day. I must confess that I probably lean a little bit more on the moderate side of that particular issue.

On the other hand, my wife and I and many of our conservative colleagues in public schools, are absolutely fed up with the federal government's illegal intrusion in the affairs of local education, and we are also appalled with the current course with which the United States is navigating, not only politically and educationally, but culturally and morally as well. For example, the liberal teacher unions, especially the California Teachers Association and the National Education Association, are dominated by pompous, leftist elitists, and they continually and unabashedly shove their liberal social agendas and policies down all of our throats whether we like it or not, and conservative teachers are forced against our wishes to pay dues to these unions that repeatedly support progressive candidates for political office who we definitely do not support! Conservative teachers, at least in the school district where I am currently employed, are also coping with prodigious bellyaches as a result of a

portion of our monthly dues being used by the California Teachers
Association to fund various television commercials that advocate
progressive social causes that are anathema to our own sincerely
held beliefs. I have been pleasantly surprised, to say the least, that
a number of my progressive colleagues have expressed to me in
private conversations, their concern not only with the political one-
sidedness that is evident with the teachers' unions, but also their
indignation with the proliferation of the "entitlement" mentality
within our schools, as well as the state and federal governments. I
have encouraged such individuals to ponder these facts when voting
in November of 2012. Many of us do have some measure of respect,
however, for our local union because at least its leadership over the
years has been willing to listen to politically diverse opinions for the
most part, and that is why I have personally volunteered to work
on various local union committees over the past several decades.

My local union is probably more responsive to the legitimate
concerns of its conservative teachers, even if it doesn't always agree
with the positions conservative teachers advocate, because it is the
one union that is directly accountable to all of us, liberal or conservative. To its great credit, my local teachers' union is not unrealistic
with regard to the harsh financial straits our school district is currently forced to contend with, courtesy of the state legislature and
governor. There is give-and-take on both sides of the bargaining
table, which is the way it should be, and that is one of the reasons
why there has never been a strike by the teachers in the community
where my wife and I proudly teach and reside. The teachers within
my school district are also not of the reprehensible mindset of many
of the teachers and other public employees recently showcased
before the American public in Madison, Wisconsin—behaving like
a bunch of spoiled thugs and bullies simply because they were being required by the governor of Wisconsin to contribute a portion
of their salaries to their own pensions and medical benefits! They
were a humiliating example for the rest of the nation to behold, and

I personally do not regard any of them to be colleagues of mine by any stretch of the imagination!

In the meantime, the state and federal governments continue to pursue educational policies that are, in the opinion of many conservative teachers and conservative parents, not only secular-progressive, but outright harmful to our nation's children. We are tragically witnessing the precipitous decline of the unique virtues of American exceptionalism consisting of patriotism, self-reliance, and a work ethic that once united this great nation regardless of one's political or religious affiliation. These remarkable attributes are no longer being emphasized and proudly celebrated as part of the regular curriculum in many of America's public schools when compared to what was taught to previous generations of American students. When my wife and I were growing up, we repeatedly participated in a variety of patriotic-oriented assemblies at school that promoted pride in our country and fostered an abiding respect for our Judeo-Christian heritage—yet today, such is often not the case. In addition, many of us question whether or not any of today's schoolchildren would even know the lyrics to traditional American patriotic songs such as *God Bless America, America the Beautiful,* or *The Battle Hymn of the Republic.* My generation was taught to sing these songs while we were attending public elementary school because they were an integral part of the school curriculum. Rarely do we hear schoolchildren singing such songs anymore, and I can't remember the last time I heard a local high school band playing other American patriotic band music at various school assemblies or evening school concerts—which begs the question, why not? Has the patriotic music of John Philip Sousa now been relegated only to the bands of our local cities or armed forces? Our public schools throughout the nation could learn a very important lesson from a remarkable teacher who is on the staff of Robinson High School in Little Rock, Arkansas. She had her high school students participate in the following activity as divulged in this inspiring true anecdote:

A Lesson That Should Be Taught in All Schools!

Back in September of 2005, on the first day of school, Martha Cothren, a social studies schoolteacher at Robinson High School in Little Rock, did something not to be forgotten.

On the first day of school, with the permission of the school superintendent, the principal and the building supervisor, she removed all of the desks out of her classroom.

When the first period kids entered the room they discovered that there were no desks.

Looking around, confused, they asked,

"Ms. Cothren, where are our desks?"

She replied, "You can't have a desk until you tell me what you have done to earn the right to sit at a desk."

They thought, "Well, maybe it's our grades."

"No," she said.

"Maybe it's our behavior." She told them, "No, it's not even your behavior."

And so, they came and went, the first period, second period, third period. Still no desks in the classroom.

By early afternoon television news crews had started gathering in Ms. Cothren's classroom to report about this crazy teacher who had taken all the desks out of her room.

The final period of the day came and as the puzzled students sat on the floor of the deskless classroom, Martha Cothren said, "Throughout the day no one has been able to tell me just what he/she has done to earn the right to sit at the desks that are ordinarily found in this classroom. Now I am going to tell you."

At this point, Martha Cothren went over to the door of her classroom and opened it.

Twenty-seven U.S. Veterans, all in uniforms, walked into that classroom, each one carrying a school desk. The Vets began placing the school desks in rows, and then they would walk over and stand alongside the wall.

By the time the last soldier had set the final desk in place, those kids started to understand, perhaps for the first time in their lives, just how the right to sit at those desks had been earned.

Martha said, "You didn't earn the right to sit at these desks. These heroes did it for you. They placed the desks here for you. Now, it's up to you to sit in them. It is your responsibility to learn, to be good students, to be good citizens. They paid the price so that you could have the freedom to get an education. Don't ever forget it."

The teacher received an award for this action in 2006 from the VFW.[16]

Conservative advocates of vouchers cite other concerns as to why they need educational alternatives for their children. As a nation, we are witnessing an alarming trend in the teaching of revisionist American history to our children with some textbooks emphasizing a progressive tilt as well as a world viewpoint of history and politics. To illustrate this very point, Texas was in the national forefront of a controversy involving the Texas State Board of Education (TSBOE) and its discussion of the framework of topics for the textbooks to be used in that state's public schools. Surprisingly, the fifteen members of TSBOE were dominated by conservatives, and they have finalized the language textbook publishers are to use to align their textbooks to current state standards. As is quite predictable, here is a partial list of suggestions advocated by the progressives serving on the TSBOE:

Removing references to Daniel Boone, General George Patton, Nathan Hale, Columbus Day, and Christmas.
Including the cultural impact of hip hop music, ACLU lawyer Clarence Darrow, and the Hindu holiday of Diwali.

Replacing the term "American" with "Global Citizen" – stating that students need to be shaped "for responsible citizenship in a global society" without any mention of citizenship in American society.
Replacing expansionism and free enterprise with imperialism and capitalism. [17]

While viewing a particular report on one of Texas's TSBOE proceedings on the Fox News Channel, I was quite amused when one of the liberal members of the TSBOE stormed out of one of the board's proceedings because the conservatives would not roll over, play dead, and simply cave to the demands of the progressives. Observing this outraged liberal lady storming out of the room in protest left me with a tremendous sense of personal pleasure and satisfaction. Now she knows **exactly** how we conservatives feel as we have had to endure for decades arrogant liberals turning a blind eye and deaf ear to issues which are important to us and our children, as well as having to endure progressive majorities running roughshod over the legitimate concerns of conservatives in our nation's schools. In any event, she is finally getting a little taste of her own medicine! Bravo, Texas!

In addition, we are also witnessing an appalling ignorance on the part of the American people in general as to their inability to accurately recall American historical facts and events, as well as the display of their increasing ignorance of the lasting influence and legacy our nation's Founding Fathers left us, especially with regard to the US Constitution. Remarkably, we have recently observed federal politicians parading their embarrassing and abject ignorance of American political science and geography before all of us on television by uttering flippant remarks publicly—attributing words that are found in the Declaration of Independence to the Constitution, arrogantly remarking to cable television news reporters that they do not "care" what our Constitution has to say with regard to the appropriate role the federal government serves in our republic, or shamefully displaying a woeful lack of knowledge of the Constitution itself.

One example I could cite is when Fox News recently reported on a particular incident whereby Democratic Senator Chuck Schumer of New York stated in an interview on CNN in 2011 that the federal government consists of three branches: the Senate, The House of Representatives, and the presidency. In the first place, both the Senate and the House of Representatives comprise one branch of the federal government, the Legislative Branch. What does Senator Schumer think the US Supreme Court and the federal courts of appeals belong to, an imaginary fourth branch? Perhaps Senator Schumer is somewhat confused about all of this as he has personally served in both chambers of Congress—when in reality the nation would have been better off had he never served in either chamber! Many of us find such ignorance on the part of elected officials who are entrusted by the American people to represent us in an intelligent manner to be most troublesome and embarrassing. Now these are the same officials who swear oaths of allegiance to the Constitution when they assume public office! Frightening, isn't it? No wonder federal politicians of the likes of Chuck Schumer are so willing to trample upon states' rights and their sovereignty and are more than content with crafting federal legislation that runs counter to the Constitution when such men and women are ignorant of the basic fundamental principles that are embedded within the very document they swear to uphold while serving in public office! Conservatives would be well within their right to call into question the quality of schools that matriculated such individuals during their adolescent and collegiate years. Were such progressive politicians educated in public schools, private schools, or both? Here are a few additional recent choice examples of both Democrat and Republican presidents that are worth sharing!

The American people were treated to another humiliating moment when former presidential candidate Barack Obama remarked publicly a few years back while campaigning in Beaverton, Oregon, that America has **fifty-seven states.** You are sorely mistaken Mr. President! America has only fifty states; therefore, this public school teacher gives you a failing grade in the area of American geography! Certainly every person is entitled to an occasional mistake now and then, since nobody is perfect, but for Pete's sake, our president should not be geographically illiterate, now should he? Then there is the fine and upstanding moment when on Friday, February 5, 2010, while speaking at the National Prayer Breakfast, President Obama repeatedly referred to Navy Corpsman Christian Brossard as **"Corpse-man."** I am sure the valiant men and women currently serving in our armed forces can take considerable solace and pride in the fact that their Commander-in-Chief is so well versed in military terminology and history!

If that were not bad enough, recall the following utterance once declared by former President George W. Bush as he spoke in Florence, South Carolina, on January 11, 2000: **"Rarely is the questioned asked: Is our children learning?"** Now bear in mind, these are the same gentlemen who dare to lecture the rest of us as to the quandary America currently finds itself in with regard to the current state of American public education. Well, if we were to look upon Presidents Obama and Bush as well as other state and federal politicians cited throughout this book as shining examples of what our nation's schools are currently producing—be they public or private—I would have to agree that our schools really are in decline. At any rate, we should be able to do much better as a nation with regard to electing more articulate men and women to political office! This is but one of many reasons as to why our nation is in serious decline: as a society, we are tolerating mediocrity at all levels. Shouldn't the American people, at the very least, hold such national figures to a much higher degree of educational standard and excellence—regardless of their political party? Honest to God, most of my eighth-grade history students have a better grasp of the Declaration of Independence, the US Constitution, and American geography than the several embarrassing political individuals just cited, and my history students can also speak proper English! Perhaps it is high time the American people propose a new amendment be added to the Constitution that would require every potential political candidate running for Congress and the presidency to pass—with flying colors—an extensive exam on the Declaration of Independence, the US Constitution, American history, American civics, and American geography before being permitted to campaign for public office, much less be elected to serve in public office. It is about time the American people give our politicians a taste of their own medicine: we could appropriately designate this new amendment The No Politician Left Behind Amendment.

The controversial issues being raised in this chapter definitely have a tremendous impact upon the education and general welfare of our children nationwide, and these issues are polarizing America and tearing our nation apart—so much so that I personally question whether or not it is too late for liberals and conservatives to come and reason together as to what is the best approach to educating our nation's children. Conservatives and liberals no longer see eye to eye on practically anything politically, economically, morally, or culturally. In addition, we are obviously no longer civil to one another with regard to our political differences, and this author and educator is certainly just as guilty of this as the next man on the street. Conservatives and progressives possess a disparate vision for America. We are on diametric ends of the philosophical and cultural spectrum to the point of absurdity, and we no longer share similar views as to what America's Constitution says or means with regard to the proper governance of our nation.

I have never personally witnessed such wide-scale anger, resentment, and disdain on the part of the majority of the American people towards our federal government as I have since the election of President George W. Bush in 2000 and the recent unforgivable display of the reprehensible Chicago-style "gangster parlor tricks" of Team Obama during the 111th Congress. From this author's perspective, the violent protests of college students against our nation's involvement in the Vietnam War of the turbulent 1960s, the ghastly Watergate scandal of President Richard Nixon and his corrupt administration during the 1970s, and the nation's collective disdain of President Jimmy Carter and his misguided policies of malaise and weak leadership during the 1970s all pale in comparison to how the majority of mainstream Americans are reacting to the policies and sophistry of our current "lead from behind" president as well as our inept and dysfunctional Congress. The current disdain being exhibited by mainstream Americans towards our federal government is eerily parallel to a couple of sobering and violent time periods in American history, and they are the Revolutionary War of the 1700s and the Civil War of the 1800s. Perhaps our current narcissistic politicians would do well to sit up and take notice, especially should our nation sink into fiscal calamity and anarchy of the type we are currently observing in Greece and other European countries. This author is certainly not advocating a reoccurrence of what transpired in America's distant past in 1775 and 1861, but if our current batch of politicians are woefully naïve as to what the American people are capable of doing in times of great distress, rightly or wrongly, then perhaps they had better spend some serious time reading and reflecting upon American history. It is worth repeating the famous quote by George Santayana: "Those who cannot remember the past are condemned to repeat it."

With regard to conservative educators and parents in this country, we are really becoming weary of and impatient with the callous indifference as well as the narrow-minded attitude and behavior being exhibited toward us by elite liberal "know-it-alls" who dominate the educational establishment at all levels—from kindergarten through college. We have simply had our belly fill of the progressive mantra that invokes the phrase "my way or the highway," as well as the obstinate and intolerant approach to how our public schools and universities should operate. It is as if all of these leftist paragons of supposed tolerance and diversity are totally oblivious of the fact that more than half of the parents of the children we teach throughout America are conservative socially and politically, yet it does not matter a pittance to any of them. The problem is that the vast majority of conservative parents simply cannot afford to fork over the thousands of dollars necessary to cover the cost of tuition required to send their own children to exclusive private schools, and that is why they are seeking vouchers to assist them with sending their children to alternative schools that represent their own ideals and values. Isn't it both ironic and quite hypocritical how liberal politicians at the state and federal levels have enough confidence in our public schools to spout all kinds of praise and platitudes of support for public school teachers and their liberal teachers' unions while the rest of us are supposed to look the other way when such liberals choose to send their own children to some of the most expensive and most exclusive private schools and preparatory boarding schools throughout the nation? As I recall, President Obama and his wife send their own two daughters to the exclusive and very expensive Sidwell Friends School in the Washington, DC, area, which charges their clients an annual tuition fee of $35,000 per child. President Obama and his liberal cohorts in government have the audacity to feign support for our public schools, so why the hell are they not good enough for their own children? What a double standard and sham being foisted upon the American people!

However, God forbid that conservative parents with less financial means be provided the same choice with their own children, especially given the present deplorable state of the nation's economy. And those parents who can afford the luxury of sending their children to similar exclusive private schools pay double in the form of their taxes being used to finance public education, while at the same time, they are compelled to pony up the funds necessary to pay the tuition for private school education without so much as being given the opportunity to deduct such private school expenses from their federal and state income taxes! At least when wealthy conservative politicians and their cohorts send their own children to exclusive private schools and academies, they don't pretend to conceal their contempt for public schools. Their general diatribe against public education is front and center for all of the American people to see on a daily basis. Even though conservative educators, such as me, occasionally disagree with this vocal bunch and **some** of their unrelenting and unfair castigation of public education, at least we know exactly where they stand. Hence, we have to give them some measure of credit for their transparency, unlike the disingenuous Democrats.

For seven years, I had the pleasure of working for a dynamic middle school principal by the name of Dr. Marilyn Kemple. Whenever teachers sat in her office to complain about some problematic situation at school, she would often respond, "Before I help you, I want you to come up with a possible solution to your own problem." I always thought there was tremendous wisdom and value in what she demanded of us. In the spirit of what this principal taught me, here are some of my own solutions as to how we might "fix" the current problems facing public education in America. You might recall that earlier in this chapter, I cautioned everyone to "stay tuned" for such suggestions. Well, some of these proposals, if given the opportunity to come to fruition, are going to be quite controversial as they will actually require all of us—regardless of the political party we are members of—to stroll onto the national stage, face the music, and replay a delightful ditty entitled, "Some Very Tough Love," a tune that was once played jointly by both Democrats and Republicans in our great nation! Only then will we actually begin to solve many of these huge problems that we have collectively created rather than dancing around them, conjuring up useless spells while pretending that these problems will somehow magically dissipate in the middle of the night. The progressives would certainly come to the stage kicking and screaming all the way, but they have had a monopoly on the control of public education for more than their fair share of time in this country's history. It is about time for conservatives to rise to the challenge, come up with some plausible solutions that do not penalize or scapegoat the nation's teachers, take control of the situation, and be given the opportunity to prove to the American people that public education can once again thrive in an environment we can all be proud of. Here are seven possibilities:

1. Before we actually resort to implementing "vouchers" for private schools, perhaps we can solve some of the problems confronting public school educators and parents within the purview of the public sector. Parents are deserving of some reasonable "choice" or options for their children. For example, there are many outstanding public charter schools around that are operating quite similarly to private schools regarding high academic and behavioral expectations of both students and their parents. Many of these charter academies are requiring parents and students to sign contracts while strictly enforcing them just like private schools do. We can continue to expand and fund such specialty charter schools in all of our school districts. We could also give more serious consideration to those school districts that would like to operate "magnet" schools of specialized instruction that target the specific needs of different categories of children rather than mainstreaming all of them into a "one-size-fits-all" educational environment.

2. The outdated agrarian structural design currently in place throughout America's schools at all educational levels that reflects a "one-size-fits-all" model is no longer feasible as it once was in our society. As this book has effectively illustrated, our society has changed dramatically over the past fifty years. Our state legislatures

and governors should establish entirely new approaches and methods towards the operation of its schools that will serve as paradigmatic models of change, innovation, and excellence. For example, many conservative teachers truly believe that students who fall within the debilitating categories previously mentioned within this chapter need to be separated from the majority of regular education students within our schools and be assigned to alternative schools designed especially for them and their educational and emotional needs. They are students who match the following profiles: those students who are consistently failing a majority of core academic classes because of outright laziness, apathy, and deliberate choice; those students who are dysfunctional and continually pose discipline problems for teachers in the classrooms; those students who choose to deal drugs on campus and abuse illegal substances while attending school and are under the supervision of probationary officers; those students who are habitually fighting, bullying, and exhibiting other symptomatic violent tendencies typical of what we see with street gangs and thugs; those students who are repeatedly defiant and disrespectful of school officials; those students who choose to engage in sexual acts and other deviant behavioral proclivities while on school premises; and those students who continually infringe upon the civil rights and proper education of regular students who really do take their schooling seriously and desire to excel in school, free of all of the mayhem being perpetrated by the aforementioned categories of misfits.

The removal of such miscreants from a regular school campus would apply to all students regardless of race, gender, family income, social status, etc. In other words, there would be absolutely no exceptions made for any student who falls within any of the debilitating categories listed above. All of us would be required to play by the same rules and adhere to the same standards. Accurate, documented records compiled by school authorities on such dysfunctional students would serve as empirical evidence proving that they should be expeditiously enrolled in publicly funded reformatory schools within every school district. Over a reasonable amount of time, any student who chooses to get his act together—one who sincerely strives to earn his ticket out of reformatory school by pulling his own weight in school, earning respectable grades, behaving respectfully and responsibly, etc.—could be given a second chance to reenroll in a regular public school and function in a normal environment. Otherwise, offending students of the categories aforementioned would remain in alternative educational facilities until graduation from high school. There would exist no third or fourth chances for these types of students.

Parents, who happen to be the taxpayers funding public education in the first place, have a reasonable right to expect that their children will be permitted to attend school free of most of the negative influence of the riffraff that is currently present in all of our schools, even the very best ones. Such riffraff is consuming an inordinate amount of time and attention of schoolteachers, counselors, and administrators. These students are wasting precious resources that could be better spent on the education of those students who sincerely desire to apply themselves in school. I will emphatically reiterate: **parents have an absolute right to send their children to public schools that are basically free of such riffraff because their taxes ought to be paying for this.** Can one possibly fathom what could be accomplished in all of our public schools if regular, decent, conscientious, and industrious children were permitted to attend school liberated of the negative influence of the very miscreants they are forced to cope with on a daily basis? In addition, the American people should seriously consider the following salient point: Forcing our children to cope with these punks on a daily basis over a period of thirteen years is a prime example of societal child abuse! As concerned and compassionate citizens who are supposed to advocate for the general welfare of all of our children, we absolutely owe to the 70 percent of

America's children who are decent and hard-working students the opportunity to thrive and succeed in an educational environment free of all hoodlums, deviants, and lazy miscreants. It is about time for the American taxpayers to unequivocally rise up and demand this of their state legislatures and governors! Enough is enough! We have simply acquiesced long enough to the philosophy, desires, whims, laws, and demands of the bleeding-heart progressives who have had it their own way with our children in the public school arena for the past fifty years—just like a bunch of spoiled and pampered brats! The time has finally arrived for spoiled conservative brats to have it their way with our nation's schools for a change!

3. We could recruit retired and active duty military personnel to help facilitate reformatory schools in all school districts, grant them emergency teaching credentials, and give them a reasonable free hand to instill some old-fashioned, military-style discipline in students by permitting them to legally and literally kick some "unruly butts." Students assigned to these schools would be required to wear military uniforms, and they would be educated in a very strict and highly regimented environment—much like a military prep school for young boys and girls. These students would be taught the core academic basics, they would be required to pass standardized tests, and they would be required to participate in school-wide activities and assemblies that would instill in them the virtues of patriotism, self-discipline, personal initiative, and hard work. Military-style physical activity such as marching and community service would also be required of all students. When necessary, students attending these schools would be subject to reasonable corporal punishment to be administered by designated school officials. If anybody could possibly accomplish this Herculean feat with any degree of success, it would be our retired and active duty men and women of the armed forces together with those civilian teachers desiring to work under their auspices. In my professional opinion, this is the final hope and chance we have left at

our disposal as a nation if we are to truly reach these students and save them from themselves and their self-destructive tendencies, especially since their parents have failed miserably to do so at home.

A very interesting development would occur as a result of all fifty states implementing this plan in every school district throughout America. I can assure the American people that if students and their parents were keenly aware of the fact that these types of very strict schools were viable certainties in their respective communities, we would actually observe significantly improved academic effort being brought to bear by much of our troubled youth as well as better deportment being exhibited by many of these chumps who are presently taking school and society for granted. Furthermore, I am willing to bet that many discouraged parents of such students would be exceedingly grateful to society ad infinitum by having their unruly kids carted off to such schools. As a nation, why not be bold and daring and give alternative reformatory military schools a gander? After all, we certainly have nothing to lose by doing so, as the current status quo in the majority of our schools is certainly not working.

4. President Obama's grandiose *Race to the Top* pipe dream, which proposes that 100 percent of our nation's children need to attend college and excel in math and science in order to succeed and be proactive citizens in a "global" society, is as farcical as George W. Bush's *No Child Left Behind Act,* with its ridiculous goal of having 100 percent of our nation's children being proficient (mastery level) in reading, language arts, and math by the year 2014! To put it bluntly, not every student is college material nor is every student college bound, and not every student should be required to attend college unless he or she truly desires to do so. Our high schools should definitely be equipped to handle a greater number of elective classes to meet the needs of those students who are not college bound. We desperately need to have sophisticated "vocational trade schools" and "technology trade schools" in operation

once again in every school district so that we may effectively train and equip high school students with the necessary knowledge and skills to survive in blue-collar careers that provide us with vital services such as auto mechanic technicians, plumbers, electricians, construction workers, warehouse workers, hair stylists and beauticians, chefs, truck drivers, service industry workers, and factory workers producing a plethora of manufactured products made in America. All of our high schools need to develop partnerships with such blue-collar businesses so that students can apprentice with these trades in order to transition into the workforce. Some people are better suited to laboring more productively with their hands in a traditional "blue-collar" work environment rather than a "white-collar" or professional environment. We have most definitely lost sight of this fact in America.

On a related note, many Americans will never completely understand why it is that hundreds of our nation's factories need to be sitting idle in our cities while we are sending practically all of our manufacturing needs overseas to China and India, propping up their economies and military-industrial complexes while we are experiencing high unemployment right here at home! We are de-industrializing America to the detriment of our own country. Our nation used to be the world's standard-bearer with regard to its manufacturing industries and creative acumen as well as our entrepreneurial prowess. It goes without saying that it is now cheaper and more profitable for various companies to outsource their work to other nations as a result of their cheap labor; however, this is ultimately not in America's best interest economically, nor is it in the best interest of our own labor force. We had better wake-up and smell the coffee before it is too late.

America is currently in serious decline, in part because we have our heads buried in the sand regarding this important issue. Donald Trump's new book, *Time to Get Tough*, hits a home run with regard to confronting this topic, and Trump's new book should be read by every American! Our government officials in Washington, DC, as well as our corporate CEOs on Wall Street had better face the reality that we are in dire trouble as a nation. We desperately need to put our own people back to work, and we need to quit stoking the economies of China and India in the name of making a quick salutary buck at the expense of our own people and national well-being. Many Americans would prefer to purchase products that are manufactured once again in our own back yard, even if such goods happen to be more expensive than those coming from China.

We have often heard politicians of both political parties quip that these blue-collar jobs are not returning and are gone forever. Oh, really? Why must this be the case? Is it no longer feasible to give the necessary tax incentives and regulatory relief to our own companies in order to encourage them to either reopen or establish brand new factories at home so that we may put Americans back to work? As a nation, can't we reduce or outright eliminate costly business regulations as well as job-destroying environmental restrictions by the EPA in order that we may lure manufacturing back to our cities where factories are sitting idle and deteriorating? Parts of Detroit resemble ghost towns, replete with abandoned and deteriorating buildings and roads that are being overrun by wild animals, weeds, and vermin! How reassuring! The EPA is completely out of control, and it needs to be reined in before we allow radical environmentalists to basically regulate the country into total oblivion! Maybe that is the EPA's ultimate solution for improving global warming!

No matter what lofty or noble educational goals we may desire to establish for our nation's children from one presidential administration to the next, the simple truth of the matter is this: Not all of our children are wired for college. There are a number of careers available to our people that do not necessarily require bachelor's, master's, or doctoral degrees in order to be successful in life. My wife's deceased father, John Shearer, built a successful multimillion-dollar trout farm business in Southern California without any college degree because both he and his wife were entrepreneurs and scintillating examples of what is possible for people to accomplish in America if they are willing to work hard enough while operating independently and free of the governmental Leviathan lurking about. As a matter of fact, there are currently thousands of college graduates with advanced degrees meandering about who are desperately attempting to secure full-time employment just like millions of other Americans, and not with much success, I might add. I have recently read numerous reports in local newspapers detailing how "white-collar" professional jobs such as accountants, lawyers, engineers, teachers, etc., are hard to come by. Recent college graduates are competing for jobs to work as regular store clerks, sales associates, secretaries, custodians, etc. In addition, precisely how are these college graduates going to pay off their exorbitant college education loans when our cities and states lack sufficient jobs to go around?

5. Here is a novel proposal. Conservatives can lobby their governors and state legislators for the establishment of competitive conservative and progressive schools in all of our communities in order that they may compete against each other not only for the purpose of winning the hearts, minds, and support of the public at large, but to also demonstrate to the country who is most adept at achieving the finest academic results with their respective student bodies. Those conservative parents who desire to have their children educated in a traditional school environment by conservative teachers—who will be more than proud to permit their students to celebrate our nation's sacred holidays while attending school; who will uphold rigorous academic standards and instruct traditional curriculum in the precise pedagogical manner of their own choosing; who will promote and maintain a strict code of conduct and safe environment for children to thrive in while operating free from all outside

interference—should be given the opportunity to do so. Likewise, progressive parents should be granted the exact same courtesy and opportunity for their own children should they desire to have them educated by progressive teachers with progressive social agendas, progressive curriculum, and progressive forms of discipline in the precise manner of their choosing. Since we are so polarized as a nation anyway—politically, culturally, and morally—we may as well consider this possibility as a viable option for parents. It certainly makes good common sense to me, and competition between these two opposing philosophies and differing approaches to the education of our children would certainly make for a most tantalizing bout. Conservative teachers and administrators operating within traditional school settings are quite confident we would do a superior job with educating our children as compared to that of the progressives. We are willing to put our money where our mouths are and put up or shut up. How about all of you progressives? Are you up to the challenge and willing to do the very same thing? In the spirit of true American competition, may the best public schools operating under the auspices of the best philosophical system prevail!

6. Conservatives can also influence the direction both public schools and various universities embark upon by flooding the profession with conservative teachers and professors. Teachers become future principals, district administrators, district superintendents, state superintendents, etc. For far too long, conservatives have basically ceded the education profession over to the progressives, so my advice is to take it back. It may take a considerable length of time to do so, but conservatives in general ultimately need to quit whining and become much more proactive in this regard. **Conservatives, unite!** Do not sit on your laurels waiting for others to bring about miracles. Become miracle workers yourselves. Furthermore, conservatives need to become even more proactive by running for vacancies on their local school boards in order to affect change locally.

7. My final suggestion is this: If the American people cannot muster the necessary courage with which to implement the six plausible solutions mentioned above that, in my professional opinion, would definitely "fix" what ails our public schools, then we have no alternative but to provide "vouchers" for conservative parents who desire to send their own children to exclusive, conservative private schools that will meet their needs and the needs of their own children. Carpe Deum!

I would like to conclude this chapter with this final, humorous anecdote:

YOU MIGHT BE A TEACHER, IF...

You believe the staff room should have a Valium salt lick.
You want to slap the next person who says, "Must be nice to have all our holidays and summers free."
You can tell it's a full moon without ever looking outside.
You believe "shallow gene pool" should have its own box on the report card.
You believe that unspeakable evil will befall you if anyone says, "Boy the kids are sure mellow today."
When out in public, you feel the urge to talk to strange children and correct their behavior and grammar.
Marking all A's on the report card would make your life SOOO much simpler.
When you mention "vegetables," you're not talking about a food group.
You think people should be required to get a government permit before being allowed to reproduce.
You wonder how some parents ever MANAGED to reproduce.
You believe in aerial spraying of Prozac.
You really encourage an obnoxious parent to check into home schooling.

You've had your profession slammed by someone who would NEVER DREAM of doing your job.

You can't have children of your own because there is NO name you could give a child that wouldn't bring on high blood pressure the moment you heard it.

Meeting a child's parents INSTANTLY answers the question, "Why is this kid like this?"

You can "hold on" until after lunchtime yard duty.

You can go to the biffy to relieve yourself, take a phone call, have a conference with a colleague, tend to first aid, and have a cup of coffee in 20 minutes.

You check for spelling and punctuation errors in every piece of writing you see.

You walk around shopping centers wearing face paint, stickers, and a daisy chain, and don't even notice the stares.

You look 50 before you are 30.

When you can't get your friends to listen to you, you put your hands on your head.

You rate the educational value of cartoons.

You count your life in periods of ten weeks (depending on term lengths).

You can sing all of the words to the "Star Spangled Banner."

You can't go anywhere without thinking "what a great place for an excursion!"

You cringe at the way bank tellers grip their pens.

You don't know the date, but know it's day 5, week 4, term 4.

When returning from a walk with your dog, you assign Fido a letter grade for the quality of his behavior while on the walk.

You get a warm inner glow when just one child says "thank you for helping me."

— Author Unknown

Conclusion

All Americans would do well to reflect upon the following factors that contributed to the fall of the ancient Roman Empire:

Political
- Public office seen as a burden
- Political unrest with the citizens

Social
- Decline in interest in public affairs
- Low confidence in empire
- Disloyalty, lack of patriotism
- Emphasis on entertainment

Education
- Decrease in general level of education among citizens

Economic
- Poor harvests
- Gold and silver decline
- Inflation

- Heavy tax burden
- Widening gap between rich and poor

Military
- Threat from northern European tribes
- Low funds for defense
- Problems with recruitment
- Decline of patriotism and loyalty among soldiers[1]

The similarities between the Roman Empire and America are quite striking, and they should send a shiver up everyone's spine. If we are not careful as a nation and begin to absorb the lessons the past has taught us, America could very well find itself following in the exact same footsteps of ancient Rome.

The chapters of this book have effectively addressed in explicit detail how the unique virtues of American exceptionalism have precipitately traversed a widening path of decline and enfeeblement during the course of the last fifty years. The question of the hour is this: Have we progressed to a point in time in our country's history where it may be an act of futility on the part of our citizenry to try and restore these virtues to their proper place in American culture and society? Many of us conservatives do not believe so.

There are three defining moments in American history when our people stood at the threshold of monumental risk and change. The first heroic moment occurred in 1775 when British-American Colonials decided to place everything they held sacrosanct at serious risk and peril in order to take a stand against British tyranny. They bravely resolved to run the gauntlet as they declared independence from Great Britain and established a new republic—the likes of which the world had never seen. The second fateful moment occurred in 1861 at the outbreak of the Civil War, the outcome of which would determine whether we would remain either one nation, the United States of America, or split into two separate nations by permanently adding the Confederate States of America. The third consequential moment is occurring right now at the dawn of the twenty-first century. Just like the previous two fateful moments cited, the American people must make a third momentous decision that is of no less significance than the other two because this third decision will also determine the future of our country. Staring us in the face while playing a game of high-stakes poker are two very disparate "hands" that are reflective of the "players" of two political philosophies that are essentially at war with one another—battling for the hearts, minds, and souls of the American people. It is time to "call" both of these hands.

First, there is the secular-progressive poker hand that is being championed by the Democrats, which has dominated American politics, our culture, and society in general for the past fifty years. The proponents of this hand are determined to mold our country into the same image of western European countries. The European Union embraces a philosophy of big government, socialism, no borders, obedience to the World Court and the United Nations, a EU currency, and a military that for all practical purposes, lacks requisite funding and is impotent. America's progressives have placed all of their Democratic cards on the poker table face up so we can see precisely what hand they are presenting. Let us quickly view the cards of this particular hand:

- The secular-progressive battle strategy will be to continue to wage its insidious war upon our Judeo-Christian heritage including its annual War on Christmas and Hanukkah.
- Progressives will most assuredly continue to mock the tenets of Christianity and traditional morality by using their willing accomplices, including the entertainment industry, the mainstream media, like-minded politicians, and civil liberties groups such as the ACLU, People for the American Way, and Americans United for Separation of Church and State, to accomplish this goal.

- Progressives will continue to exhibit infidelity to the Constitution and continue to weaken it by insisting it is a "living Constitution." In other words, this is code for straying from the Founding Fathers' original design, intent, and wording of that precious sacred contract so that liberals may either rewrite it or tweak it to support their nefarious agenda.
- They will continue to press for the unconstitutional power-grab being perpetrated by a monolithic and tyrannical federal government that basically blurs the lines of delineation of constitutional principles such as Limited Government, Separation of Powers, Checks-and-Balances, Republicanism, the Rule of Law, Federalism, and Individual Rights (Bill of Rights).
- They will continue to push for a national economy that lists more and more socialistic, and they will continue to weaken and undermine our armed forces and national security.
- Progressives will continue to trumpet a public school system that is under their tightfisted control, while at the same time arrogantly raising the middle finger of that fist as they salute the rest of us who dare to question their tactics and secular-progressive agenda in our nation's schools.
- They will continue to cheer a university system of higher education that is also dominated by intolerant secular-progressives, thereby offering their students very little in the area of diverse political thought and discourse.
- They will permanently set in stone a society that promotes their crippling virtue of governmental dependency based on an "entitlement mentality" that will perpetually enslave all Americans on their liberal plantations of cradle-to-grave government cotton fields while assigning more federal agency "overseers" to whip all of us into submission. This national nightmare is also analogous to the oppressive and tyrannical "Borg" of *Star Trek-The Next Generation*. The Democratic "Borg" will continue to "assimilate" all of the rest of us into "the collective" where "resistance is futile."

• Progressives will continue to justify and make excuses for a dysfunctional society that is also in serious decline because of the deleterious impact fatherless homes as well as the feminization of our schools, our boys, and our men in general are exerting upon our culture.

• They will be perfectly content with defending and supporting like-minded parents who are increasingly ceding their authority over their own children to all elements of the "nanny state" or "the collective."

• They will see fit to appoint liberal magistrates to a judicial system at all levels that values the rights of criminals over those of victims, and such magistrates will continue to make a mockery of our Constitution as they shamefully run roughshod over it with absolute impunity.

Second, there is a common sense, constitutionally conservative poker hand, championed by the majority of Republicans as well as Tea Party patriots, which has prevailed now and then during the past fifty years. The proponents of this hand desire to restore the virtues of American exceptionalism that have made this country unique and truly great for several centuries. We have absolutely no desire to emulate western European nations. This is one of the reasons why America rebelled against Great Britain in 1775 in the first place! Throughout this book, this author has offered a poker strategy as to how traditional American virtues can be restored to our society. Conservatives have placed our cards on the poker table face up, and we are now calling the secular-progressives' bluff. Let us quickly view the cards of this particular hand:

• Conservatives will be proud to acknowledge and advocate for the tenets of our Judeo-Christian heritage and its traditional morality, and we will do so boldly without making apologies.

• We will not be ashamed to publicly acknowledge and celebrate our country's vibrant and sacred holidays such as Christmas, Easter,

Thanksgiving, Hanukkah, Passover, etc. We will not ignore these sacred holidays within our public schools either.

• We will continue to use our own legal advocacy groups such as the American Center For Law and Justice, the Alliance Defense Fund, etc., to promote and defend our traditional customs, our mainstream religious values, and our religious civil rights guaranteed all of the American people in the First Amendment of the Constitution. We will strike a mighty blow for liberty and religious freedom rather than bow to the intolerant bigotry being promoted by the secular-progressives of this nation and their minions within the Democratic Party!

• Conservatives will restore fidelity to the Constitution by remaining faithful to the original design, intent, and wording of our Founding Fathers when they crafted that sacred covenant between the American people and their government.

• We will restore limited government and common sense back to our federal government that has been permitted to run amok these past fifty years as evidenced by its incessant trampling on the constitutional rights of individuals as well as states' rights. Our federal government has shamefully betrayed the American people as well as our Constitution by continually violating the principles of Limited Government, Federalism, Checks and Balances, the Rule of Law, Separation of Powers, Republicanism, and the Bill of Rights. Our Founding Fathers would be absolutely appalled with the current behavior and tyrannical heavy-handed tactics being utilized by our federal government that is increasingly displaying the very same attributes of old Great Britain and the tyrannical power it once perpetrated upon the American people during the 1760s and 1770s! Our Executive Branch now resembles and functions similarly to that of the old British Monarchy while our Legislative Branch resembles that of the House of Lords in Parliament! Our British ancestors of Old England would be so proud of us now as we have managed to come full circle! Contemporary Brits would be well within their right to seriously question why America rebelled against them in the first place during the 1700s!

• We will untangle all small business entrepreneurs from the snare of burdensome state and federal business regulations so this country may once again thrive economically.

• Conservatives will reduce confiscatory taxes on all individuals and businesses so additional mom-and-pop shops can be created and employ out of work Americans. Families will thrive as they too will be able to retain a larger share of their income that can be better spent in their own homes and local communities rather than being wasted on a plethora of federal programs that should not exist in the first place. The government that governs least governs best.

• We will restore free market principles to our economy rather than continue to travel down the road of European-style socialism. Conservatives will be more than content to bury the debilitating liberal philosophy of "social justice" which has crippled this nation and created a "class of dependency" whose members continually feed upon the state and federal government gravy trains at the expense of the rest of us. We will once again restore the American virtue that basically states, "You cannot help men permanently by doing for them what they could and should do for themselves." Contrary to what progressive "social justice" advocates would have us all believe, the traditional American virtues of individual responsibility and duty to oneself and society is neither heartless nor selfish. We can assist and care for the nation's poor without confiscating the wealth acquired by industrious American individuals and families and without engaging in vile class warfare and class hatred! Our conservative space battleships will be armed in order to fight the "Borg" as we refuse to be "assimilated" into the Democratic Party "collective." We will also avoid the other Democratic "Talosians" who would like nothing better than to imprison the rest of Americans in their "menageries" only to have our thoughts and actions controlled and manipulated by such powerful and elitist pseudo-intellectuals!

- We will reindustrialize America so we can once again be the envy of the world with regard to our manufacturing prowess and business acumen, while at the same time putting millions of Americans back to work. We will rein in the abusive power of the EPA. The federal public employees currently working for that job-killing agency had better be prepared to join the ranks of the unemployed! Only then will such radicals be in a position to better appreciate what the rest of Americans throughout our great nation are currently experiencing economically as a result of the EPA's unchecked and uncontrolled tyrannical stranglehold upon America.

- Conservatives will see to it that we become energy independent once and for all by tapping a huge new geyser spewing forth vast natural resources within the boundaries of our own country in order that we may gradually wean ourselves from the teats of OPEC and the Middle East.

- We will eventually wrestle public education from the headlocks of the secular-progressives by exerting a significant and much-needed conservative influence on the current system or by implementing "vouchers" and "school choice" in the very near future if all else fails.

- By shrinking the scope and power of the federal government, we will significantly reduce our people's dependence on the government gravy train so they can once again take care of themselves and their own families with a renewed sense of pride rather than perpetuating the repugnant philosophy of "spreading the wealth." Secular-progressive Robin Hood and his band of liberal Merry Men need to be confined exclusively to their hideout in Sherwood Forest. Nevertheless, basic safety nets such as Social Security and Medicare will be maintained, adequately funded, and strengthened so that they too can become solvent and operate in the capacity with which they were initially designed to serve the American people.

- Conservatives will see to it that our armed forces are sufficiently funded so that our men and women in uniform are well equipped to confront any foe with a crushing blow. No one will dare cross us without paying a dear price for doing so!

Well, there it is my friends. These are the two poker hands Americans must openly present upon the national card table. Which of the two opposing hands would you desire to play? Which hand do you believe should prevail while reeling in all of the "chips" of traditional American virtues? Which poker hand is ultimately in the best interest of the American people and the nation at large? Given the choice of replicating the fate of the ancient Roman Empire or rekindling the majesty of "A City upon a Hill," I believe the majority of Americans would choose the latter. Needless to say, my fellow poker players, the choice is ultimately up to you!

Notes

Introduction
1. Napa valley register.com/business/columnists/tom-mills/article.

Chapter 1
1. Ann McGovern, *If you Sailed on the Mayflower*, p.21, Scholastic Inc.
2. John Winthrop, "Model of Christian Charity."
3. Robert Dallek and Terry Golway, *Let Every Nation Know*, Sourcebooks, Inc., pp. 68-70.
4. Ibid, pp. 69-70.
5. The American Presidency Project, www.presidency.ucsb.edu/ws/index.
6. "Freedom Forever," Opinion Page, The Press Enterprise, Riverside, Ca, 2007.
7. McDougal Littell, *Creating America*, pp. 98-99.
8. Ibid, pp. 94-95.
9. Ibid, pp. 94-95.
10. Emma Vandore, The Associated Press, The Press Enterprise, Riverside, Calif., Sunday, Sept. 2, 2007.

11. 96029: Homosexuals and U.S. Military Power, ROTC and Campus Policies, Harvard University and ROTC, CRS Issue Brief, Dec. 12, 1996.
12. Greg Jackson, *Conservative Comebacks to Liberal Lies,* p. 166.
13. Ibid, p.166.
14. "History of Boston Latin School," www.bls.org/efml/13tmpl_history.cfm.
15. Ibid.
16. Peter Marshall and David Manuel, *The Light and the Glory,* p. 188
17. Ibid, p. 182.
18. Ibid, pp. 170-171.
19. Kitty Purington, "Not All Are Pleased at Plan to Offer Birth Control at Maine Middle School," www.newyorktimes.com/2007/10/21/us/21portland.html.
20. Bill O'Reilly, "Culture War Over Boulder High School Panel That Encouraged Students to Have Sex; Break the Law," Thursday, June 14th, 2007, FoxNews.com, The O'Reilly Factor.
21. Greta Barclay Lipson, "Singapore Whipping," In *Hard Choices: Ethics Dilemmas, and Points of View,* Frank Schaffer Publications, 1995.

Chapter 2

1. Deborah Kent, *Lexington and Concord,* p. 15, Grolier Publishing, 1977.
2. Ibid, p.18.
3. Ibid, p. 18.
4. Ibid, p. 22.
5. Robert G. Ferris and Richard E. Morris, *The Signers of the Declaration of Independence,* p. 4.
6. *Creating America,* McDougal & Littell, p. 160.
7. Arthur M. Schlesinger, Jr., *John Hancock, Revolutionary War Leaders,* Chelsea House Publishers, pp. 20-21.

8. *Creating America*, McDougal & Littell, p. 160.

9. Ibid, p. 160.

10. Ibid, p. 161.

11. Arthur M. Schlesinger, Jr., *Samuel Adams, Revolutionary War Leaders*, Chelsea House Publishers, p. 26.

12. Ibid, p. 26.

13. *Creating America*, McDougal & Littell, p. 161.

14. Arthur M. Schelsinger, Jr., *Samuel Adams, Revolutionary War Leaders*, Chelsea House Publishers, p. 28.

15. *Creating America*, McDougal & Littell, p. 160.

16. Arthur M. Schlesinger, Jr., *Samuel Adams, Revolutionary War Leaders*, Chelsea House Publishers, p. 45.

17. Creating America, McDougal & Littell, p. 165.

18. Ibid, p. 166.

19. Ibid, p. 170.

20. Ferris and Morris, *The Signers of the Declaration of Independence*, p. 27.

21. Ibid, p. 27.

22. Ibid, p. 28.

23. Ibid, p. 30.

24. Ibid, p. 31.

25. Ibid, p. 31.

26. Ibid, pp. 31-32.

27. *Documents of Freedom*, Celebration U.S.A., Inc., pp. 54-55.

28. Ibid, pp. 56, 57.

29. Ibid, pp. 58, 59, 60.

30. "Little Berkeley House of Horrors: Taking It To The Pink," *Contra Costa Times* Website for Night Owl, October 30, 2007.

31. "Activists Talk Love, Not War, With Iranian President," by Jennifer Lawinsky, FoxNews.com, September 25, 2008.

32. Ibid.

33. http://pol.moveon.org/petraeus.html.

Chapter 3

1. Lori Borgman, *The Death of Common Sense*, lori@loriborgman.com.
2. *The Bill of Rights and Beyond*, Commission on the Bicentennial of the United States Constitution, 1990, p. 2.
3. Ibid, p. 2.
4. Ibid, p. 2.
5. Ibid, p. 3.
6. Ibid, p. 9.
7. Ibid, p. 12.
8. Ibid, p. 12.
9. Ibid, p, 13.
10. Joseph Loconte, "Why Religious Values Support American Values", Heritage Lectures # 899, Heritage Foundation, May 26, 2005.
11. *The New England Primer*, www./~7/neprimer.html.
12. Ibid.
13. New England Primer, 1777 edition; www.sacred-texts.com.
14. www.mcguffeyreaders.com/1836-original.htm.
15. Engel V. Vitale, www.oyez.org/cases/1961.
16. Abington V. Schempp, Ibid.
17. JAJ Publishing, Gregg Jackson, *Conservative Comebacks to Liberal Lies*, p. 49.
18. Ibid, p. 49.
19. Ibid, p. 49.
20. Ibid, p. 45.
21. Everson V. Board of Education, www. oyez.org.
22. Stephen Mansfield, "The Founders Got It Right," *USA Today*, July 16, 2007.
23. Ibid.
24. Alan Reitman, "American Civil Liberties Union," Encyclopedia Americana, Grolier, Inc., Volume One, p. 681.
25. Ibid, p. 681.
26. Ibid, p. 681.

27. www.aclu.org/freespeech.

28. www.pfaw.org./pfaw/general.

29. Ibid.

30. Ibid.

31. americansunited@au.org.

32. Ibid.

33. Ibid.

34. Ibid.

35. www.aclj.org/News/Read.

36. Ibid.

37. Ibid.

38. Ibid.

39. "The Great Awakening," *Creating America,* McDougal & Littell, p. 139.

40. Ibid, p. 139.

41. Ibid, p. 139.

42. Ibid, p. 139.

43. Ibid, p. 172.

44. Ibid, p. 433.

45. Ibid, p. 439.

46. Ibid, p. 433.

47. Ibid, p. 434.

48. Ibid, p. 435.

49. Ibid, p. 435.

50. Ibid, p. 436.

51. Ibid, p. 441.

52. Ibid, p. 441.

53. "Martin Luther King Jr.," biography, Nobelprize.org.

54. Ibid.

55. Martin Luther King Jr., "I Have A Dream," americanrhetoric. com/speeches/ mlkihaveadream.htm.

56. Dinesh Ramde, "Protesting Pastors Endorse Candidates," The Associated Press, 2008.

Chapter 4

1. Ralph Waldo Emerson, *Concord Hymn*, national center.org/ConcordHymn.html.
2. *Creating America*, McDougal & Littell, p.171.
3. Les Adams, Chapter Four, *The Second Amendment Primer*, Palladian Press, Birmingham, Alabama.
4. Ibid, p.70.
5. Ibid, p. 70.
6. Ibid, p.71.
7. Ibid, p.71.
8. Ibid, p.77.
9. *Creating America*, McDougal & Littell, p. 177.
10. Ibid, p.179.
11. Les Adams, Chapter Four, *The Second Amendment Primer*, Palladium Press, Birmingham, Alabama.
12. Ibid, p.87.
13. Ibid, pp. 87, 91-93, 95.
14. Ibid, pp. 97-102.
15. Stuart Taylor Jr., *National Journal*, www.intrnet.hereford,ac.uk/Subject/Politics/Tippingpoint.doc, June 9, 2000.
16. "A Mixed Verdict," Steven Greenhunt, The Orange County Register, July 13, 2008.
17. Ibid.
18. Ibid.
19. Ibid.

Chapter 5

1. "The Stuff of Legends: The Way of the Mountain Men," xroads, virginia.edu/~hyper/HNS/Mtmen/lifestyle.html.
2. jedesmith.html and Jim Clyman, "The West," Geoffery C, Ward.
3. Ibid.
4. Ibid.
5. Ibid.

6. Ibid.

7. Ibid.

8. Ibid.

9. "Jedediah Smith," *Creating America,* McDougal & Littell, p. 394.

10. animalliberationfront.com/Philosophy/Bill of Rights.htm.

11. stopsunstein.com.

12. worldpolicy.org/projects/globalrights/econrights/fdr-econ.

13. stopsunstein.com.

14. Ibid.

15. www.peta.org/about/faq.asp.

16. Harry Cline, Farm Press Editorial Staff hcline@farmpress.com, Sept. 15, 2007.

17. New York Times News Service, the Press-Enterprise of Riverside, Friday, October 23, 2009.

18. MyHeritage.org:Crime.

19. Thomas Sowell, Creators Syndicate, Press-Enterprise, Riverside, Wednesday, October 28, 2009.

Chapter 6

1. Christian D. Stevens, "There Was No Room For Subtlety in '30's," *Great Falls Tribune,* 1988.

2. National Fatherhood Initiative's Mission & Accomplishments, https://www.fatherhood.org/mission.asp.

3. Ibid.

4. Ibid.

5. Ibid.

6. Patrick F. Fagon, "The Child Abuse Crisis: The Disintegration of Marriage, Family, and the American Community," May 15, 1997, The Heritage Foundation, http://www.heritage.org/Research/Family/BG1115.cfm.

7. Maggie Gallagher, "Fatherless Boys Grow Up Into Dangerous Men," *Wall Street Journal,* December 1, 1988, http://www.fathermag.com/news/2770-WSJ81201.shtml.

8. "Study Finds Teen Pregnancy and Crime Levels are Higher Average Kids from Fatherless Homes," men@menhotline.org and www.fathermag.com/news/2776-UCSB.shtml.

9. "Fatherless Homes Statistics," www.fathermag.com/news/2756-suicide,shtml.

10. "Bill Cosby's Address at the NAACP's Gala to Commemorate the 50th Anniversary of Brown V. Board of Education," 17 May 2004, www.mishalov.com/bill-cosby-NAACP.html.

11. Ronald Kessler, "Jaun Williams Assails 'Phony Black Leaders,'" Thursday, July 27, 2006, NewsMax; archivenewsmax.com/article/2006/7/27/90631.shtml.

12. Ruben Navarrette, "Spoiled Kids Will Doom This Country," Washington Post Writer Group, March 3, 2009, The Press-Enterprise, Riverside.

13. www.snopes.com/humor/iftrue/palisades.asp.

14. Deborah Lambert, "Squeaky Chalk," *Campus Report*, April 2007, Volume 22, number 4, Accuracy in Academia.

15. Christian Hoff Sommers, "The War Against Boys," *Atlantic Monthly*, May 2000.

16. Jonathan Rauch, "Face New Gender Gap," *Press-Enterprise*, January 27, 2008.

17. Lambert, "Squeaky Chalk."

18. Don Closson, "The Feminization of American Schools," Probe Ministries, www.Leaderu.com/orgs/probe/does/fem-schools.html.

19. Bill Barnwell, "The Feminization of Men," www./ewrockwell.com/barnwell/barnwell23.html.

Chapter 7

1. Thomas Sowell, "Government Programs Can't Fix Irresponsible Behavior," Creators Syndicate, August 25, 2009.

2. Lyndon B. Johnson Library and Museum, National Archives and Records Administration.

3. Biography of Jimmy Carter, www.jimmycarterlibrary.gov.
4. Redlands Unified School District, Redlands, Ca.
5. California Teachers Association, "The Seven Myths of No Child Left Behind."
6. Notice published by the U.S. Department of Education in the Federal Register on October 19, 2006.
7. The National Center for Research on Education, Standards, and Student Testing, "Fixing the NCLB Accountability System."
8. Notice published by the US Department of Education in the Federal Register on October 19, 2006.
9. "Moving Beyond the Basics! Why Reading, Math and Science Are Not Sufficient for a 21st Century Education," Thomas B. Fordham Institute, December 12, 2006 conference.
10. Neal McCluskey, "Feds in the Classroom: How Big Government Corrupts, Cripples, and Compromises American Education," Cato Institute, Washington, DC.
11. Robert B. Bluey, "Another Revolt on the Right," Townhall.com.
12. *Dallas Morning News*, November 4, 2009.
13. Ibid.
14. www.cta.org/issues-and-Action/Teacher-Shortage/Index.aspx.
15. Ibid.
16. http://www.snopes.com/glurge/nodesks.asp.
17. Matthew Staver on the Huckabee Show, February 5, 2010, Liberty Counsel, www.LC.org.

Conclusion

1. "The Rise and Fall of Rome," *Creating America*, McDougal & Littell.

Endnotes